SCHOOL
of
WOKE

SCHOOL

of

WOKE

HOW CRITICAL RACE THEORY
INFILTRATED AMERICAN SCHOOLS AND
WHY WE MUST RECLAIM THEM

KENNY XU

**CENTER
STREET**

NASHVILLE   NEW YORK

Center Street
Hachette Book Group
1290 Avenue of the Americas, New York, NY 10104
centerstreet.com
twitter.com/centerstreet

First Edition: August 2023

Center Street is a division of Hachette Book Group, Inc. The Center Street name and logo are trademarks of Hachette Book Group, Inc.

The publisher is not responsible for websites (or their content) that are not owned by the publisher.

The Hachette Speakers Bureau provides a wide range of authors for speaking events. To find out more, go to hachettespeakersbureau.com or email HachetteSpeakers@hbgusa.com.

Center Street books may be purchased in bulk for business, educational, or promotional use. For information, please contact your local bookseller or the Hachette Book Group Special Markets Department at special.markets@hbgusa.com.

Library of Congress Cataloging-in-Publication Data
Names: Xu, Kenny, author.
Title: School of woke : how critical race theory infiltrated American schools and why we must reclaim them / Kenny Xu.
Description: First edition. | New York, NY : Center Street, [2023] | Includes index. |
Identifiers: LCCN 2023008689 | ISBN 9781546003656 (hardcover) |
ISBN 9781546003670 (ebook)
Subjects: LCSH: Critical pedagogy—United States. | Critical race Theory—United States. | Discrimination in education—United States. | Racial justice in education—United States.
Classification: LCC LC196.5.U6 X82 2023 | DDC 370.11/5—dc23/eng/20230313
LC record available at https://lccn.loc.gov/2023008689

ISBNs: 9781546003656 (Hardcover); 9781546003670 (ebook)

Printed in the United States of America

LSC-C

Printing 1, 2023

This book is dedicated to Barbara and Jack Tapping

Contents

PART III
The Parent-Led Revolt

What Is Critical Race Theory?

Critical Race Theory (CRT) is the idea that racism is inherent in America's laws and institutions insofar as they continue to perpetuate divides between whites and nonwhites, particularly Black Americans.[1] It questions America's moral progress and the color-blind foundations of our liberal order.[2] Meaning, CRT is skeptical that America has truly eliminated racism as triumphalist versions of American history proclaim, and cites our continuing disparities between white and Black people as evidence. Hence, CRT teaches that racism is present and should be uprooted even in institutions that explicitly profess no racism—such as schools—as long as the outcomes between Blacks and whites continue to be unequal.

Some variants of Critical Race Theory place an emphasis on each American's individual responsibility to confront racism. "Racist and antiracist are like peelable name tags that are placed and replaced based on what someone is doing or not doing, supporting or expressing in each moment," writes Ibram X. Kendi in his popular primer on racism in America, *How to Be an Antiracist*. People who believe in Kendi's logic, which he calls "inspired by Critical Race Theory,"[3] are encouraged to track down racism in institutions so that they can prove they are on the "antiracist" side of history—an ally against racism, so to speak.

Other variants emphasize the ways in which racism has wormed its way into the minds of white people through our education system. "White people raised in Western society are conditioned into a white supremacist worldview," Robin DiAngelo claims in her number one *New York Times* bestselling book, *White Fragility: Why It's So Hard for White People to Talk About Racism*. According to some prominent Critical Race Theorists, even when racism is not explicitly stated or evidenced, it is still present in the thoughts and feelings of white people, nourished by schooling that deemphasizes race and mistakenly teaches that we are a color-blind country and that racism barely exists. Gloria Ladson-Billings, the author of an article entitled "Just What Is Critical Race Theory and What Is It Doing in a Nice Field Like Education?," claims that our current educational system is reinforcing a "white supremacist master script."[4] This master script controls the narrative about America and convinces white people that they are morally neutral people when in reality they are complicit actors in the fight for or against racism based on their schooling and conditioning.

There is no one definition of Critical Race Theory, but all variants assume that racism is somehow present in our national institutions and that injustice will prevail until we root it out. It is the intellectual progenitor of the activism that is currently dominating our discourse about "systemic racism." That includes our education system.

Introduction:
Merrick Garland's Wedding

In the summer of 2018, Merrick Garland, who had just lost his bid to become a Supreme Court Justice, walked his daughter Rebecca Garland down the aisle of the luxurious St. Vrain wedding venue in Longmont, Colorado, her arm clutched in his. He was leading her to her about-to-be husband, Alexander "Xan" Tanner. Xan Tanner, then twenty-seven, was the wunderkind cofounder of Panorama Education, a *New York Times*–profiled full-service "analytical software and services company" based in Boston, Massachusetts.[1] A millionaire and a Mark Zuckerberg acolyte, Xan Tanner sat at the pinnacle of what was increasingly becoming the height of liberal fashion—Yale grad, big-tech CEO, education activist.

But what was behind his fortune? The *New York Times* may have described Panorama in cagey language in its coverage of the Tanner-Garland wedding, but the reality is that Panorama Education is not a software company at all but rather an educational technology company whose lead business model is *data*, particularly data about *children*.

Along with his fellow Yale graduates Aaron Feuer and David Carel, Tanner created a student-surveying platform that focuses on the mysterious concept of "social-emotional learning," which Panorama defines rather vaguely as "supporting the whole student."[2] Yet what's curious is his quick rise to riches. There's nothing technologically savvy about Tanner's product, which could have been created on SurveyMonkey.[3] Yet strangely, Zuckerberg chose Tanner out of many potential investment opportunities and elected to fund *him*. Tanner ended up raising more than $16 million personally from the tech billionaire and $76 million from others by using Zuckerberg's name between the years 2017 and 2021, as *Forbes* reported.[4]

Zuckerberg had a very intense interest in "fixing" public schools, and his $1 billion Startup:Education fund, which he established in 2012, was actively looking to invest in educational do-gooders like Tanner. The fund was made to "[improve] education for the nation's most underserved children."[5] Zuckerberg and his wife, Priscilla Chan, believed that they could "solve" education in America by leveraging what he knew best— the power of big business.

But the Facebook CEO needed loyal servants for his cause. And Xan Tanner, with his prestigious background and social-justice bona fides, fit the profile.[6] Tanner himself had plenty to gain from a partnership with Zuckerberg—in particular, money, and lots of it. His path to riches was to run a child research firm with Mark Zuckerberg's money attached to it!

But as soon as Tanner took the job, Zuckerberg asked him to tackle what had previously been an intractable problem: how to persuade America's public-school boards to give the fund access to private data about their children. After all, the last time Zuckerberg spent big money on education—in a widely publicized takeover of the Newark public schools, in 2012—he watched his $200 million disappear into a black hole of mismanagement and graft. "There was $20 million that went to consultants who received, in general, a thousand dollars a day for carrying out various management reform efforts," wrote Dale Russakoff, a journalist who documented Zuckerberg's attempt at school reform. Another $89 million went into a teachers' contract, which had little direct effect on learning. The *New York Times* excoriated Zuckerberg's gift as one that "slowly melt[ed] into an ocean of recrimination."[7] The national embarrassment convinced the fledgling philanthropist that he should exert his influence in subtler, more under-the-table ways in the future. And one of those ways was through conduits such as Tanner.

Still, how was the young Yale grad going to get his foot in door with the notoriously hard-to-crack school boards? After years of keeping his nose to the grindstone, pitching, and trying to persuade school boards to adopt his Zuckerberg-backed surveying product, Tanner found the answer: go woke.

Tanner's pitching strategy was to convince schools that they needed data on "racism" at their institutions to help children with their "social-emotional health." (The 2015 Every Student Succeeds Act mandated that schools find some way to address social and emotional wellness in students.) The company targeted the most progressive districts in the nation, such as those in El Dorado County, California, the city of Boston, and Washington, DC.[8] Promising that the districts would gain insights into the state of racism among local fourth graders, Panorama secured the contracts, which ranged in value from the hundreds of thousands to the millions of dollars, by asking questions such as "How clearly do you see your culture and history reflected in your school?" and "How often do you feel that you are treated poorly by other students because of your race, ethnicity, gender, family's income, religion, disability, or sexual orientation?" These questions, when answered by emotional nine- and ten-year-olds, would usually swing toward the direction of Critical Race Theory— averring that our institutions and our schools retain and abet racism.

As revealed in new documents leaked from Fairfax County Public Schools (FCPS), in northern Virginia, Panorama had signed a five-year, $2.4 million deal with FCPS to conduct surveys among students about ways in which they were being targeted because of their race and gender.[9] This included transgenderism: Panorama asked questions such as "Some people describe themselves as transgender when their sex at birth does not match the way they think or feel about their gender. Are you transgender?"[10] The surveys were not optional for students, meaning that students had to sit down for at least an hour, probably more, to take this survey, conducted on behalf of a for-profit business.

But because Tanner positioned himself as the ur-woke surveyor, progressive school boards let him in. In fact, local governments eventually showered Panorama with more than $27 million in payments between 2017 and 2020.[11]

Other organizations quickly noticed Tanner's business model and followed him. In Loudoun County, Fairfax County's immediate neighbor, students were asked to take "social-emotional" surveys conducted by the University of Virginia and the Virginia Department of Education. UVA went even further than Panorama when it came to injecting sensitive political issues directly into the bloodstream of the school day, asking Loudoun County ninth graders: "During the past 12 months, did you ever seriously consider attempting suicide?" and "During the past 12 months, did you ever feel so sad or hopeless almost every day for two weeks or more in a row that you stopped doing some usual activities?"[12]

Data-mining children by asking traumatizing questions may appear to be an exercise in futility. But rest assured, the progressive school administrators had a purpose for these surveys. Coincidentally enough, soon after the contracts were signed, school boards, including those in the District of Columbia Public Schools, started reporting things such as "Black and at-risk students were less satisfied with their schools than their White, Asian, and not at-risk peers."[13] Their evidence? Right there in the footnote: Panorama Education.

Armed with "data" on "racism," activists and special interests could walk up to the front of the aisle and loudly crow "systemic racism" at the district and demand reparations and policy changes—usually to persuade weak-willed administrators to give them more money and power. Rest assured, you're going to see this in action in chapter 1 of this book.

Panorama Education promised to obtain data based on Critical Race Theory in order to secure contracts with woke school boards. This data was subsequently used to propel the nationwide narrative that racism is a "health crisis" and an "education crisis" in America. All the while, the Garland family, woke educational bureaucrats, and billionaire elites cashed in on the grift. Elite progressives got rich and politically influential by going woke.

So Merrick Garland must have been very pleased that his daughter was going to marry Xan Tanner. He fit every quality that Garland must have wanted in a son-in-law: elite, liberal, a natural at playing at the elite liberal game of kowtowing to the forces of social justice and bowing down to the

Zuckerbergs of the world. Most important, Tanner understood the business purpose of propagating Critical Race Theory: to *land the contract.*

This book is about the complex interweaving of radical activists, school-system bureaucrats, and social justice–oriented businesses such as Tanner's as they form a symbiotic economy propped up by the racism narrative in the United States. The activists get their ideology. The school systems get power over children. The businesses get profit. It's a neat arrangement for everybody—except the children themselves.

PART I

THE INVERSION OF THE SCHOOLS

CHAPTER 1

Ground Zero for Critical Race Theory

I n America, we're taught to not be on the side of the guys holding the pitchforks. So when a throng of parents from wealthy Loudoun County, Virginia, showed up at the county school board meeting on June 22, 2021, waving signs and talking about removing objectionable material from their school classrooms, one could have been forgiven for thinking "town of Salem" or "Hester Prynne."

The Loudoun County school board would certainly like you to think that way about the parents. "I'm deeply concerned about the rise in hateful messages and violent threats aimed at progressive members of the school board," said the board president, Brenda Sheridan, to the *Washington Post* about the parent protesters surrounding the Loudoun County Public Schools (LCPS) offices.[1] Her use of the words "hateful" and "violent" was intentional. It was meant to draw our attention to the age-old trope that the guys holding the pitchforks are reactionaries preying on marginalized peoples.

But the story is deeper than the LCPS spin. Loudoun County is not Hicktown, USA. It is educated, blue-ish, and rapidly diversifying—mostly with new immigrants. The high level of splendor in the county brings with it certain expectations of academic excellence, particularly from upwardly mobile, striving middle-class families who have the most to gain—and lose—from the public education system. They have real jobs: they wouldn't just waste their time protesting at a school board meeting unless the stakes were very high. Clearly, whatever had happened in

LCPS over the previous months—perhaps years—had sparked a profound sense of concern among the county's industrious residents.

"Stand up, Virginia!" the parents chanted at the brick administrative offices. Some climbed onto makeshift stages and gave speeches. Others exchanged phone numbers, networked with other parents, even did work while waiting to get into the board meeting. It was part protest, part tailgate, part business conference. These were novice protesters armed only with megaphones and a sense of conviction.

Who are these parents who stood at the doors of LCPS, the center of a national controversy over Critical Race Theory? What did they want from the school board? And why would Brenda Sheridan take the unusual step of actively campaigning against her own constituents—not just chiding them but also accusing them of being fundamentally "hateful" people with bad intentions?

These are just some of the questions that were swirling on that muggy day in June, when a local parent protest lit up the discourse about schools and exposed to a national audience—finally—what our trust in the magnanimity of the public education system for the past fifty years has brought us.

Downward Spiral

In 2021, Loudoun County's reputation for excellent schools was already going downhill. The district's budget in 2021 was $1.56 billion, which was double what it had been just thirteen years previously.[2] The district was getting more money from the state (specifically, from its Democratic governor, Terry McAuliffe, and his successor, Ralph Northam) than it could possibly spend directly on a child's education. In fact, even adjusted for inflation, the per-child spending in Loudoun went up 29 percent in just the thirteen years between 2010 and 2022.[3]

Yet over that period of time, Loudoun County math and science scores remained stagnant. Between the years 2012 and 2019 (before the COVID-19 pandemic made scores even worse), the county's grade 4 standardized test scores barely budged.[4]

Seeing that test scores were not improving and that school districts were not doing anything substantial with the exorbitant budgets they had been given under three governors—including Republican Bob McDonnell and Democrats Terry McAuliffe and Ralph Northam—one could reasonably ask what the Loudoun County superintendent of schools had been doing over those years. But one would not get a straight answer from the school district: the truth is that the superintendent manages an educational empire, complete with business contractors, government liaisons, lawyers, nonprofit grifters, and, somewhere below all these people, teachers. And when this empire stagnates or fails to deliver, a superintendent's job is to try to find ever more ingenious ways to paper over the district's failure so that it can present the most glossy appeal for government funding.

Critical Race Theory and wokeness simply help superintendents and school boards deflect blame from themselves. What's in it for them? The answer is that evangelizing CRT allows them to blame "society" and "white people" for their own mismanagement. Stagnation in outcomes? Blame it on "racism." Lower scores for Black kids? It's the fault of implicit bias. In response to research that found that Loudoun County's Black kids continued to struggle compared to their white peers, LCPS published a report blaming the issue on "a low level of racial consciousness," encouraging the schools to individually publish statements denouncing white supremacy.[5]

So Loudoun County's progressive school board, presiding over a stagnating system, was licking its lips indeed at the possibility of injecting CRT into the lifeblood of its curriculum. Finally, the ultimate unaccountability machine had arrived—blaming everything on racism and white people.

Loudoun County's crusade to imprint CRT in the school system started in earnest in early 2019 with the enlisting of a local activist named Michelle Thomas. Thomas, the chapter president of the Loudoun County NAACP, had spent a long time being a Black rights activist. Her raison d'etre was activism: as a child growing up in Reverend John Lewis's district in Atlanta, Georgia, she participated in marches sponsored by

Reverend Jesse Jackson and Coretta Scott King. Her biography says that her track record as a "revolutionary thinker, business innovator, prolific communicator and prophetic voice has established as a leader of leaders."[6] But journalist Luke Rosiak's investigation of Thomas's boastings reveals that her business achievements came from "money from government contractors (which are required to subcontract some of their work to minority-owned businesses). Though it was an IT-related business, MCA's (now-archived) website was comically primitive."[7] In other words, she knew how to take advantage of the racism narrative for her own personal gain. And as president of the Loudoun County NAACP, her promise to her donors and nonprofit friends was that she would turn Loudoun County into the site of a racial turf war in the middle of which she could put her favorite person—herself.

These were the mutually aligned incentives facing both the woke ideologues and the school system based on the racism narrative. All either side needed was an opportunity. And in early 2019, it came. Or, more precisely, Loudoun County giddily manufactured it.

A PE teacher at Madison's Trust Elementary School, in Loudoun County, had given the class an "Underground Railroad" obstacle-course assignment in which the children's objective was to "assist each 'slave' to complete the obstacle course without ringing any attached bells, which would alert 'catchers,'" according to a sample lesson plan.[8] Now, for most students, the exercise was playful and completely nonthreatening. In fact, it *was* standardized and published in several educational-games textbooks *as an antiracist exercise*—hence the reason the school district was discussing it. However, for one Black student, the exercise was not funny. The PE teacher happened to assign this student the role of the "slave." Aggrieved, the student complained, and the complaint somehow reached the Loudoun County chapter of the NAACP—and Michelle Thomas.

Immediately, Thomas hastened to expose the incident to the *Loudoun Times-Mirror* and other local publications. "We are in a racism crisis in Virginia, and the school is where it starts," Thomas complained to the paper before admonishing the district in person at the school board meeting on

February 12, 2019.[9] "Slavery was not a joke; you don't get to choose!" she exclaimed with righteous indignation. "Stop giving those insensitive exercises to our children. They don't need to relive slavery—they've done enough; they've paid enough."[10]

Sadly, the elementary school principal listened to Michelle Thomas. Shortly after the Underground Railroad incident, the Madison's Trust principal created an "equity and culturally responsive team" to reteach the Underground Railroad lesson and future lessons in a more inclusive manner. He vowed that the team would be made up of "school staff and parents."[11]

But the LCPS administrators, seizing the opportunity, did not keep this vow. Instead, the district attempted to find "professionals" to advise the school about racism—professionals who were expert CRT agitators. The LCPS superintendent at the time, Eric Williams, sent his assistant superintendent, Ashley Ellis, as an envoy to meet with an "outside facilitator" group called the Equity Collaborative about professional equity trainings. The LCPS signed sight unseen with the group, paying a grand total of $314,000 over the course of one school year, a sum that would pay the annual salaries of at least five teachers.[12] LCPS then spent $120,000 of that $314,000 to produce a "Systemic Equity Audit" that described the state of "systemic racism" in Loudoun County.[13]

The audit of LCPS, naturally, found shocking structural racism embedded in the county. "School site staff, specifically principals and teachers, indicate a low level of racial consciousness and literacy," the consulting group wrote.[14] It shared anecdotes of parents who bashed LCPS teachers with "racism" allegations and gave teachers no opportunity to respond to the claims. The report also attributed the startling 50 percent increase in hate crimes between 2016 and 2017 to increased racism. (The real reason is likely because there was an increase in the *reporting* of hate crimes during those years.)

Oh, and you thought Michelle Thomas was out of the picture? Following the publication of the report (which, if you remember, was written at the directive of LCPS), she filed a lawsuit alleging "systemic racism" in LCPS—with the Equity Collaborative's Systemic Equity Audit *used as evidence of her allegations*. That's right: Michelle Thomas used evidence that

LCPS *commissioned and paid for* against it in a lawsuit. It's almost as if LCPS *wanted* the idea that it was a racist community to get out there without having to say it themselves!

But back up. What, in fact, was Michelle Thomas's specific premise for her legal claim of LCPS's "racism"? It was that *Asian Americans* were over-represented at the top school in Loudoun County, the Academies of Loudoun, where they made up 48 percent of the student body, while Blacks made up a mere 2 percent. Her allegation was that the school system and *Asian Americans* were "structured" to deny opportunities to Black kids at the county's top high school for gifted and talented students.

So incoherent is this point about racism that if you look at the admissions statistics for the Academies of Loudoun, you'll find that white children are also underrepresented. Are Asians prejudiced against Blacks *and* whites? Any judge would have laughed this lawsuit out of court in normal times.

But these are not normal times, and this was not a normal lawsuit.

Pause here for a moment to breathe and reflect. Loudoun County could have avoided the sudden debacle it found itself in during the summer of 2019 if it had just responded to the Underground Railroad incident by saying, "We love and support our teachers and parents. We trust our teachers and do not believe they are racist, and any allegation that a PE teacher is peddling racism in a child's game is ludicrous." But it didn't. It *invited* the racism narrative into its doorway. The county practically rolled out a red carpet for it.

The lawsuit's sham premise wasn't even the real point. Asian Americans became convenient scapegoats in the Systemic Equity Audit, designed to establish a legal precedent that LCPS was systemically racist. What's even more unbelievable—or possibly conspiratorial—is that the state judiciary bought this argument.

The Democratic Office of the Attorney General, under then governor Ralph Northam, decided to jump in to arbitrate a "conciliation" between the NAACP and LCPS. Now, we need to appreciate the political context of the moment. Donald Trump was president, already setting many liberals on edge. Virginia was reeling from the exposure of a blackface incident involving Northam at a party he attended in the 1980s. (Northam first admitted his participation, then later denied it, then still later said he wasn't sure. At issue was whether he was pictured in a photo that showed two people at a party—a man in blackface and someone else in a KKK wizard costume. Whichever one he allegedly was, even in 1984, seems irrelevant.)[15] After facing calls to resign, Northam refused. But to appease his critics, he vowed to do more for "diversity and equity" while in office. So after the blackface scandal, he was desperately searching for ways to look as woke as possible. He *needed* to regain the Black support he had deservedly lost in the midst of political scandal.

CRT in schools was the opportunity, he decided. After a year of deliberation, Northam asked his senior assistant attorney general, R. Thomas Payne, to issue a document called the "Final Determination of the Office of the Attorney General Division of Human Rights," which it did on November 18, 2020.[16] With titular finality, the executive branch of the Virginia state government recommended (read: ordered) Loudoun County Public Schools to comply not only with the admissions revisions demands at the Academies of Loudoun but also with nearly the entire scope of the organization's demands.

These were among the orders:

- establish "mandatory equity trainings" for teachers;
- institute a "systemic racism audit";
- change the name of the Hillsboro Academy to something else;
- hire more "diverse staff" across the county;
- change current "admissions practices" to a "merit-based lottery" system dictating bare-minimum criteria that would heavily lower the percentage of Asian Americans in the school; and
- lower the "discipline and office referral rates" for Black students.

You might think that there's no way all these demands could be taken seriously in a court of law as a response to an admissions issue in one Loudoun County school. Sadly, the matter never made it to an evidence-based trial. The Northam government arbitrated the agreement itself, settling it out of court. The district was then forced to apply a "racial equity" lens to nearly everything it did. That meant preferential hiring and promotion practices were put in place in order to achieve "equitable outcomes" in racial representation among the workforce. That meant discriminating against Asian Americans in the admissions process for math and science programs designed for gifted and talented students—the imposition of a *truly* racist policy. That meant changing the names of schools and training teachers in the Equity Collaborative's radical teaching philosophies. It also meant that the NAACP and the Equity Collaborative got everything they wanted and more. *And* Loudoun would need to report its progress directly to the governor's office. This was back when many assumed that the Democratic governor-to-be, Terry McAuliffe, would arrive in office in January of 2022 and issue more directives to further plunge Loudoun County and the state of Virginia into the bath of antiracism. (The election of Republican governor Glenn Youngkin obviously upset this particular plan.)

CRT in schools had arrived.

The point of the Michelle Thomas lawsuit against LCPS was not to truly root out and fight real racism. The unverifiability of the Equity Collaborative's report and the misguided assertion that the Asian kids in the Academies of Loudoun were evidence of "systemic racism" proves that point. Instead, the lawsuit was meant to provide an "in"—a means to get Critical Race Theory injected into the veins of Virginia's educational system. That was the goal, and it worked.

The Immediate Consequences of the 2020 Settlement

The consequences of Loudoun County's settlement with the NAACP under Ralph Northam's supervision had the immediate effect of pouring CRT—and its corresponding labeling of white people as the "oppressor"—into the district.

One of the witnesses to this stark change was Xi Van Fleet, a Chinese American Loudoun County mom married to a white man. In an interview with me, she spoke about a young Loudoun County man close to her, most likely her son, but she referred to him as her "friend." "In high school, he came back with comments like 'America is awful,'" she said. "And he started to say, 'White people!' [in a derogatory sense]. I said, 'What do you mean? Your dad is white!'"

Instead of being taught that all people are fundamentally equal and that you shouldn't care about the color of a person's skin, Xi's "friend" was taught that white people had inherent privileges in society and that skin color is an ardent, stubborn fact about the way people treat one another. To be color-blind was useless and even racist, he sputtered to her. Xi would get into arguments with her "friend." The arguments would turn nasty. They contributed to the gray hairs on Xi's head. Every time Xi got the upper hand in the argument, her "friend" would retreat back to the pithy lines first delivered to him in high school classes. "You don't understand race in America," he would say to her. "You're an Asian woman. How come you don't see racism?"

"It's because I've never faced discrimination in this country," Xi retorted. But her "friend" wouldn't buy it. He would insist that he, an Asian American man, was the victim of widespread systemic racism and that Xi was, too. He said she was too stubborn and drugged up on America—*especially* white people—to admit it. He had particularly choice words for the white man who literally conceived him.

"He became so embarrassed that half of him was white," she said. "And he cut me off." The two are no longer speaking—she and her own half-Asian "friend."

———

Soon the Equity Collaborative had its fingerprints all over Loudoun County. CRT went right into the school curricula for a number of teachers in the name of "fighting racism." At John Champe High School, English teacher Gurinder Badwal showed students a PowerPoint presentation called "4 Criticisms," in which she specifically outlined four ways to analyze a text: Historical Criticism, Ecocriticism, Queer Theory, and Critical Race Theory.[17] She called CRT "a lens that examines the appearance of race and racism across dominant cultural modes of expression." Tying racism to "dominant cultural modes" is the modus operandi of CRT—to show that that the United States maintains a racist enterprise that suppresses the truth about its inherent racism. Critical Race Theory is de facto the only lens children are being taught about race and racism in Badwal's class.

In a 2019 memorandum to district superintendents called Superintendent's Memo #050-019, the Virginia superintendent of public instruction, James Lane, wrote, "Our leaders have left our communities hurt and left our students seeking deeper understanding."[18] To that end, he continued, "as educators, we have an obligation to facilitate meaningful dialogue on racism and bigotry with our students, staff, and school communities." District superintendents were advised to include in school curricula various resources directly addressing perceived racism, such as *White Fragility*, by Robin DiAngelo, and *Foundations of Critical Race Theory in Education*, coedited by Gloria Ladson-Billings. Under the description of the books, Lane wrote, as guidance to the state's district officers, that "CRT has proven an important analytic tool in the field of education."

In *White Fragility*, DiAngelo repeatedly makes the case that Black people are not to blame for their problems. Rather, white people must bear the burden of attempting to rectify the deep racism of our country and society: "It is white people's responsibility to be less fragile; people of color don't need to twist themselves into knots trying to navigate us as painlessly as possible."[19] And this is the lens from which district superintendents were instructed to analyze race and racism—one that shifts all the blame to white people and places no shared responsibility with Black people or the system's own leaders.

And yet in 2021, the incoming Loudoun County school superintendent, Scott Ziegler, denied that Critical Race Theory was being taught in class, saying at a school board meeting, "LCPS has not adopted Critical Race Theory as a framework for staff to adhere to. Social media rumors that staff members have been disciplined or fired for not adhering to the tenets of critical race theory or for refusing to teach this theory are not true."[20]

Ziegler, of course, was lying through his teeth. He was so wrong that even the previous superintendent, Eric Williams, contradicted him. Williams wrote in a 2019 memo, "While LCPS has not adopted CRT, some of the principles related to race as a social construct and the sharing of stories of racism, racialized oppression, etc. that we are encouraging through the Action Plan to Combat Systemic Racism, in some of our professional learning modules, and our use of instructional resources on the Social Justice standards, *do* align with the ideology of CRT."[21]

The emphasis on *do* is his.

Across Loudoun County and all over Virginia, the term *Critical Race Theory* sprang from curriculum materials, school-official guidance, and academic conversation in and about schools. It did not simply emerge out of nowhere in 2020 and 2021; it had been lurking in the educational sphere for many years before then.

Depress to Possess

So quiet, so lawyerly was the hum of efficient infiltration that most teachers and administrators did not notice it. In fact, before the outcry surrounding CRT in 2021, it took very special kinds of people to even perceive that something was going wrong. These were the kinds of people who had experienced very acutely the process of politicization occurring in Loudoun County, the kinds of people who had heard the same rhetoric and seen the same machinations elsewhere—specifically, in their home countries. They had a sensitivity to Marxist thought that would swoop right over the head of an average American.

Xi Van Fleet's short-cropped hair radiated feminist defiance, but her darting, suspicious eyes demonstrated sensitivity—and in this case, those eyes were trained on the Loudoun County public school system, which reared, and eventually damaged, her "friend."

In Cultural Revolution–era China, Xi had lived in a Beijing compound as part of a relatively affluent family of legacy Communists. She was taught the party line of endless conflict with people different from her and was inculcated with the Marxist lexicon of "oppressor" and "oppressed." However, since her parents were military officers in the Communist Party, she was also taught to believe that her family, despite being wealthy, was on the "good" side waging war against the evil "capitalist" bourgeoise. Mao's class philosophy was particular on not just eliminating wealth inequality, but on eliminating anyone hostile to him and his political beliefs. Because of this, Xi's Mao-aligned family could get away with being wealthy and even getting special treatment. They lived in a guarded compound with a swimming pool, and they ate meat every day, albeit just a little bit, during a period when the rest of China was suffering through a food shortage. "It was like a different world," she said. It was a world in which the separation between rich and poor was between those who professed enough appreciation for Mao and those who didn't. It was a world where division between the good Maoists, the "Red" classes, and the bad imperialists, the "Black" classes, was stressed in every facet of society, from literal walls to the mental walls put up by the education system.

One time, Xi went out a little beyond her compound and came across a poor girl. The poor girl screamed, then threw mud at Xi's face. Having just washed her hair, Xi was infuriated and chased the girl all the way back to her home. The poor girl lived in a hut down the street. Xi was astounded to discover that whole families lived just outside the compound. The girl ran to her mother. Xi expected the woman to reprimand her daughter for throwing mud in Xi's face. But the mother did not. She only scowled at Xi, as if she were looking at a reprehensible object. "I thought she would scold her daughter, but no, she did not say a thing," Xi told me. So ingrained were the social divisions that neither party could muster even a modicum of politeness toward the other. There, in that moment, was a gap in understanding so wide, a perception of the Other so severe, that there was no possibility they could get along or even be polite to each other. There, in that moment, was class consciousness—the *true* consequences of class consciousness. Xi was taught to think the people outside of her compound were capitalist scum, and the poor girl was taught to think that the people inside the compound were also capitalist scum. In other words, there was no truth in Maoist society, except the wall.

"I couldn't even talk to her," Xi said about Lily Tang Williams, another Chinese immigrant to America who came from the other side of the tracks.

Growing up in the same city as Xi, Lily experienced hunger in a way that Xi couldn't even think about. She lived with eight family members in a house with no bathroom. She had to do her business in a ditch outside the hovel. But, Lily recalls in an interview with me, she figured that at least she belonged to one of Mao's five favored Red classes. Wrong. The so-called peasants, the inheritors of socialist civilization, were made to get by on meal tickets for a couple tiny portions per day. They were promised the world and got dirt. Furthermore, they faced social indoctrination so severe that they had to worship Mao, lest he (in reality, the Red Guards, Mao's radical activist militia) smite them. "We had to write diaries to confess to ourselves [our faults for not being sufficiently aligned with Mao]," Lily said.

The kids in Lily's town were forced to undergo rigorous social indoctrination to ensure compliance with Maoist values. The Chinese Cultural Revolution witness and author Rae Yang writes in her memoir, *Spider Eaters*, about the academically useless indoctrination she received in a physical labor course at her school, Beijing 101 Middle School:

> The aim of the [physical labor] course, I was told, was to help us cultivate proletarian thoughts and feeling...For an entire afternoon, all we did was carry coal cinder from one corner of the schoolyard to another. A few weeks later we might be carrying it all the way back. What a waste of time! The work made me dirty and uncomfortable.[22]

Embracing Mao and supposedly being part of his favored class did not help Lily escape hunger and poverty. It did not put food on her family's table. It did not save her from the drudgery of the working class, even as Mao promised more than enough to eat for everyone. All Mao Zedong ultimately did for Lily was teach her to hate rich people and Rightists as well as her own living conditions. It depressed her and sent her into a frenzied hatred of those who lived inside the walls—people like Xi, who ironically was taught the same about her.

Lily, raised in Maoist indoctrination, said that "the school pushed me to chant 'Long live Mao! For ten thousand years,'" Lily said. "And then he died. I was so sad."

The social indoctrination took a toll on Lily. Her response to the death of Mao was this: "At first I cried my eyes out. My god had just died. I could see him smiling down at me from heaven." But Lily was of strong intellect. "Thank God I had some brains. I eventually realized I was being lied to." Mao was not a god, and he was not smiling down from heaven. The Communist Party was just trying to force her into adhering to a party line—and becoming a loyal slave to the party.

Adds Lily, "That's what Communists do. They want you to hate, to not love, to protect the leaders, the state, and to think everyone else is your enemy. Divide and conquer. That is the Marxist tactic for slavery."

Now take a look at what LCPS has been championing: in the Systemic Equity Audit of LCPS, schools were asked to "condemn white supremacy, hate speech, hate crimes, and other racially motivated acts of violence." Individual schools would be required to "include this message on their websites and in communications to parents twice a year, and not only in response to an incident."

Obviously, twice a year wasn't good enough. The CRT cognoscenti would have the schools recite the white-supremacy condemnations twice a day if they thought they could get away with it.

It was in America where the two women, Xi Van Fleet and Lily Tang Williams, from different classes taught to hate each other, could really come together and bond as equals. Together, they overcame their petty antagonisms toward the other side. And together, they discovered a new form of garbage in their adopted country. In Loudoun County.

With Devastating Effect

In the span of the four years between 2016 and 2020, progressives fundamentally changed education across America by using Critical Race Theory to imbue Maoist principles of oppressor and oppressed into the school system and teaching the kids of various races to hate each other. But why?

It is because Critical Race Theory is a cudgel to deflect blame from themselves while forcing an army of woke ideologues and business partners into the school system. In Maoist China, party leaders could easily blame their failures on the other side. In the new politburos being established in American schools, school administrators can now do the same. The yawning racial achievement gap could be blamed on "racism." The raging anxiety epidemic facing teenagers was now a problem of "white supremacy." Critical Race Theory did not simply facilitate unaccountability and hatred. It facilitated unaccountability by hatred.

In capitalism, there is an age-old idea: if it works, keep doing it. And in racial capitalism, in those Trump-tinged years, the progressive media narrative that a school was racist unless it did X, Y, and Z could not be disputed—at least not initially, not when there were emotional liberals running our schools. So the woke kept doing it. They kept bombarding the school systems with devastating narratives, accusing anyone and everyone of systemic racism. By the time the smoke cleared, they had already taken Little Round Top, Stalingrad, and Okinawa. They had already taken over some of our most prominent school districts, and we're living in the midst of their oppression.

Let me lay out the model of Critical Race Theory's entrance into public schools in full.

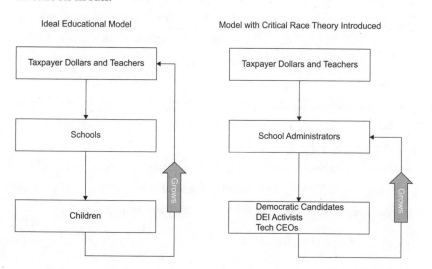

On the left side of the diagram above is our ideal educational model. It is the model of democratic, publicly funded education that we as Americans have dreamed of and worked hard to build. In this model, taxpayer funds and teachers pool resources to create schools, which act in service of our children, growing and developing them to the point where they can contribute to society and become the taxpayers and teachers of the future.

On the right is the inversion of that model. The kink is the introduction of Critical Race Theory and all its bureaucratic partisans. It could start with a single Diversity, Equity, and Inclusion officer, such as the chief equity officer of Loudoun County. It could be a powerful principal or vice principal with an ideological agenda who wants to prove that America is a racist country. It could also be a person in such a position cynical enough to embrace that narrative for his or her own personal gain—such as Michelle Thomas. You let a single person with these intentions into the system, into a place of power, pulling the levers of a well-funded school system, and you give the opportunity for them to invite all their lackeys, their woke allies, and businessmen partners into the schools—people whose careers are not based on merit but on preserving the racism narrative. You let the viper hatch her young. And watch as the offspring consume the institution from the inside out, just as they have been doing at Loudoun County.

And notice what party is not in the second model: the children. The children and their growth and educational development are left out of the Schools of Woke. They are practically irrelevant from the standpoint of aiding and abetting the taxpayer-funded grift—except as props to get more money.

This inversion happens when you let an unaccountable ideological bureaucracy infiltrate your schools. If nothing is done about it, it won't be the schools serving the children anymore. It will be the "children," in the form of government money and moral capital dedicated to the premise of helping them, serving the woke triangle of government bureaucrats, activists, and the social justice–industrial complex instead.

CHAPTER 2

The Beginning of Parents' Rights

What does a school superintendent do? Perhaps the most basic answer might be: protect children from physical harm and sexual violence. Maybe we can't ask a superintendent to take full responsibility for declining test scores. Or a rise in mental health issues. Or, for God's sake, solving "racism." But we can demand full accountability from a superintendent in at least one of his or her capacities: to protect children from harm. If superintendents lie about incidences of physical and sexual aggression, they should be fired in disgrace. That we can demand if we live in a civilized country.

So when a fifteen-year old girl is sexually assaulted in the girls' bathroom by a "gender-fluid" biological male wearing a dress, and the Loudoun County Public Schools superintendent, Scott Ziegler, denies in a public forum that this ever occurred—while quietly shipping the predator off to another school, where he proceeds to sexually assault another girl, and the LCPS school board nods along in approval—you know something is deeply, deeply sick in our school systems today.

This is the story of how it happened and why it got covered up—and what wokeness has to do with it.

No Adults Allowed

"I have a theory that public schools would actually be better if adults didn't show up," Jamie Almanzán, a consultant and trainer from the Equity

Collaborative who was paid $5,500 a day for a four-day "diversity" training session, said to a crowd of masked-up teachers at LCPS.[1] "I certainly don't think [teachers] offer learning per se. I think what [they] offer are relationships... actually the internet's better than the high school is [at disseminating information]... Truthfully, the teacher in relation to dissemination of information is obsolete. But the teacher in relationship to *relationship* is the thing."[2]

Almanzán is a disciple of a Marxist educator named Paulo Freire, who devised something called "critical pedagogy"—the idea that a teacher's job is to develop a student's "critical consciousness" about his place in the world. This critical consciousness inevitably takes the form of the student's realization that he is an oppressed being and that his purpose is to rebel against the systems that try to oppress him.

The Equity Collaborative, right before teachers' very eyes, was attempting to change the relationship between teacher and student from one of learned and learner to one of friend, facilitator, and caretaker, so that the student could recognize his own oppression à la Paulo Freire.

And Loudoun County liked what it heard from Almanzán. So much so that it paid him a $90,000 annual salary to stay on the payroll as an "equity consultant."[3]

There's a very specific reason why LCPS wanted Almanzán's "relationship-focused" theory of education embedded into its teacher and administrator trainings. It's because LCPS needed to redefine its purpose to justify its exorbitant spending—on guidance counselors, mental health programs, lawyers, nonprofit contracts, and DEI initiatives, all of which were largely responsible for the rapid growth in school-system budgets since 2000.

As taxpayers, we traditionally believe that a school system is designed for the specific purpose of helping students *learn* essential subjects such as math, reading, and science, things we are too busy or uninformed to teach kids ourselves. According to this model, the school should *teach*, and the parents should provide emotional and financial support.

Well, scratch "emotional" from that formula. Now school systems just want your financial support as they seek to push agendas that encroach upon greater and greater aspects of a child's life, including mental health, social awareness, and even coping with discrimination. As school systems have gotten bigger and more bloated, they bring in ever more administrators who serve each of these purposes—*all for the overall goal of helping the child.* In fact, since 1950, the number of administrative staff at public schools has increased at six times the rate of their student populations.[4]

Administrative staff justify their presence in the school system in terms of their caretaking purpose for kids. The mental health counselor, the IT support specialist, the Diversity, Equity, and Inclusion officer—all of them are employed because they can point to evidence that they are helping the students. If a mental health counselor or trainer can trace a student's problem back to something he or she said on a survey, even better. That's, of course, why businesses like Panorama Education exist.

Understand that Almanzán's "relationship" ideology completely justifies the administrative bureaucracy. If a school's job is to build a relationship with its children, then it is assumed that the school should be allowed to discuss and guide children through sensitive moral and identity-based issues—to be their friend.

This may seem nice at first. But what all this jockeying for the right to care for the student does, in fact, is create a funnel effect in which administrators and bureaucrats are increasingly competing for children's attention. The mental health counselor needs time during the school day to evaluate children for disorders. The social-emotional learning expert needs time in the middle of math class to conduct seminars about taking care of yourself. The lawyer needs more laws about students to be passed so that he can continue his legal work. Increasingly, the role of the student has been fundamentally transformed from pupil and learner to carrier of all the burdens and job security for the rest of the school system. This is yet another consequence of the inversion of schools—the student becomes the justifier rather than the justified.

As increasingly bloated staffs compete for the attention, affection, and authorship of the student experience, one critical party is left out: the parent. That's because the parent historically has had the ability to say to the counselor, operations officer, or DEI expert, "Hell, no—don't touch my kid!" If a parent can intercede on behalf of her child, then the various beneficial-sounding agendas pushed by specialists eventually have to halt. This creates a problem for the careers of these specialists. To preserve their jobs and justify their exorbitant bureaucratic spending, they need to find a way to get parents out of the picture and get children to listen to them instead. Perhaps even *turn children against their own parents.*

Say hello to opportunity.

Queer Theory

LCPS believed it had found a cheat code that would rapidly accelerate its transformation of the school system into a magnet for a child's complete dependency. That cheat code, unbeknownst to all but the most perceptive academics, is called Queer Theory.

Queer Theory—or, more precisely, Critical Queer Theory—is the assertion that kids should self-determine their choices in life, especially when it comes to the sexual choices that they make with other people, including adults. Queer Theory gives unlimited agency to the child, including the right to determine his or her gender and determine whom he or she wants to have sex with. The adult's responsibility to correct, inhibit, and socialize the child is reduced to nothing, because the child is his or her own conduit of self-determination and meaning in life—no adult necessary except to facilitate.

I considered writing this book without going into details about Queer Theory, a sort of subdivision of CRT. But the events in Loudoun County and all over the nation in response to the sexual assaults of teenagers forced me to change my mind. It is impossible to fully comprehend what is going on in the underbelly of the school system without understanding how Queer Theory activism is transforming the schools under the guise of LGBTQ affirmation.

Let me draw your attention to a 2004 book called *Curiouser: On the*

Queerness of Children, a primer and collection of essays edited by Mount Saint Vincent University professors Steven Bruhm and Natasha Hurley.[5] In the first chapter of the book, author James Kincaid argues that we currently define childhood by what *"it doesn't have"* instead of by its liberty. According to Kincaid, we have created a false construct of a child's "innocence" by focusing on what he *hasn't done* (i.e., had sex) rather than what he would have done if he were free to pursue his desires.[6] Rather than allow the child to "speak for himself," we ask the parents to be the child's voice. We construct narratives of innocence and acceptable sexual behavior that need to be deconstructed. Once we deconstruct them, we can create a freer, more liberated world and a freer child. It is assumed that this freedom will permit the child to sexually experiment.

For Queer Theorists, legalizing gay marriage wasn't enough—in fact, marriage itself is just an artifact of "sanitized middle-class worlds where the children are evacuated of any desires but those of creature comforts."[7] Rather, we have to go further, go younger. We have to eliminate the barriers to sexual self-determination from the whole idea of childhood. Decrying the concept of rearing a child away from sexualization, Kincaid asks the reader to consider that little boys and girls just might *want* to be more sexually available. In other words, we have to kick adults and adult mores out of the room. Let the kids decide for themselves what they feel like. Male? Female? Sexual? The child gets to decide. No adults allowed.

To illustrate how sexual self-determination is impressed upon children, let us take a look at the Governor's School of North Carolina, a prestigious publicly funded five-week summer retreat for talented students away from their families. At this retreat, students received a pamphlet entitled, and I'm not exaggerating, "The Flying Gender Unicorn."[8] The pamphlet has a depiction of a unicorn with a vagina along with a set of terms (Gender Identity, Gender Expression, Sexual or Romantic Identity, Physically attracted to, and Romantically attracted to) adjacent to the picture. It also has a section called "External Genitalia (At birth)" that depicts a sliding scale of pictures, from what is clearly depicted as a penis to what is clearly depicted as a vagina. However, there are three "in-between" pictures, showing the "spectrum" nature of the genitalia. The implication is that children can be whoever they want to be and they choose to engage in whatever sexual contact they wish.

Don't overthink this one. This is the ideology that most fundamentally threatens the traditional authority of parents over their children—when preached to children, it gives them the feeling of being totally free from the need to obey their parents or to conform to long-established social norms. And this ideology has been entering our school system—welcomed and invited by school administrators who have much to gain—at a breakneck pace in the name of fighting "anti-LGBTQ oppression."

Weaponizing LGBTQ Issues

It was June of 2021—LGBTQ Pride Month at Loudoun County Public Schools. And Queer Theory was on the classroom agenda.

In addition to teaching the theory to high schoolers (Gurinder Badwal's English class comes to mind), LCPS had just ordered a truckload of books to stock in its libraries in an effort to support "diverse" and "underrepresented communities." Prominent among them were books aimed at LGBTQ young adults.[9] Among them were books like *Lawn Boy*, *Gender Queer*, and *My Princess Boy*. The first two are famous, but *My Princess Boy*, which is written by Cheryl Kilodavis and illustrated by Suzanne DeSimone, is more explicit and targeted at younger children—those between the ages of four and eight.

In *My Princess Boy*, the narrator tells the story of a boy who wears a dress but whose father and brother love him unconditionally, playing with him and doing all sorts of fun things together. At first it seems like a generic gay book. But then the story takes a dark turn: "He is the happiest when he looks at girls' clothes. But when he wants to buy a pink bag or a sparkly dress, people stare at him. And when he buys girls' things, they laugh at him." Now you can see Queer Theory inserting itself: it's not *just* that the queer kid feels happy in a dress; it's also that the world hates him for it, wants to impose its social norms on him. He is not only queer but also oppressed because of his queerness.

Then comes the admonition: "If you see a princess boy, will you laugh at him?...Will you like him for who he is?"[10] Implied: Will you support the princess boy's feelings as the ultimate source of his self-determination? Or are you a bigot?

"Our princess boy is happy because we like him for who he is," the narrator says, the implied consequence being that "if you don't like him for who he is, our princess boy will be unhappy." And what eight-year-old reading this book wants to make a friend feel unhappy?

As it turns out, this literary device—shaming the reader for making someone unhappy—is used to shame more than children. It's used to shame *adults* into conformity with LCPS's sexual agenda.

Karen Lithgow is an elementary school teacher in Fairfax County, Virginia. Specializing in English as a second language, the thirty-three-year-old teacher started seeing things in the latter part of her ten-year teaching career that she had never seen before. "I had a student say that he was gay. And I never had a student say that to me ever before—and that's fifth grade," she said in an interview with me about an incident that took place in 2021. What became increasingly apparent was that there was a broader cultural effort in her school to force everyone—including her—to openly praise that student for being gay. "If he wants to wear women's clothing, we can't say anything about it. We have to use whatever name [students] want. They can go to whatever locker room...they want." This student became some kind of symbol of pride and joy and even worship, and Karen lived under a gag rule that effectively scripted all her talk about sexuality into generic affirmations—or else. If a teacher so much as messes up a pronoun, the administration could be called in. She could face discipline for her behavior as "anti-gay"—as well as the shame of that label.

An hour into our conversation, the ESL teacher started talking about the social-justice terms used to privilege queer kids, and with a loud of burst of emotion, she said, "*Equity* and *inclusion* are two buzzwords, and I'm tired of it!"

The Gender Sledgehammer

Loudoun County's policy 8040 was a parent's nightmare. The comprehensive gender policy reads, in part: "School staff shall, at the request of a student or parent/legal guardian, when using a name or pronoun to address the student, use the name and pronoun that correspond to their gender identity."[11] It also specifies that transgender students are to be given bathroom accommodations in conjunction with their preferred gender identity and should be allowed to participate in sports in their preferred gender-identity category—and all this without the express consent of their parents. (The "or" in "at the request of a student or parent/legal guardian" does a lot of work.)

No surprise: the kids who persistently claim to want to be a different gender are already struggling in several ways—in need of their parents more than ever. Children with gender dysphoria are often some of the most depressed children at schools. Since 2015, the year gay marriage was legalized across the United States, the portion of LGBTQ teenagers who reported feelings of "persistent sadness and hopelessness" jumped from 60 percent to a staggering 75 percent in 2022.[12]

In other words, if there are any kids who can be emotionally manipulated into serving an agenda they don't fully understand, it's LGBTQ kids. But instead of having their parents take care of them and discuss their issues with self-awareness, the LCPS teachers and administrators take the opportunity to do it themselves. Would you let your kid go through a crisis of self-identity guided by a schoolteacher or a principal—without even knowing about it? I certainly hope not.

In North Carolina's largest school district, Charlotte-Mecklenburg, students can fill out a "gender support plan," allowing elementary school children to "come out" in school without telling their parents. In fact, "school staff, caregivers, and the student work together to complete" the document, which asks what gender a student would like to switch to and *whether or not* the parents should be informed.[13] The fact that the district even gives the option of not notifying the parents is scary enough.

But beyond that, there is a clear motivation here to hide a child's gender transition, to secretly work with and encourage children to keep secrets from their own parents. In doing so, LGBTQ activists in Charlotte-Mecklenburg schools—and in other districts across the United States—are attempting to lead children down the road of separation from their parents' authority.

New surgical and medical techniques can insert hormones into children's systems to semi-effectively block puberty, preventing the growth of male and female genitalia during the teenage years. According to the Mayo Clinic, "Transgender and gender-diverse children might choose to temporarily suppress puberty through the use of prescription medications called pubertal blockers."[14] These are just some of the things that schools and hospitals can now recommend to children who merely express a wish in writing to transition to another gender.

By simply accepting a child's word that he or she is meant to be of a different gender, schools are quickly stripping from parents the right to have any say over their children's transition (about which, let's be honest, the *vast* majority of parents would say, "Hell, no!"). Make no mistake: Queer Theory is the sledgehammer with which the school system is wielding its ultimate authority over parents and their children.

As it turns out, people who think this is ultimately about LGBTQ rights or even LGBTQ health are not seeing things through the correct lens. Transgender individuals make up a reported 0.5 percent of the population. Their health is important, and the long-term effects of both transgender medication and surgery are worth discussing. But school boards and administrators do not lie or push political propaganda on behalf of transgender individuals because they really care about that 0.5 percent of the population. They do it because the policies that are enacted regarding transgender people affect the power and control school administrators have over the *other* 99.5 percent of the population—control that will extend long after the transgender moment in our history is gone.

Ironically, in the name of liberation and freedom from oppression, Queer Theory in schools represses more than ever.

To Loudoun County's progressive school bureaucracy, policy 8040 and Queer Theory are the system's best bet for wrenching control of children out of the hands of parents and into the hands of the state. If the LCPS woke could force teachers to bow to the will of transgender students, easily some of the nation's most vulnerable and mentally unstable kids, and force people to allow them into bathrooms of the desired gender— especially when the most common age of a male sexual predator is sixteen and the most common age of a female sexual assault victim is fourteen— then the woke could do anything with these children.[15] They could turn kids into wards of the state.

The Transgender Sexual Assault and a Superintendent's Failure

Everything—policy 8040, Queer Theory, the LCPS school system— coalesced in a perfect storm when the choices of a compromised superintendent turned a tragic event into the biggest school disaster in the history of Loudoun County.

Questions arose about what happened on May 28, 2021, in that girls' bathroom at Stone Bridge High School. The boy's lawyers claim he stopped the assault after seeing his victim in pain. The girl's lawyers say he only stopped because "his knee-length skirt got caught in his watch."[16]

A teacher noticed two pairs of feet—one male and one female—in the girls' bathroom while the assault was occurring but did nothing about it. Later on, she justified her inaction by saying that "somebody could have their period. They might need a tampon." Or, shedding insight on the rather normal situation of boys walking into girls' bathrooms in Loudoun County, "somebody had a boyfriend they had a fight with."[17]

What is clear is that the practice of boys and girls entering each other's bathrooms to talk, flirt, or even have sex was shrugged off by Loudoun County teachers. The connection between this look-the-other-way culture and the LGBTQ affirmation brought about by Queer Theory cannot be denied. Teachers were afraid to step on the toes of an LGBTQ child, the pride of Loudoun County Public Schools and a critical element in the effort to wrest control of students away from their parents.

The first LCPS heard about the incident was from the girl herself, around an hour after the assault occurred. The principal of Stone Bridge High School met with the chief operating officer, who then forwarded his concern to the superintendent, Scott Ziegler. Notably, the COO caught Ziegler's attention by stating in his email correspondence that "the incident . . . is related to Policy 8040."[18]

The boy was already a problem case. On May 12, two weeks before the assault, a Loudoun County teacher confessed in an email to her superiors that "if this kind of reckless behavior [from the boy] persists, I wouldn't want to be held accountable if someone should get hurt."[19]

Notice immediately the teacher's feelings of exasperation. She felt she didn't have the authority to discipline the child herself, so she told her superiors that she didn't want to be held accountable for his misbehavior.

Could it be because of the child's self-identified gender and the protections the school felt it needed to put in place? The parents of the girl referred to the boy as "gender-fluid."[20] Yet the *Daily Mail* wrote: "It remains unclear if the boy is transgender and if that is how he was allowed into the bathrooms that day."[21] We have every reason to believe, however, that even if a teacher had caught him entering that bathroom, she would have been greatly discouraged from calling him out on it. The teacher who saw the male feet in the bathroom sure did jack squat about it. Nobody wanted to be *that* teacher in a climate like this, where LGBTQ affirmation is simply everywhere. So laden in ideology was the school that a teacher denied what was going on before her very eyes.

Back to Superintendent Ziegler: after he had the meeting with the COO about the assault, he typed an email to the LCPS school board about the matter—but he *didn't mention policy 8040 or the fact that the assaulter was wearing girls' clothing.* According to the special grand jury eventually convened to rule on this incident, LCPS displayed a "remarkable lack of curiosity" about the details of the bathroom assault and even a lack of willingness to discipline the male child. In fact, the boy's own mother had begged school staff to discipline the boy for his tendencies, only for the staff to respond by "siding with him and trying to be the fair and neutral party, often discounting my approach and recommendations," according to the mother. At every turn the school's disciplinary and advisory staff dismissed voices of concern and rationalized the child's behavior.

All the while, the Loudoun County school board was debating policy 8040—and parents were *livid* about it. Many of them held demonstrations in front of the LCPS administrative offices to protest exactly what I've covered in this chapter—the withholding of information about their children in the name of LGBTQ advocacy. Ziegler, who was on the side of passing the new policy, needed to find a way to end this debate. If he informed the school board about the transgender sexual assault, the school board—which still had one or two conservative members—might not pass the policy, the biggest infringement of parents' rights in the history of public schooling. Ziegler's fundamental rewriting of the relationship between school, parent, and child for the purpose of justifying his fiefdom of wokeness was at stake. He had to protect his nest.

So when the school board requested his presence to calm the nerves of the protesting parents, Superintendent Scott Ziegler did what he was advised to do: openly lie.

In that June 22 board meeting, he declared, on advice from the PR firm the Donovan Group, that transgender students presented no menace to society or to Loudoun County. "The issue of…transgender students assaulting other students in the restroom—*Time* magazine in 2016 called it a red herring, that the data was not simply playing out that transgender students were more likely to assault cisgender students."[22]

Ziegler insisted, "The predator transgender student does not exist." He even added, "We don't have any records of assaults occurring in our restrooms."

Even as LCPS was actively sitting on a case of a gender-fluid teenager allegedly sexually assaulting a fourteen-year-old girl in the girls' bathroom, the superintendent openly lied about having no record of assaults in bathrooms—while one was *directly staring him in the face.*

Parents were left in the dark about the event until it was too late. On August 11, 2021, the Loudoun County school board passed policy 8040 in a 7–2 vote. The policy forced teachers to adhere to a script about transgender students and allowed students to submit gender-change requests to the administration without the consent of their parents. No one in the public caught wind of the transgender assault, which was kept under wraps. Scott Ziegler could breathe a sigh of relief, at least for now.

But secrets cannot keep themselves.

As it turns out, the way the transgender assault became public knowledge was sheer poetic justice. Scott Smith, a man dragged out of that fateful school board meeting, screaming, by the Loudoun County police department—a meeting that eventually descended into chaos—was the father of the girl assaulted by the gender-fluid teenager. In an exclusive interview with the conservative publication the *Daily Wire*, he confirmed that the victim of the attack at Stone Bridge High School was in fact his daughter.

Meanwhile, the male predator was quietly transferred to another high school, Broad Run High School, also in Loudoun County, where he was allowed to roam in search of his next victim.[23] No parents at either high school were notified that a boy accused of sexual assault was hanging out at the school with their children. Scott Ziegler knew all this during that June 22 meeting and later. None of this he chose to make public.

Why is this so horrifying? It is not as if the teenager assaulted the girl because he was transgender. It is not as if the only conclusion is that gender-fluid individuals are predators exploiting soft policies for their own carnal pleasure. But the fact that a Loudoun County administration would go to such pains to deny the existence of an assault that they themselves were investigating shows how little they cared about parental transparency, especially if it violates their social agenda. These parents who are campaigning against the sexualization of their children must be so oppressive, the school board thought, that they should be resisted rather than trusted. *Don't tell them anything*, whispered the voice of Queer Theory in their ears.

On October 6, 2021, the same gender-fluid teenager was found to have yet again sexually assaulted another young woman, this time at Broad Run. On that day, he allegedly forced the female victim into an empty classroom, where he held her against her will and inappropriately touched her.[24] Loudoun County hurried through the case, sending it to a juvenile court judge for ruling. The county had already passed the policy it needed, and there were no takebacks.

On October 25, 2021, the judge found the alleged predator guilty of both the May 28 charge and the October 6 charge of sexual assault.[25]

What's sad is that the October 6 charge could have been avoided if the school had properly notified parents about the incident. Teachers could have spoken out about the boy's suspicious behavior if the transgender gag policy hadn't been passed. Policy 8040 could have been properly reconsidered if parents had known the facts at the time of its passage.

That same day, the litigators representing the victim, the Stanley Law Group, issued a statement saying, "We will pursue federal Title IX actions against the local government and all officials who are responsible for allowing this harm to come."[26]

A special grand jury was convened to deliberate the case. They found gross negligence on the part of Ziegler, writing that "LCPS Administrators were looking out for their own interests instead of the best interests of LCPS." Let me be specific: LCPS administrators were looking to rapidly push Queer Theory into the social agenda of the county for the purpose of transforming the school-child relationship into one in which children are wards of the state—parental transparency and student health be damned.

On December 7, 2022, one day after the grand jury report, Scott Ziegler was fired in disgrace. And he deserved to be. I would go further: LCPS administration should be defunded by the state government into near austerity until by instilling parent-transparency protections and rescinding the gross policy 8040 it can clean up the mess it made. Loudoun County's incompetent and ideologically fanatical administrators cannot be allowed to hold children hostage in service of their child-possession agenda. Move the kids to another county or pay the teachers directly to teach in makeshift offices: the administrators need to go. All of them.

In a slipup, Ziegler even admitted in a confidential email to school board members that he didn't believe the stuff he said publicly about transgender individuals, referring to the gender-fluid child who was alleged to have assaulted the girls as a male rather than as a self-identified female.[27] But he felt like he couldn't say what he really believed. There was the agenda of totally possessing the child to protect.

The superintendent *manages an educational empire*, and it's his responsibility to fend off the political party operatives, friendly business connections, and activist nonprofit organizations trying to make a career out of their advocacies. It's *his* responsibility to push a school out of its lethargy and demand achievement. When he doesn't, the school system fails to educate kids. It instead becomes a fiefdom of patronage that subordinates education to administration for the benefit of the people running the schools.

Scott Ziegler was supposed to fend off the vipers. Instead, he became a viper himself.

He got on board the one-way train to the School of Woke.

CHAPTER 3

The Invention of Critical Race Theory

Critical pedagogy and its influence over the school system in America did not develop overnight. It has been lurking in the background in sheltered academia, taking little opportunities to advance where it can, waiting for the right time to strike.

Since the 1970s, Marxists have been developing an educational philosophy based on their dialectic way of viewing the universe. *Dialectic* means the interplay between thesis and antithesis. Marxists envision a form of child pedagogy in which everything, including reading and math, is framed within the dialectic of the privileged and the oppressed. In every place they have tried it, their pedagogy has failed, but that has not stopped them. What we will see is a band of ragtag Marxists, kicked out of their own countries for their failed philosophies, who came to the richest country in the world—America—to take advantage of its wealth and government largesse and incubate a new form of Marxist education that, when combined with the unique racial dynamics of our country, creates a potent poison that soon spread through our teacher's colleges into our schools: Critical Race Theory.

Paulo Freire and the Creation of Critical Pedagogy

In the 1920s, the state of Rio Grande do Norte, in northeastern Brazil— "the poorest and most underdeveloped area in the whole of Brazil," according to one writer—was a pit of depression and starvation. Nonetheless, it was a pit from which a star emerged.[1] In an accursed place where five hundred out of every one thousand babies died every year, Paulo Freire, the son of a police officer, lived and worked within this rigid feudal structure of paternalistic landlords, masses of illiterate, landless laborers (campesinos), and petty, deprived peasants. It was there where he wrote a book called *Pedagogy of the Oppressed*, which was published in 1968 and became a worldwide bestseller distributed in schools all over the world, especially in America.

What is *Pedagogy of the Oppressed*? It is a treatise that posits a radical alternative to traditional education. Its inspiration was Freire's own life: as a boy growing up in Pernambuco, Brazil, adjacent to Rio Grande do Norte, he saw his upper-class family fall into steep financial troubles during his youth. It was through this experience that he came to resent his former upper-class peers and found solidarity with the poor and working class instead. The introduction to the 2000 edition of *Pedagogy of the Oppressed* says: "It is the realization of such class borders that led, invariably, to Freire's radical rejection of a class-based society."[2]

In many ways, Freire's story resembles Lily Tang Williams's and Xi Van Fleet's. Both came from a society in which the lines of class, and of minority rule by an aloof elite, were drawn in permanent marker. And both women became profoundly cynical about those class lines. The difference between Freire on the one hand and Williams and Van Fleet on the other, however, is that Freire internalized those divisions while Williams and Van Fleet came to America and followed a different path—the American dream, which transcended the class-conflict philosophy of Karl Marx.

Freire was a lawyer for all of thirty days before he decided he'd had enough; his first client was a dentist who offered everything short of his eighteen-month-old daughter to pay his legal bills.[3] Moved by his client's destitution, the young idealist refused the dentist's payment, quit his profession, and set out to be an adult educator in a very poor part of northeastern Brazil called Angicos, in Rio Grande do Norte.

Angicos, a valley of death where no product beyond sugarcane was produced, was absolute hell on earth. It was there where Freire discovered the distressing moral and physical conditions of the working class. Born halflings, stooped from birth by poor diet and nutrition, dead at forty if not younger from overwork and exhaustion, these adults were not only uneducated, he realized; they also had no motivation to learn. The idea of learning did not speak to their experience as campesinos, beady-eyed slaves who sleepwalked between their labors and their tents day after day, survived on a starvation diet, and had nothing to live for and nothing to give them hope.

Freire began his mission of radically reforming education in Angicos—specifically, he taught skills-based education for underperforming adults—and his teaching methods became legendary within and beyond his native Brazil. The Brazilian educational savant held that he was able to teach a pack of illiterate adult sugarcane laborers how to read and write in just forty-five days, impressing the local authorities. He did so through a technique he developed called conscientization.

Freire started off by immersing himself in the lives of the campesinos in the area. He and his fellow educators lived the life of the poor, working long hours in the cane fields, experiencing the frustrations of the campesinos' daily grind. Then he began to collect an inventory of the campesinos' most common phrases—those using words such as *água* (water) and *beber* (drink). Then he selected among this inventory a few fairly complex words that spoke to the campesinos' living conditions. In fact, he selected only seventeen words in all. Among them was "favela" (slum), a core example used by Freire to demonstrate to the campesinos their plight.

Then Freire and his educators would draw a provocative illustration on a chalkboard of something resembling a "favela." The illustration would get the campesinos talking, a process Freire called decoding. The intention was to have the campesinos develop an emotional connection to the word "favela," knowing that it described and in fact encapsulated a lot of the peasants' deepest feelings and fears. Only then would "favela" be written on the chalkboard. The educators would strip the word down into its phoneme families, and the peasants would take apart those phonemes and form new Portuguese words. By the end of the first session, some people had already written other words down, and by the end of the fifth night, one peasant was already writing sentences.

It was a truly incredible achievement. Forty-five days later, the campesinos were literate. They could read and write and even start to compose full paragraphs. And Paulo Freire felt his conscientization campaign was vindicated. He was certain that only by motivating the peasants to *emotionally* connect the words with their class story could they truly learn. And the results suggested to him that this was in fact the case.

There's no doubt that Freire found in the German-born Karl Marx the proper tools for analyzing and deconstructing prevailing conceptions of class and society. In Brazil at the time, social classes were separated by level of education to a vastly greater degree than they are in modern-day America. It would have been totally natural for a young intellectual to find the vocabulary for deconstructing a truly class-based society such as Brazil's in the works of Marx, who analyzed social change in terms of large-scale, sweeping movements. "It was [the favela's] facts that led me to Marx," Freire admitted in an interview. "The hard facts."[4]

Freire viewed the world as a hostile, oppressive place where "oppression narratives" were deposited into children's minds, just as money is deposited into a bank. He believed that the only way to break free from this enslaving mindset was to activate children's political consciousness, their sense of estrangement from the world.

Later conflicts with the Brazilian government led Freire to be kicked out of his own country, forced to flee to America because of the radical nature of his ideas. But not before he produced a work of literature that permeates our educational discourse today.

This was his great work, *Pedagogy of the Oppressed*.

How Do Teachers Colleges Execute Freire's Theory?

A 2003 study conducted by education studies professors David Steiner and Susan Rozen found that all fourteen of the top-ranked teachers colleges in the country frequently assigned Freire's *Pedagogy of the Oppressed* in graduate-level philosophy of education courses.[5] The book has since sold a whopping 750,000 copies (in academia, that qualifies it as a world-altering bestseller), making it impossible to have a fully contextualized conversation about the modern education system without referencing this seminal work.

But the reasons why the Brazilian's tome entered the teaching curriculum are varied and often related to political interests. Stereotypically middle-class, obedient strivers with good grades cherry-picked Freire for insights that conformed to their own ways of looking at the world. I know this because some of these strivers have come out and said as much. In a remarkably self-reflective account of her own experience reading Freire, Latina American educational activist Blanca Facundo admitted, "We [educators] were not so much attracted by Freire's literacy method, but by the educational practice of liberation and struggle against oppression implied by Freire's educational philosophy."[6] In other words, she didn't really care for Freire's actual *method of teaching* but was instead interested in his ideological struggle against oppression.

Turns out Facundo was rather influential in exporting Freire to America. An organizer of a group of around three hundred candidates for a master's degree in "education, the humanities, or social sciences," the Latina educator felt enticed by Freire's liberatory education model and sought to execute it in America. Her account of her experience, although long and self-indulgent to the point of rambling (and certainly not worth printing in any kind of book that aims to have entertainment value), gives incredible access into the minds of teachers-college graduates around the time of Freire's peak notoriety.

"We felt indebted to the oppressed because we had been privileged, even if (and perhaps because) some of our families had been themselves oppressed and had 'made it' within the system. We did not have a very clear idea as to where we were going or precisely what kind of change we wanted, but surely enough we wanted change," she wrote.[7]

Change. Change NOW. Does this sound like a popular campaign slogan that rallies youth in the modern age? That's because it is. But it's a slogan and nothing more. The youths turned Freire's lifework into a marketing cliché.

As a result, nearly every liberatory education program started by Facundo and her social cohort in the 1970s bombed by the 1980s. The adult-education practitioner Thomas Heaney sat on a board overseeing these liberatory education programs and finally observed: "Most attempts to develop liberatory education in the United States have failed."[8] The federal government rescinded the grants for almost all these social-justice programs by the time Ronald Reagan came into national office, in 1980. Of course, the leftists would blame Reagan, but they hardly gave any presidential administration a reason for sticking around.

For one, they weren't teaching the students what the students actually wanted to learn. "It has been our field experience that, while we wanted to develop critical consciousness with learners, they wanted a high school diploma, or to learn English as a second language; and very rapidly, to get a job," Facundo writes sourly. Damn, Blanca—American students are more interested in finding a job than in learning about theoretical Marxism! And instead of catering to what these students wanted, Facundo and other self-anointed executors of conscientization told these students what they *should* want, then were surprised that they didn't want what the anointed thought they should want (which is being told they're oppressed). Who knew? "It was an exhausting and very frustrating endeavor. All our premises had been proved false by the learners," Facundo finally admitted.[9]

But let's say these students really did want to get inspired by the Marxist framework. The way these leftist educators went about teaching it was, well, astoundingly lazy. They basically did not follow any professional method of teaching at all.

They described themselves as "unplanned" and "spontaneously enthusiastic," but the better characterization might be "hippie." Only two of the twenty-four Latino Freirean educators given grants to do such work with children even *had* structured literacy programs for poor children; the rest basically relied on God and perhaps LSD to deliver reading and writing skills to their students.[10]

Maybe the left would be better at being the left if they worked harder at being leftists.

Look, even if we gave these educators all the excuses they wanted—Reagan, good intentions, and the like—American education was not the only sphere in which Freirean conscientization had been tried and failed. One of the biggest studies on conscientization as an educational literacy method—and one that is very similar to Facundo's efforts—was conducted in 2007 in Nigeria and involved three groups of around twenty illiterate residents outside of Ibadan, the country's third-largest city. All three parts of Freire's method were scrupulously applied basically to a tee: the insertion of the political situation into the minds of the students (through words such as those for "crude oil," "begging," and "poverty"), the creation of pictorial images that are explained through the lens of politics, and the translation of the pictorial images into phonemes.

Oh, the students achieved political consciousness, all right. So intently did they absorb the political imagery that they refused to learn literacy. Kester Ojokheta, a professor of education at the University of Ibadan, writes:

> After the completion of stage two [of the Freirean method], it came as a great surprise to the facilitators, that the discussants were not willing to participate in the literacy teaching/training process. They were in a state of emotional wreck. They were furious, angry, shouting and restless. They were shouting Change! Change! Change![11]

The students wept and gnashed their teeth, "cursing" the wind, screaming, "Why! Why! Why! Why!" blaming the instructors for not using their erudition to solve the massive problems of poverty and national corruption that pervade their society. They flatly refused to learn an inch of phonics. The instructors evacuated under threats of violence from the destitute, radicalized peasantry, who were hurling insults at the researchers on their way out.

Whatever Freire did in Angicos was a unicorn. By the late 1980s, it became apparent that Freirean "critical conscientization" was not going to help students learn, and grants previously made for that sort of effort dissipated in America: even a rich country like ours couldn't bear the weight of its failure. Yet the death of the liberatory education movement embittered a generation of formerly idealistic educators. In fact, it was the astounding tailspin of their idealism that gave birth to the mainstreaming of a new ideology to explain the predicament of poor, Black, and Latino children—Critical Race Theory.

Marxist Critical Theory Enters the Consciousness

In June of 1934, a German Jewish intellectual named Herbert Marcuse landed on Ellis Island to take a job at Columbia University in New York. He was part of the Frankfurt school, a culturally Marxist group of scholars predominantly composed of German Jews in exile who escaped from the burgeoning Third Reich and found asylum in New York City at Columbia's Teachers College and other elite universities.

The Frankfurt school was known for developing a new Marxist project called critical theory. In the wake of several failed Communist revolutions in the early twentieth century across Europe (and the disappointment in the wake of the one revolution that really worked, the Russian Revolution), the Marxists of the Frankfurt school began to rethink Marx's original theories to explain why the proletariat had been hitherto unsuccessful in bringing about its planned utopia. As exiled German Jews, they turned to their experiences within the fascist state of Nazi Germany for answers.

For Marcuse, the Nazi Party (or the National Socialist German Workers' Party) was a class-consciousness experiment gone horribly wrong. Part of what Communists tried to incite was a kind of seething class resentment in the working-class public. During the worldwide Great Depression, the Communists in the Weimar Republic gained many seats in the German Reichstag because of this political strategy. But what the Communists did not anticipate was that another party that preached resentment would also rise—except this party would preach resentment based on race rather than class.

Calling Jews a "race-tuberculosis of the peoples," ambitious political leader Adolf Hitler defined the Nazi Party in terms of a racial conflict rather than the class conflict that the Frankfurt school believed *should* be going on between the German workers and the German industrialists.[12] Invoking common stereotypes of Jews, Hitler asserted that the "Jew's feelings are limited to the material sphere," creating the illusion of a divide between what he viewed as greedy Jews and the rest of the supposedly innocent, victimized German people.[13]

Stop targeting Jews, Marcuse must have thought during some of Hitler's diatribes. *Target the industrialists and capitalists instead!*

America, however, was keen to look past that second thought of Marcuse's just because the Communist scholar was adamant about the first. The United States welcomed Marcuse and his supposedly antifascist Frankfurt school into its well-funded, ivy-encrusted academic halls and affluent neighborhoods. The US government even gave him a job: it let him help make anti-Nazi propaganda. Little did the bureaucrats know, however—or maybe they didn't care at the time—that they were welcoming a group of thinkers who were interested not only in intellectually fighting the fascist state but also in fighting what they perceived to be capitalist hegemony in America.

The Frankfurt school's theory was fundamentally anchored around a reimagining of Marx's capital power as social power—the idea that capitalism in America would be deconstructed by cultural rather than economic forces. Marcuse's fellow Frankfurt school thinker Max Horkheimer challenged us to see "the relationship that exists between intellectual positions and their social location."[14] That is, people at the top of the social hierarchy create a variety of supposedly rational and reasonable (in their view) justifications that sound good but whose real purpose is to legitimize upper-class power. If they can get people at the bottom of the social hierarchy to believe those justifications, all the better for the bourgeoisie.

This theory of social critique, in which the upper class seduces the lower classes with propaganda designed to keep them docile, Horkheimer calls *hegemony*. The theorists argue that the cultural institutions of the West at the top of the social hierarchy had preached a "hegemonic" narrative of hard work, individualism, and job seeking to poor people that undermined the Communist cause by giving optimism to those who worked *within* the system of capitalism rather than working to overthrow it, as Horkheimer wanted.

The Frankfurt school's solution to this problem was something its members called critical theory: an examination and infiltration—a *Kritik*, or critical analysis—of Western hegemonic interests to figure out how to ultimately take them down.[15] The assumption was that higher social classes were actively trying to keep lower social classes down—subtly, conspiratorially, but validly all the same.

If this sounds like an ideology of paranoia, it's because it *is* an ideology of paranoia. The dogged efforts of woke ideologues at your local school to "root out" racism, even where it doesn't exist, comes out of this critical-theory paradigm.

And no one better embodied this paranoia than a Harvard Law School professor named Derrick Bell.

Merging Marxism with Race

As the first Black professor of law ever hired by Harvard, Derrick Bell could have been grateful for the opportunity. Instead, he felt bitterness and rage at what he perceived to be the oppressive white establishment that had kept his people down for so long. Ironically, while Marcuse fled the racialized consciousness in Germany, Bell began to work on a new racialized consciousness in America—and who better to borrow from than the patron saint of dichotomization himself, Marcuse?

Bell was a street-smart thinker who followed the political current. Out in the streets, a Nation of Islam leader named Malik el-Shabazz, better known as Malcolm X, preached: "The white liberal differs from the white conservative only in one way: the liberal is more deceitful than the conservative."[16] Bell used Shabazz's rhetoric in his harsh critique of northern liberal desegregation initiatives, writing in a 1976 legal article that "civil rights lawyers were misguided in requiring racial balance of each school's student population as the measure of compliance and the guarantee of effective schooling."[17] Bell had a point. Northern desegregation initiatives in the South, prompted by *Brown v. Board of Education* and, more precisely, by *Brown II* (the follow-up to *Brown*, which mandated that desegregation had to be enforced with "all deliberate speed"), did not pan out as many people had hoped. In this sense, Bell was just speaking to ordinary Black frustrations with northern liberalism and integrationism.

But he used the fact that Black people increasingly opposed forced desegregation of the public schools as an excuse for him to deconstruct *all* of Western liberalism, including the greatest Western triumph of them all, *Brown v. Board of Education*.

In a 2004 speech at Stanford University, Derrick Bell shocked the intellectual world when he articulated his sincere belief that *Brown v. Board of Education* was a bad decision. "What *Brown* did for many African Americans was legitimate the status quo" of white hegemony, he said. "From the standpoint of education, we would have been better served had the court in *Brown* rejected the petitioners' arguments to overrule *Plessy v. Ferguson*."[18]

Yes, America would have been better off under *Plessy v. Ferguson*, the famous ruling that legalized racial segregation! There was a murmur of surprise from the listening crowd. But they shouldn't have been surprised.

Bell, significantly influenced by Freire and Marcuse, had been writing about America's secret racist conspiracy against Blacks for a long time, seeing most of America's major decisions as attempts to legitimize white supremacy underneath a veneer of color blindness. To Bell, all *Brown* did was replace overt racism with covert racism, and the most lauded Supreme Court decision in the history of the twentieth century was a mistake because it created a *false* unity, a unity that legitimized rather than attempted to overthrow white social hegemony.

The idea of covert racist hegemony influenced many young Black leaders at Harvard Law School during the time Derrick Bell was teaching, especially between the years 1986 and 1990. Hmm. What young Black male was studying at Harvard Law School in 1990?

Okay. I won't keep you guessing. It was Barack Obama.

Obama attended Harvard Law School during the period in which Bell abandoned his tenured faculty position in protest against the university's unwillingness to hire a Black female professor. In fact, Obama went so far as to *be the introductory speaker* at a rally where Bell formally announced his resignation. He said of Bell, after lauding his record of achievement: "How has he accomplished all this?... He hasn't done it simply because of the excellence of his scholarship, although his scholarship has opened up new vistas and new horizons and changed the standards of what legal writing is about."[19]

Obama concluded, "Open up your hearts, your minds, for the words of Professor Derrick Bell." The crowd roared as he embraced his Harvard Law professor in 1990.

In the following chapter, I will explore the ways in which Obama turned Derrick Bell's academic theories—now known as Critical Race Theory—into public policy. But notice this right now: as a young man, Obama admired Derrick Bell. He admired him because of the audacity of his scholarship. Bell and his Critical Race Theory acolytes were celebrity Black intellectuals seemingly beyond reproach. If even *Brown v. Board of Education* could be deconstructed and hung out to dry as an example of a white supremacist country covering its tracks, then every American government policy was ripe for the picking. This range gave Bell—and consequently Obama—a feeling of power, a high of superiority over even the Constitution and a beloved Supreme Court precedent. It is in this grand moral superiority, mixed with seething racial resentment, where we see the true of origins of Critical Race Theory.

Going Mainstream

Finally fully evolved, with its own deity (Freire), its own prophet (Marcuse), and its own evangelist (Bell), Critical Race Theory and the oppressor-oppressed dichotomy conquered the academic discourse surrounding race in just a couple of years, disproving critical race educator Gloria Ladson-Billings's famous 1998 lament that "I doubt [CRT] will go very far into the mainstream."[20] On the contrary, in just a few short years, CRT became the prevailing mode of legal scholarship at Harvard Law School before being promulgated by Teachers College, Columbia, and other academic institutions as the dominant mode of educational scholarship. Because these ideas were coming out of Harvard and Columbia as preferred paradigms about society, they were also the ideas that elite aspirants would adhere to in order to gain an edge in their careers.

The spread of CRT in education proved profitable for its early adopters. Ladson-Billings even became head of the influential American Educational Research Association, which disseminated her ideas to graduate schools of education everywhere. By the time the 2010s rolled around, CRT had not only gained a foothold in teachers colleges nationwide but had also become the central framework within which teachers were to think about *every* problem. "The proper mindset was...that America was inherently racist, and that was the message we should be giving to students, too," said teacher Daniel Buck, who was deluged with CRT philosophies at the School of Education at the University of Wisconsin–Madison before graduating in 2016.[21]

While CRT was consolidating its power over academia, it was also pushing out other modes of racial analysis that didn't rely upon the hegemonic premise once advocated by the Frankfurt school. (This is a good place to note there are indeed other racial analyses out there besides Critical Race Theory.) One such analysis was performed by social scientists Charles Murray and Richard Herrnstein at Harvard. In the 1994 book *The Bell Curve: Intelligence and Class Structure in American Life*, they argued that differences in IQ can explain a fair percentage of the differences in household income and level of education between white and Black Americans. Their analysis was directly extracted from data in the 1979 National Longitudinal Survey of Youth, which assessed around twelve thousand Americans. It found that Black Americans with similar IQs as whites were also as likely, if not more likely, to get a high-paying professional job and that the reason why more Black Americans than white Americans were at the so-called bottom of the socioeconomic ladder was centrally a result of IQ, with racism only being a minor factor.[22]

This book sold more than three hundred thousand copies and rocked the social-scientific world, but it especially challenged the Critical Race Theory view of America as a hegemonic, racist society. If differences in outcomes can be mostly explained by nonracial characteristics such as intellect, then CRT loses its luster as the defining theory of racial differences in America.

Obviously, people who thought that discrimination still played a large role in American racial differences felt threatened, and some lashed out to attack *The Bell Curve* as well as Murray and Herrnstein themselves. *New York Times* columnist Bob Herbert wrote that the book was "a scabrous piece of racial pornography masquerading as serious scholarship...a genteel way of calling somebody a n★★★er."[23] But even Herbert acknowledged that the central basis of Murray and Herrnstein's claims—that a Black person on average scored around fifteen points lower on a standard intelligence battery than a white person—was "a point that was widely known and has not been in dispute." Mainly, then, Herbert wrote his article to impugn the motives and character of the *Bell Curve* authors, and he wasn't the only one.

Threatened, Critical Race Theorists started to gang up on the Harvard social scientists like pack animals. Derrick Bell wrote, "Better one more libel of blacks as an inferior people than a truth posing a greater threat that could lead to racial atrocities and class warfare."[24] In 2022, nearly thirty years after *The Bell Curve*'s publication, Kimberlé Crenshaw, a Bell apprentice and official coiner of the term *Critical Race Theory*, even brought up the book in an interview about banned books, saying, "When I look at the list of topics now banned because they're discriminatory, I can't help but notice what's not there: eugenics, *The Bell Curve*, things that if there really, really was concern about teaching our children ideas that are divisive and that cause us not to share in our common heritage as Americans, it would be a whole different list."[25]

Eventually, the book became an academic pariah, and even mentioning its kind of analysis in an academic environment today will cause one to get whacked for upholding "scientific racism." Meanwhile, CRT embedded itself in the academic framework as the defining mode of racial analysis in America.

I don't deny that *The Bell Curve* is a provocative piece of reasoning, and it definitely does not offer the full story about racial disparities in America. But *The Bell Curve* has already been socially and academically ostracized. Meanwhile, the theory that white people are to blame for Black people's current problems—the practical purpose of CRT—only gets more popular and more ingrained in our culture.

So CRT advocates won that battle—the popular consciousness battle between cultural and genetic explanations of racial disparities and explanations based on a theory of a prejudiced and discriminatory country. The problem is, they didn't win the battle by arguing the theory's intellectual merits but by employing sheer thuggery and bullying. That leaves the debate between race and culture in our society today still, as a matter of fact, unresolved. In the chapters ahead, I will attempt to resolve this debate—both by showing that CRT's explanations for racial disparities are wrong and how and why CRT's solutions produce epidemic failure wherever they are tried.

When an intellectual opponent comes to you and argues, "Critical Race Theory is a theory found in academia," you can respond, "Yes. That's where ideas typically begin. And then spread."

CHAPTER 4

Fertile Ground for Critical Race Theory

B ut Kenny," you might ask, "isn't it true that Americans *have* oppressed Black people for a very long time? And isn't it true that that oppression can still manifest itself in the unequal educational outcomes of Black versus white kids today? Don't we have *some* obligation to help these Black kids, even if it comes at the temporary expense of the freedoms and satisfactions of white people?"

My short answers to these questions are, respectively: yes, yes, and maybe (my long answers will be revealed later in the chapter). But to what extent our efforts to ensure stronger outcomes for Black people have actually helped, especially in the field of education, remains an open question. The results suggest that there's a difference between answering these questions honestly and promulgating a Critical Race Theory viewpoint that posits that Americans are still secretly, conspiratorially racist.

The Gap

This is a chart showing the reading achievement gap in NAEP scores between Black and white kids for those Black and white Americans born between the years 1954 and 2000.[1] (The National Assessment of Educational Progress is a widely administered standardized test of fourth and eighth graders in the United States.)

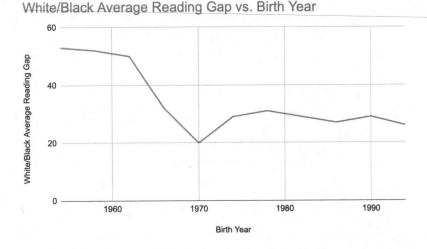

White/Black Average Reading Gap vs. Birth Year

Up until around birth year 1970, the gap between races on these nationally standardized metrics had been narrowing steadily, so that Americans could take comfort in the hope that one day Black children would be fully assimilated into American academic life, showing no differences from their white peers. Until birth year 1970, economists widely accept the idea that the closing of the racial achievement gap could be attributed to declining discrimination, the end of segregated schooling, and the increased availability of resources for Black Americans—changes that the civil rights movement was *supposed* to effect. But something happened around 1970—the testing years between 1980 and 1992—that has continued on into the twenty-first century: the racial achievement gap stopped closing. In fact, the evidence points to its starting to widen again—a horrifying, dispiriting trend for people who prize the ideal of fully equal outcomes in education.

(A similar trend could be witnessed in math NAEP scores.)[2]

Every three years, an international organization called Program for International Student Assessment (PISA) comes up with a standardized exam for fifteen-year-olds across the world.[3] Although there are issues regarding how much we should trust the countries that report PISA scores—the major cities of China, for example, report a rather high 579 on the assessment—it is still the best way to compare relative educational outcomes on basic math, reading, and science skills.

At face value, it looks like America is doing rather poorly on the PISA exams—in 2018, out of all "developed countries" taking the exam, we ranked a paltry twenty-third, behind Australia, Norway, and Slovenia, with an average score of around 495. However, if you look deeper, you find that our statistics have a glaring asterisk—one so jarring that PISA refused to refer to it in their in-depth report on America's PISA scores, leaving skilled researchers to nose through raw data to find it.

The average performance of Asian Americans is 549—highest in the world among all other developed countries except China (if China is to be believed). The average performance of white Americans is 521—good for third highest in the world, behind Estonia and China. The average performance of Black American fifteen-year-olds is 436, comparable to the scores of students in most developing countries in Africa and the Middle East.[4]

It's the most frustrating gap in recent American history because it shows a concerning stagnation of the movement toward the truly color-blind society we were hoping for, one in which we cannot predict differences in educational outcomes by race.

There are no easy answers to the question of why this gap remains. Some people have speculated that the decline of the Black family is a factor. As early as 1965, New York Democratic senator Daniel Patrick Moynihan wrote a report called "The Negro Family: The Case for National Action," widely called the Moynihan Report today.[5] And the situation described in its pages has gotten much worse since the report's publication. In 1969, the percentage of "illegitimate births" (out-of-wedlock births) among Black Americans was 29, while the percentage of illegitimate births among white Americans was a mere 4.5. Now, the proportion of such births among white Americans is the same as it was among Black Americans in 1969, while the proportion of out-of-wedlock births among Black Americans has reached a staggering 72 percent.

Moynihan pointed to a quotation by economist Edward Wight Bakke on the inability of the Black male to find meaningful work, thanks to white subjugation, and to the transfer of children, especially male children, to the care of two females (one being the government caseworker): "Already suffering a loss in prestige and authority in the family because of his failure to be the chief bread winner, the male head of the family feels deeply this obvious transfer of planning for the family's well being to two women, one of them an outsider. His role is reduced to that of errand boy to and from the relief office." By Moynihan's politically incorrect analysis, gathered from his government-sponsored work with Black Americans in their communities, the strip-mining of Black masculinity caused by racism and slavery results in a loss of pride so great that it impedes his ability to function in the world and consequently to raise his children. Consequently, the female takes on the twin burdens of raising children and working outside of the home, a burden so great that she can do neither with any real passion; thus the relationship between the sexes sours, and the family collapses. The man is deprived of his prestige, which drives his motivation to work, while the woman is deprived of her luxury, which drives her child-rearing. And this ruinous landscape still dominates certain sectors of Black America that drag down the community.

Other people, including Charles Murray, have suggested that IQ distributions in an IQ-stratified society are the main cause of poor educational outcomes in Black Americans. The IQ-centered analysis would argue that racism *has* hindered Black achievement—but has since become less of a factor—and that the current achievement gap is IQ-related (which does not imply that Black people are genetically inferior, because IQ is both genetic *and* environmental). The evidence that supports this is the IQ testing of a large random sample of white and Black people (more than ten thousand) as part of the National Longitudinal Survey of the High School Class of 1972. Murray found in 1994 that the average IQ of Black people in that sample was 85, while the average IQ of white people was 100.[6] Since then, the news has gotten (slightly) better: his new estimate, based on new tests and data he examined for his 2021 book *Facing Reality: Two Truths About Race in America*, places the average IQ of white people at 103 and the average IQ of Black people at 93, a significant improvement for Blacks. (The higher number for non-Latino whites is attributable to the influx of low-education Latinos into America starting in 1990.)[7] But as Murray argues in both books, a lot of things regarding IQ we *simply can't change*, at least not quickly—because IQ is at least in part genetic.

Critical Race Theory pushes back on both fronts, saying that all this—the IQ gap and the out-of-wedlock-births gap—is the result of racism and slavery. This is the most sympathetic argument Critical Race Theorists make. It is a powerful one, because we *know* that large swaths of America were truly racist for a long period of time. We *know* that that racism, spread out over centuries, could have profound consequences on the psychology of Black people. And we *know* that it would not be unreasonable, given these facts, for *someone* to shoulder the blame. But is it all of us non-Black people?

We Have Shared the Blame...and Here Are the Results

America has absolutely tried to solve the racial achievement gap. We tried with money, with accountability, and now we're trying with Critical Race Theory.

Total spending on public K–12 education has gone up at three times the rate of inflation since 1972[8]—and Black and Latino kids disproportionately benefit. In fact, University of Pennsylvania educational analyst Ericka Weathers modeled per-pupil spending by race between 1993 and 2014 and found that schools on average spent $229.53 more on Black children than on white children and $126.15 more on Latino children than on white children.[9] And President Barack Obama's 2015 Every Student Succeeds Act mandated that districts continue to be funded in a way that drives more money to Black and Latino populations.[10]

That money went to some of the most progressive districts in America, which then increased administrative bloat and promulgated an industry within the school system that uses taxpayer money to launch businesses, nonprofit organizations, and "equity" measures designed to take even more taxpayer money—without helping kids.

Example 1: Maryland Public Schools

The state of Maryland passed the Bridge to Excellence in Public Schools Act in the year 2000. The act called for roughly $1 billion in additional taxpayer funding to support "equity"—specifically, to close the achievement gap between Black and white children in Maryland, a gap that lawmakers attributed to "disparities" in funding. (Notice that attributing the achievement gap to funding disparities allowed school boards to avoid blame for shirking their responsibilities to these kids.) Representatives for the school districts told sob stories about kids who just need a little extra bump to achieve their biggest dreams. They waxed poetic about all these little children in need. They promised to establish career-preparation academies and hire better-educated teachers who would be well compensated.

The Bridge to Excellence program increased per-child spending per year from $8,921 in 2002 to $16,835 in 2017, raising state taxes an average of $1,000 per person annually during that period.[11]

"An analysis of trend data reveals that performance gaps by race and ethnicity have not narrowed over time across most of the measures considered," stated a report produced by the Office of Legislative Oversight of Montgomery County, Maryland's largest county, in 2019, nineteen years after the act was passed. The gap between Black and white scores did not decrease, countywide or statewide. The gap between Latino and white scores did not decrease. If anything, these gaps widened. Even the liberal *Washington Post* editorial board wrote: "The state's previous experience also demonstrated the shortcomings, if not outright failure, of increased education expenditures to produce better outcomes."[12]

We now have some data about where all this money went. According to the budget of Montgomery County Public Schools (MCPS), around a third of the allotted funds went into salaries for teachers based on teachers-union contracts.[13] The rest went into initiatives such as new facilities, the reduction of class size, and the salaries of new administrators. In fact,

Maryland is home to six of the top ten counties in America as measured by public-school-administrator spending. The money given by the state as part of the Blueprint for Maryland's Future seemingly disappeared into a vacuum and emerged in the contracts of hundreds, even thousands of new directors of technology, mental health counselors, and secretaries.

This is a hard pill to swallow. It demands scrutiny. But nineteen years later, in the face of their failure to close the gap with funding, a supermajority of Democrats in Maryland came right back to the well with a $4 billion proposal that would pour more money into "equity." They outright overrode Republican governor Larry Hogan's veto and forced a $3,000 average tax increase on Maryland families to fund it.

Increasingly desperate for money, the commission went full-bore into woke language—the icing on the cake. The new woke MCPS school board wrote that the district needed "a clear systemwide comprehensive approach to anti-racism."[14] Montgomery County schools superintendent Jack Smith, a witness in support of the proposal, even went so far as to say, "Research shows that the achievement gap disproportionately affects students of color and students affected by poverty," proposing an "Equity Accountability Model" as a solution. He demanded $450,000 from the state for an "anti-racist audit" in the wake of George Floyd's death.

Example 2: An Analysis of Nationwide Trends Between
Progressivism and the Racial Achievement Gap

Montgomery County, Maryland, is not an isolated county—it is an example of the overall effect that money has on progressive school districts nationwide. In other words, the more progressive a district is, the *higher* its racial achievement gap.

Perhaps this isn't shocking to you, but in the United States, the more people there are who vote with the left in any given county, the bigger that county's achievement gap between Black and white students is, in both math and reading.

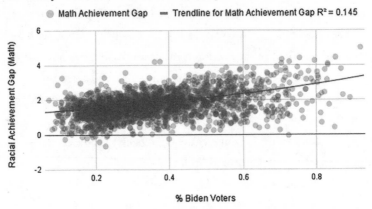

Above is a graph of the racial achievement gap in math in every county in America, gleaned from the Educational Opportunity Project at Stanford University, which produces one of the nation's most widely trusted databases of educational statistics.[15] Through this very simple comparative analysis, one can see that there is a weak but substantial correlation between how Democratic-leaning a school district is and how wide the achievement gap is between Black and white students.

Note that there is a slight upward trajectory in the racial achievement gap in math as the percentage of Democratic voters increases. In reading achievement (see below), the line is flatter but still worth noting.

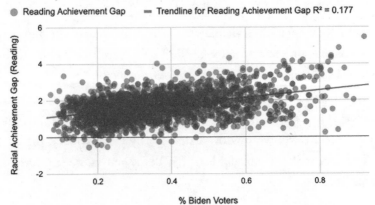

These graphs, at the very least, reflect the failure of progressive public-school governance to produce meaningful results for Black and Latino kids over time. If progressives continue to blame Black people's problems in America on "systemic racism," they must confront, then, their dispro-portionate responsibility in this "systemic" educational disparity.

It's time for America to have the wool pulled from their eyes. It's not enough now just to say, "We've tried." We have to carefully and ruthlessly evaluate what we have tried—and make changes when our trying has only led to more failure.

Example 3: No Child Left Behind—Equity Without Critical Race Theory

No one—no one—tried to effect a federal overhaul of the education sys-tem to help Black children quite as much as the Republican forty-third president, George W. Bush.

I'm serious. "America must close the gap of hope between communities of prosperity and communities of poverty," said Bush in a speech before the NAACP in 2000, just weeks before his election. "We have seen what happens—we've seen what happens when African American citizens have the opportunity they've earned and the respect that they deserve. Men and women once victimized by Jim Crow have risen to leadership in the halls of Congress."

The president was on tour to preach his particular brand of Republican politics, known as compassionate conservatism. To W, the problems faced by the Black community could be summed up in one word: respect. If African Americans (the overlong and now obsolete term for Black people used during the early 2000s) gained the "respect that they deserve," they would become leaders. Innovators. They would attain the highest posi-tions of power and, most important, would close the racial achievement gap between Blacks and Whites that had of course been around since the time of slavery and Jim Crow.

This is the definition of *equity*, a new word I will introduce formally in this chapter: it means that racial achievement outcomes should be equally balanced, and the reason why they aren't is because of lack of opportunity—even racism.

No Child Left Behind was politics' first response to *The Bell Curve*, which presented the possibly cynical view that true educational proficiency—the ability to meet a "grade-level" bar in performance objectives—was simply not a reality for a solid portion of the nation's students, particularly Black and Latino students. Bush said no to that viewpoint and sought to aggressively get Black and Latino students' scores up to the level where they would indeed catch up with those of white students.

It was W's Texas promise—the promise of the convergence of racial outcomes in education—that kicked off the twenty-first century, a staggeringly high bar set in an earnest southern drawl. But if people dismissed the Texan for his accent, they sure didn't dismiss the swipe of his pen. No Child Left Behind (NCLB), the landmark 2001 law signed by Bush, pledged to fulfill every single one of the president's promises made at the NAACP convention. In a sweeping preamble, it pledged to "close the achievement gap with accountability, flexibility, and choice, so that no child is left behind."

Bush's No Child Left Behind did several things: first, it greatly increased federal funding to schools, contingent upon schools achieving a proficiency objective based on standardized test scores. Basically, for schools to be eligible for certain federal funds, they needed to raise the students' average scores to a certain acceptable level.

The act also specified a punishment for schools that did not get those averages up in short order. From withholding federal funding to such measures as sacking a school's entire leadership department, it put teeth into the law and basically said: "We're not putting up with your bullcrap. [Exactly as W. would say it.] Do it or get cut."

Naturally, despite the increased federal funding for inner-city schools, No Child Left Behind became immensely unpopular with teachers unions and the administrators running them, forcing them to straighten out and raise test scores in order to increase their salaries. It was effectively a kick in the rear for them—and the lethargic, already bureaucratized educational industry flush with new money was not used to being kicked. Some schools straightened out right away: a significant portion of low-performing schools right below the threshold requirement whipped into shape and reached the goal in a year or two. Other schools, low on confidence, sank lower and lower. Overall, reading and math scores did improve during the first seven years of No Child Left Behind: math scores among nine-year-old Black students, for example, improved significantly on the National Assessment of Educational Progress, from 211 to 226, between the passage of NCLB in 2001 and 2012, but those gains were not sustained into high school and dissipated into insignificance by the time those nine-year-olds reached the twelfth grade. Thus the gains were too modest and too weak to weather the political damage No Child Left Behind did to a formerly core constituency—Republican suburban parents.

By inflicting a barrage of standardized tests on children, No Child Left Behind angered the wealthy, well-connected parents who would otherwise have been reliable conservative Bush voters. By 2008, then presidential candidate John McCain was unwilling to defend the law wholesale, and then presidential candidate Barack Obama made political hay by attacking it, winning suburban educated voters and later the presidency. "[Obama] has said [NCLB] relies too heavily on poorly designed tests to gauge progress in reading and math at the expense of a well-rounded education," stated a 2008 report on the National Public Radio program *All Things Considered*, an example of the nonstop barbs the Democratic candidate would direct at Bush's signature law.[16]

People think Iraq and the economy were the reasons why the GOP lost to an upstart Barack Obama in 2008. And both issues were factors—but people often forget that education was the third-most-important issue among all voters in 2008, according to the Pew Research Center.[17] It was also the issue that most energized Democratic and Obama-leaning voters: 83 percent of Obama voters thought education was an important priority, while only 61 percent of McCain voters thought the same. Education was becoming an issue in which Democrats were gaining a significant edge, largely because of the brimming frustration surrounding NCLB's testing provisions.

All the while, the Critical Race Theorists' characterization of the issue as an artifact of slavery and racism continued to pick up steam. Linda Darling-Hammond, then Obama's campaign adviser on education policy, quoted Ladson-Billings's framing of the educational issue as a "debt" in a 2007 article on No Child Left Behind. The fact that such a prominent educational figure, once considered by Obama to be the secretary of education, would echo the framework of a critical pedagogist on the campaign trail signals the mainstreaming of the Critical Race Theory narrative among the intellectual elite during Bush's presidency. Even as the country itself was at a zenith in its race relations (a time when 60–70 percent of both white and Black adults, the highest share ever, said that "relations between white and black people are very or somewhat good"),[18] the educational establishment was quickly and zealously putting forth an intentionally divisive narrative that pinned racial inequalities directly on systemic racism. Why? Because they wanted to ice the president they distrusted—the evangelical, anti-intellectual Texas hillbilly George W. Bush.

And they did. As soon as Obama took office, his policy advisers began to chip away at No Child Left Behind: by 2015, all that remained of the law was its federal money. The dismantling of No Child Left Behind's accountability provisions was Critical Race Theory's first major policy victory. The race-obsessed educational establishment, with the help of the newly elected Barack Obama, was able to lift the onus of blame from schools and clear the way for it to be placed on "America" and "racism" instead—exactly the way the school systems wanted it. With the end of Bush's signature law, schools lost nearly all their accountability metrics, and state bureaucracies and educational activists were able to choose their own direction without molestation—even if that direction was down.

In the Face of Lack of Progress, Obama Foments a Critical Race Theory Resurgence

The community organizer Barack Obama talked a good game about education during his speech in Thornton, Colorado, in 2008:

We don't have to accept an America where we do nothing about the fact that half of all teenagers are unable to understand basic fractions. Where nearly nine in 10 African-American and Latino eighth-graders are not proficient in math . . . This kind of America is morally unacceptable for our children. It's economically untenable for our future. And it's not who we are as a nation.[19]

On the campaign trail, Obama derided in moral terms the lack of progress in math education among Black students in the public schools, demanding a change that his administration promised to bring.

Did he bring change? He definitely did—just not in the way he promised. Eight years later, the entirety of his term, 87 percent of Black eighth graders were still not proficient at math, the same percentage as before he took office.[20] And the twelfth-grade scores during Obama's tenure are even worse: only 7 percent of Black and 12 percent of Hispanic children scored as "proficient" in math.

Rather, the Obama administration, guided by Critical Race Theory ideas that were quickly mainstreamed within the academy, did things that were counterproductive and set back the education system a great deal. The consequences continue to ravage children today. Based on the idea that America's educational system is racist, as argued by his law school professor and Critical Race Theory progenitor, Derrick Bell, Obama made it possible for Critical Race Theory in education to become a mainstream opinion during and especially after his tenure as President.

Let's talk about the forty-fourth president's guidance on school discipline during his tenure, for example. Critical Race Theorists have been arguing for decades that school disciplinary measures are responsible for the high rate of Black incarceration in American jails. As *Vox* editors Libby Nelson and Dara Lind elucidated in a 2015 article, the "school-to-prison pipeline" is a pejorative term meaning that when schools insist on "zero-tolerance" discipline policies and the presence of SROs (safety resource officers, also known as police on campus), it contributes to a military culture in the school and often increases juvenile detentions and suspensions, especially among Black kids.[21] Critical Race Theorists argue that "currents and stereotypes that flow in significant part from the long history of stigmatization in the United States affect school decision making," as law professor David Simson writes in the *UCLA Law Review*.[22]

Through his education secretary Arne Duncan, Obama initiated one of the biggest overhauls of school disciplinary policies in modern history, hinged on a narrative of systemic racism unprecedented in his time. Duncan announced on January 8, 2014, that the Department of Education (DOE) would be "investigating"—i.e., looking for civil rights violations—in schools that were disciplining Black kids at a higher rate than white or Asian kids.[23]

The government started prosecuting districts like mad, going after Anne Arundel County, Maryland; Lafayette Parish, Louisiana; Hillsborough County, Florida; and more than three hundred others as of January 3, 2017. If the government found one of these schools guilty of a Civil Rights Act violation based on a policy's "disparate impact" on Black kids, it could lose all its federal funding—around 8 percent of an average school district's total budget. So disastrous would the consequences of not complying be that schools resorted to active discrimination in favor of Black kids (willingly choosing to direct them away from detention or suspension, even when they need it) in order to avoid the risk of such funding losses. Legal theorist and University of California–San Diego professor Gail Heriot, in conjunction with scholar Alison Somin, wrote:

> School districts wishing to avoid costly investigations would need to avoid the kind of disparate impact that would attract OCR's [Office of Civil Rights] attention. The easiest and safest strategy would be clear: Reduce suspensions for minority students in order to make your numbers look good.[24]

The consequences of this DOE guidance on school discipline, especially for Black kids, have been severe. In some school districts, elaborate procedures were set out, requiring an "Equity Team" to ensure "social justice for all students" in disciplinary matters, increasing the power of ideological racism peddlers to determine whether students should be suspended based on the perception of "systemic racism." In other districts, as outlined in a settlement agreement between the DOE and the Oklahoma City public school system, for example, districts pledged to conduct "meetings" to "consider steps that can be taken to eliminate the disproportion to the maximum extent possible."[25]

Are these schools or prisons? One Black teacher with fourteen years' experience told the *Pioneer Press* of St. Paul, Minnesota:

> The students of [St. Paul public schools] are being used in some sort of social experiment where they are not being held accountable for their behavior. This is only setting our children up to fail in the future, especially our black students. All of my students at [John A. Johnson Elementary School] were traumatized by what they experienced last year—even my black students. Safety was my number one concern, not teaching.[26]

When personal safety is the number one concern for a teacher, learning and education are not likely to be priorities in the classroom.

The Obama-era guidance on discipline, informed by Critical Race Theory, produced massive, game-changing consequences for disorderly conduct in public schools across the nation. And the numbers speak for themselves: disorderly conduct complaints about school-age kids spiked 45 percent between 2011 and 2016 in Virginia alone, from 360 to 523. Unfortunately, Black kids were the subject of 62 percent of all such complaints.[27] Discipline issues are going up in schools across the nation because teachers and schools are afraid, or unwilling, to use disciplinary methods on Black students. And all this based on the insidious idea that schools and teachers are implicitly racist.

As the new era of Critical Race Theory in education dominates the public schools, we will see more blame shifted to teachers for failing to correct misbehaving kids, eventually creating a catch-22: don't discipline the kids, and they wreak havoc on your classroom; do discipline the kids, and the principal wreaks havoc on you.

Critical Race Theory Is Not the Solution

The persistence of our unequal education outcomes laid fertile ground for Critical Race Theory, and it is understandable why some people would buy into it. We as a nation should carry some motivation to improve, even some blame for, the position that Black kids are in in America. We've tried, and failed, as a nation to close the racial achievement gap between Black kids and white kids. We've really *tried*. And it would be tempting to blame this failure on hidden, conspiratorial racism on the part of the white elite.

But it's wrong. These are people with good intentions—and bad ideas. There are better ones. We've seen all-Black schools survive and even thrive in our country when parents and families buy into it. The Sisulu-Walker Charter School of Harlem, in Manhattan, is just one of many examples. A 2015 study conducted by Stanford University professor Caroline Hoxby found that the predominantly Black and Latino students who attended New York City charter schools like Sisulu-Walker from kindergarten to eighth grade could close around "86 percent of the 'Scarsdale-Harlem' gap—the difference in scores between students in Harlem and those in the affluent New York suburb—in math and about 66 percent of the gap in English."[28] Or, as economist Thomas Sowell pointed out, most of the students at the all-Black Dunbar High School in Washington, DC, continued on to college between the years of 1870 and 1955, even as "most Americans—white or black—did not."[29]

Making a claim that the administrators are secret racists, or that America *doesn't want* Black kids to succeed, undermines the success stories that exist in our country. Furthermore, these claims distract from the *real* problems that exist in our educational institutions today. It is not racism that explains why Black kids aren't succeeding at the level we wish them to. It's differences in intelligence, failed leadership, and forced change.

Which leads me to answering the question, Don't we have *some* obligation to help these Black kids, even if it comes at the temporary expense of the freedoms and satisfactions of white people?

The answer is that even if we do have such an obligation, we can't be guilted into making additional liberal or progressive calls for more money, more resources, and more power and legitimacy for the sake of "equity." Every time a Critical Race Theory–influenced pedagogy (or really, any idea that cites race as a justification for money and power) reaches the policy level, it fails, usually in an epic manner.

We have to work on the two central issues among low-income Black kids today: the decline of the family and the lack of discipline in the schools.

We cannot indulge these Critical Race Theory temptations any further.

An Economy of Victimhood

Although the accountability to No Child Left Behind stopped, the money didn't. In short order, between the years 1970 and 2012, the average cost to educate a child in the public school system from kindergarten to twelfth grade ballooned from an inflation-adjusted $56,903 to $164,426—and funding based on the ideological tenets of "equity" is among the chief reasons why.[1] State legislatures led the way in using the sob stories of Black and Hispanic children to demand ever-more-outrageous tax increases to fund "education" for the "disadvantaged."

That is a threefold increase in the cost of educating a child, but the child sees precious little of that money. So where did it go? Woke contractors and businesses adhering to Critical Race Theory have benefited from the nearly blank check that state and federal governments have given school systems over the course of forty years. When it rains, it pours.

As a result, we as a nation currently have the most bloated, least accountable education system in the history of the country—in other words, we live in a bubble.

What exactly is a bubble? According to *Investopedia*, an economic bubble occurs "any time that the price of a good rises far above the item's real value."[2] I'm going to take a few liberties with the term here to describe something that's not purely economic in economic terms: America's "investors" (the government) have put so much new cash into the system, even though the returns (skills and learning) don't come close to reflecting the value of the investment, that they've created a bubble. The money is disproportionately going to businesspeople and activists positioning themselves as woke.

With the deconstruction of No Child Left Behind and Obama's guidance on equity allowing alleged racism to control and shame the straggling bureaucrats, school districts and their woke patronage allies are effectively free to do whatever they want, leaving the ballot box as the only line of defense. During the 2010s, they proceeded to cultivate an embarrassingly large interschool economy rooted in the ideology of victimhood and based in Critical Race Theory.

This economy consists of an alliance among consultants, race-based nonprofit organizations, school systems flush in money from recent federal interventions, public speakers, teachers unions, and Democratic political bosses who facilitate an ever-more-permeable membrane of barter and trade within the public school system and outside the public consciousness—because, as they all realize or are cynical enough to believe, the racist public doesn't deserve to know what's going on in the school systems it funds.

Antiracism, Inc.

Before 2020 and George Floyd's death, Ibram X. Kendi—born Ibram Henry Rogers to a family of accountants—was at best a niche speaker and author whose most well-known book was called *Stamped from the Beginning: The Definitive History of Racist Ideas in America*. In this book, he claimed that that scientists Robert Boyle and Isaac Newton used their studies of light and color to establish that white was the "chiefest color." He wrote:

Isaac Newton took it upon himself to substantiate Boyle's color law: light is white and white is standard...Newton created a color wheel to illustrate his thesis. "The center" was "white of the first order," and all the other colors were positioned in relation to their "distance from Whiteness." In one of the foundational books of the upcoming European intellectual renaissance, Newton imaged "perfect whiteness."[3]

Kendi wasn't a premier intellect. But he was the man of the hour, one whom our school system raised up in a post–George Floyd 2020, when discussion about race in America reached its highest fevered pitch. During the protests surrounding Floyd's death, at the hands of a Minneapolis police officer, Kendi's 2018 book, *How to Be an Antiracist*, reached number one on the *New York Times* bestseller list.

And progressive school boards lavished him with taxpayer money.

Fairfax County Public Schools paid Kendi $44,000 in speaking fees and book purchases to conduct an hour-long Zoom webinar for teachers about "antiracism," according to *The Federalist*.[4] Charlotte-Mecklenburg schools, in Charlotte, North Carolina, paid Kendi $25,000 in taxpayer money for the same speech.

When questioned about the sum, Charlotte-Mecklenburg school board member Carol Sawyer responded, "To the extent that systemic racism appears in our culture, it also appears in our schools, and we need to root it out." Even Republican board member Rhonda Cheek, while disagreeing with Kendi's view that capitalism arose from the slave trade, supported bringing him in during the racial reckoning that surrounded Floyd's death. She believed— or was persuaded to believe in the emotional climate of the time—that Kendi's antiracism advocacy was fundamentally good and honest. She said, "I'm not thinking that there's a lot of people here that I would agree with on everything they say…but that doesn't mean that there are not parts of his work that would be very valuable on improving student outcomes."[5]

What we see here is a shift in language from the early 2000s. Although the 2000s political climate placed extraordinary focus on Black and Latino kids, even that era of American politics did not actively seek every opportunity to blame those problems on racism. That all changed with the economy of victimhood, led by pro-CRT advocates like Kendi, who realized that stoking the fires of racism was not just social justice—it was also good business.

Diversity, Equity, Inclusion, and Their Consequences

Enter the Diversity, Equity, and Inclusion industry. It started in the 1990s as a face-saving measure used by companies to show that they were complying with affirmative action laws. It has since evolved into an industry whose job is to *tell* companies they are racist—so that they can make face-saving, widely publicized changes to help them avoid discrimination lawsuits and public pressure from progressives. For example, in 2021, the credit-card company American Express brought in Khalil Muhammad, a sought-after DEI speaker, to train its employees in the theory that capitalism is racist.[6] Perhaps the irony that these employees worked for a credit-card company was lost on management.

The pay for Diversity, Equity, and Inclusion chairs at big companies and universities is simply enormous. Google reportedly spent $114 million on its diversity program in 2014; it employs a chief diversity officer who makes north of $190,000 a year.[7] The University of California–Berkeley's first head of "Diversity, Equity, Inclusion, and Belonging" made an astounding $200,000 a year.[8]

But it's not just about the pay—rich though it may be. It's also about the immediate gratification one gets from being in a position where—finally—people have to kiss up to *you* or you can say, "Off with her head."

Let's not kid ourselves: the power to control your company's narrative on race *is* an attractive position to be in, and not just for a sociopath. Have you not felt, at least at one point in your life, the lust for the power to tell somebody to *just shut up*? That's what DEI officers are able to do at these schools and companies: they are able to control the narrative and use moral righteousness to shut people down—using the power of the word "racism" to zip the trap of anyone they disagree with.

And our top Black talent is increasingly choosing DEI career paths, a choice that inspires resentment against them, rather than career paths in math, science, or law, which afford respect based on productivity. A 2019 survey of the top 250 companies in the United States revealed that 63 percent of them had filled new Diversity, Equity, and Inclusion positions in the previous three years—most of them with Blacks.[9] Meanwhile, the number of Black lawyers has not increased since 2011.[10] Even with preferential admissions policies, the number of Black males in medical school in 2022 is lower than it was in 1978.[11]

Although plenty of Black students initially *want* to pursue these high-value STEM and law professions when they come to college, they disproportionately end up without the requisite degrees. Peter Arcidiacono, a Duke University economist, found that Black students admitted to Duke have a higher rate of *wanting* to declare a STEM major than white students do. But Black students graduate with a STEM major way less frequently than white students do—a 62 percent expected STEM graduation rate versus a mere 29 percent final STEM graduation rate.[12]

Some of this is the result of affirmative action mismatching Black students into overcompetitive pools at universities, a policy extensively covered in my book *An Inconvenient Minority*. But another reason is because of the "pull factor" of the social advocacy majors—the same pull factor that lured a young Barack Obama into social-justice advocacy. Not only did he feel like he was "making a difference," he was also rewarded immediately by the institutions that praised him for doing it—in particular, Harvard University.

And these same institutions are still pulling the highest-tier Black students away from STEM and into social justice with greater-than-ever incentives. Harvard announced the creation of a $100 million fund to "atone for [its] role in slavery." The massive fund would be spent on "teaching, research and service" and would aim to discover and publicize Harvard's role in perpetuating slavery and racism in America. Its supporters, such as the Harvard president, Lawrence Bacow, called the fund "a moral responsibility to do what we can to address the persistent corrosive effects of those historical practices on individuals, on Harvard, and on our society."[13] Harvard plans to spend the money on "dialogue, programming, information sharing, relationship building, and educational support." Its recommendations include: "1. Engage and Support Descendant Communities by Leveraging Harvard's Excellence in Education" (i.e., hire social-justice educators and social-justice administrators); "2. Honor Enslaved People through Memorialization, Research, Curricula, and Knowledge Dissemination" (i.e., build buildings and monuments dedicated to opponents of slavery and racism); and "3. Develop Enduring Partnerships with Black Colleges and Universities" (i.e., establish social-justice coalitions and hire their directors).[14] Each of these recommendations requires the institution to dole out jobs to college graduates who come from the social-justice arm of the elite-college industry.

Meanwhile, business schools are now creating Diversity, Equity, and Inclusion majors—majors specifically intended to recruit Black kids into business schools and pump up their diversity numbers. Are these affirmative action programs even helping the larger Black community succeed? Some Black leaders—leaders that hardly anyone would call right-wingers—think not. The Black civil rights leader W. E. B. Du Bois wrote in 1903 that for Blacks to achieve true equality with whites, a "Talented Tenth" must lead them—a gifted minority of the Black population that attends college and can reform the uneducated masses of Blacks in America. Yet Du Bois stressed that these Black students must be educated in a certain moral manner: "[Education] must strengthen the Negro's character, increase his knowledge and teach him to earn a living," he proposed.[15]

The current way that our "higher" education system is deliberately treating young, talented Black people—as weak minority tokens capable only of social-justice degrees—is appalling. It is antithetical to Du Bois's ideals. It is harming the "Talented Tenth" of Black America by driving them to the economy of victimhood, which seeks division and failure rather than color-blindness and improvement.

The Cost (in Dollars) of Critical Race Theory

Now I should attempt to answer the question, How much does CRT's economy of victimhood, built into our educational bubble, really affect our K–12 public schools? This is, of course, an impossible question to answer exactly or even reasonably. But I feel obligated to at least put some numbers behind what I'm asserting so the quantitatively inclined people among us can wrap their minds around the true costs of CRT entering the schools.

In total, Loudoun County Public Schools spent between $1 million and $2 million on addressing the fallout of the Underground Railroad incident in the school year 2019–20. The money was spent on equity consultants, antiracism reports, and the diversity trainers profiled in chapter 1. But that does not include all the indirect spending, such as fees paid to lawyers for writing briefs, fees paid for office space to shelter this economy of victimhood, and the cost of the human and capital resources it took to bring these corporations in to do their work in the district. It also does not include the hours spent by administrative staff who were morally navel-gazing and indulging the whims of the diversity industry. How many millions of dollars does that add to the calculation? A conservative estimate, based on an average legal billing of $250 an hour for a fifty-hour project, would be around $125,000 for the briefs. Then consider the hiring of a chief equity officer. He or she needs a room, a secretary, and other resources. That's another $50,000-plus.

Still, a defender of LCPS might argue that even if the total cost of all these initiatives was around $2 million a year, that's just a tiny fraction—0.1 percent—of its total annual budget, which stands at $1.5 billion.

But now we have to get into the second-order effects.

First, we have to consider the learning time lost because of businesses like Panorama Education and the teaching time lost because of training in Critical Race Theory. In Loudoun County, teachers went through three-day seminars in "critical pedagogy," and students took one to two hours of their class time to complete Panorama surveys. Yet the total learning hours lost doesn't count the number of hours children spent thinking that their lives are a mess because of their sex and race rather than learning and really engaging with educational content. A teacher paid $60,000 a year who has to spend three days learning Critical Race Theory probably costs the district $500 for those three days, and with six thousand teachers in the district, the cost for the training comes to something like $3 million.

Second, regarding the decline in performance attributed to Critical Race Theory: an Ohio State researcher named Vladimir Kogan found that student performance in some five hundred school districts nationwide declined during periods of intense political controversy, a phenomenon he labeled the "Loudon County Effect."[16] He found that the "relative downward movement" in learning attributed to school controversies "accounts for about 5 percent of a full year's growth in the subject," losses that persisted even four years later. Now, liberal publications will spin this as "when parents meddle in the affairs of teachers, learning declines," but we know that Critical Race Theory in schools is a deep, entrenched issue that involves more than just complaining parents—and we know that Loudoun County walked itself into this controversy with its mismanagement and political pandering.

A 9–11 percent learning loss in math over the course of one year, if allowed to remain permanent, is estimated to be equivalent to a roughly $43,800 per person loss in lifetime earnings, according to Harvard University's Center for Education Policy Research.[17] So a 5 percent learning loss, if scaled linearly, would amount to $22,000 a person. Multiplied by LCPS's 81,000 students, that would total $1.78 billion in lifetime earnings loss.

I'm not going to prognosticate that CRT will cost Loudoun County students $1.78 billion in lifetime earnings; there are too many other factors at play to make a rigorous assessment. But I'm showing you that small but persistent effects have gigantic second-order repercussions. As long as CRT and the economy of victimhood is allowed to stay within the school system, superintendents and school boards will make bad decisions that will have millions—and indeed, *billions*—of dollars' worth of repercussions. From failing to hire meritocratically because of racial goals in hiring to failing to discipline unruly children because of equity-related guidance to setting low expectations for Black kids because of reluctance to look like a racist, the effects are difficult to measure, but we know they can occur in a school system as a result of Critical Race Theory. China's Marxist Cultural Revolution, for example, precipitated a "brain drain" in which the country's top talent was persecuted and excellence diminished. That Cultural Revolution caused China to enter a deep economic depression and eventually led to a technological and infrastructural disadvantage from which the country is only now recovering. Today, China is still walking out of the hole that Mao Zedong created.

A nearly $2 million price tag for incorporating Critical Race Theory into the pedagogy of a single school district is just the start if the ideologues are left unencumbered. In fact, the costs of just one or two DEI consultants will become costs associated with learning loss, distraction, and lack of discipline if these consultants come into power. Because the leaders make it clear: Critical Race Theory is an ideology that enriches its practitioners by oppressing everyone else. Unless school districts get back on track and eliminate every CRT position under their jurisdictions, the ideology will continue to fester until it costs tens of millions of dollars and the learning lives of thousands of students.

When Will the Bubble Burst?

At the beginning of this chapter, I described the economy of victimhood within the education industry as a bubble. I described it this way because the level of investment in it is far outpacing the value of its services. Sadly, because public education is largely a government expenditure, the bubble can be sustained theoretically indefinitely. Of course, these expenditures, without subsequent policy reform, will reduce our country's investments in infrastructure, health care, the military, and social services. Meanwhile, our children are not benefiting from the massive increase in education spending. The woke businesses, contractors, and other actors wedded to Critical Race Theory are. The bubble will not burst like that of a stock market. But the declining quality of educational services will be reflected in the decreased competence of teachers, administrators, and, ultimately, students. By nourishing the economy of victimhood, we are nourishing our country's worst instincts, taking advantage of Americans' liberal generosity and desire to help Black and Hispanic kids. But the economy of victimhood only enriches people and woke structures that will do neither.

This is what's at stake with the inversion of our schools. In part 2, I will examine how the woke phenomenon is affecting the most critical task we face as a nation—the education of our kids.

PART II

DYSFUNCTIONAL CHILDREN

CHAPTER 6

Maiming Childhood

Three hundred miles south of Loudoun County, in wagon wheel country, the Republican lieutenant governor of North Carolina, a five-foot-eleven, three-hundred-pound Black man named Mark Robinson, confronted a gaggle of reporters at his mansion. Clutching a towel to wipe the sweat pouring from his face, he had just declared a massive investigation for the purpose of ridding North Carolina schools of books such as *Gender Queer*, which he called "pornographic," as well as any CRT-influenced history textbooks.[1] "We are not going to stop until the schools of North Carolina are safe from this kind of filth!" he steamed. His tirade against the books broke practically every rule of politically correct 2020s America, including the first one, Don't insult the LGBTQ community, and the second one, Don't try to ban books.

At his front porch, where the press conference was being held, Robinson held a prop—a wooden board that had on it an enlarged page from *Gender Queer*. In the book, by cartoonist Maia Kobabe, the protagonist explores her relationship with her gender-nonconforming identity, ultimately coming out as gender-fluid. Borrowing its sexual themes from the Queer Theory book *Curiouser: On the Queerness of Children*, *Gender Queer* is a sort of teen-pop explication of Queer Theory, positing the notion that "heteronormative" society is oppressive and that things like innocence, modesty, dress codes, and chastity are constructs used to oppress the queer child's inner self.

A *Publishers Weekly* review writes in a parenthetical aside that *Gender*

Queer contains "some sexually explicit content." That's a bit of an understatement. In the scene Robinson displayed, the protagonist blows into the erect penis of his sexual partner, with all the genitals explicitly drawn. Although Robinson used this obscene image to rally his Republican campaign supporters, his feelings about the book, which was found in libraries of North Carolina's Wake County, among others,[2] reflected a larger populist upheaval against books adhering to new forms of gender- and racial-oppression ideology first promoted in America by Critical Race Theorists and Queer Theorists.

Robinson's focus was on LGBTQ issues, but other North Carolina officials fixated on Critical Race Theory. A school superintendent removed from the English curriculum at Tuscola High School, in Haywood County, a book previously assigned to a tenth-grade English class, *Dear Martin*, by Nic Stone. The book is about a Black teenager at a white prep school who, on track for admission to an Ivy League college, finds himself in a difficult run-in with the police. The parent who suggested the book's removal said the book contained too many s-words and f-bombs. A close reading of the book, however, reveals other disconcerting issues besides the language. On the first two pages, the protagonist, a Black male teenager named Justyce, describes his ex-girlfriend in artless physical detail, particularly her curves and sexual organs. You're not reading *Lady Chatterley's Lover* so much as you're reading the degenerate mind of a seventeen-year-old. Then, within the next ten pages, the boy is assaulted by a police officer while trying to help his ex-girlfriend drive home. The situation depicted in this scene is probably the worst police altercation one could dream up for a Black teenager short of lynching. The officer (Officer Castillo, an obvious nod to the half-Latino officer who shot Trayvon Martin, in 2012) accosts Justyce, pins him to his car roughly, then locks him in burning-hot handcuffs, foul-mouthing him with all kinds of slurs and racist tropes. It's a nightmare that would enrage any kid and perhaps strike intense personal fear in the Black kids reading the book, especially since Justyce was clearly written as a kind of representational stand-in for young Black males everywhere. Throughout the book, Justyce grapples with racial stereotypes, including those in his own family, concluding in an imaginary conversation with Martin Luther King Jr., whom he address in his journal, and tells that he does not want to be like him.[3] He repudiates King's color-blind dream, claiming he wants to see the world his own way, based on his own experience.

Yes, the book speaks to very real racial anxieties that Black teenagers have across the United States. In one scene, Martin, after witnessing the death of his friend (shot by a police officer), visits the leader of a Black jihadist gang. Although he quickly leaves, he realizes that the temptation to completely cut himself off from American society is there, lingering in his head, as it lingers in the head of many Black teenagers.

But this doesn't mean that the book helps assuage any of these anxieties or channel them in productive ways. Because race *is* a reason that many Black boys don't even bother trying to assimilate into American society, the school system has a special responsibility to handle these issues with care. These are not issues to be taken lightly. If a Black boy comes out of a book like *Dear Martin* thinking: *Man, no matter what I do, this country will always be against me,* his outlook on life is devastated. And if that message is endorsed by the school via a classroom assignment, it could crush him.

"If you still think of attachment in the most simple way...it's [about] how you feel about yourself [and] how you feel about the world, and it's either good or bad," Natalie Mroz, a Florida-based clinical psychologist, said in an interview with me. "If from an early age, people are telling you the world is dangerous, the world is bad, don't go close to strangers or go out in public, you develop a very clear 'others are bad, the world is bad' [mentality]. And so you either develop an avoidant attachment style if you think [of] yourself [as] bad...or more of a narcissistic style...to be able to think 'I'm good; everyone else is bad.'"

Natalie touches on things here that are essential to early childhood education. Yes, a child's feelings, including those of marginalization and lack of self-respect, should be validated. But they need to be validated in a way that makes the child feel comfortable in the world and society rather than at odds with them.

Lieutenant Governor Mark Robinson was saying rather bluntly what could be said with sensitivity. But the principle is the same: "Everything is permissible for me—but not everything is beneficial," said the apostle Paul.[4] We can say that pornographic books have a right to be published while also criticizing the content and intentions behind them.

After all, if words truly can affect children's lives and outlook on life, why don't we offer children the words that truly build them up and help them see a world of opportunity? Rather, Critical Race Theory uses language that compels children to see the opposite.

The Way Things Ought to Be

Every moment in Mark Robinson's life could have come from an episode of a long, emotional television show about Critical Race Theory.

He was the ninth of ten children born in a poor East Greensboro, North Carolina, neighborhood. And Mark Keith Robinson had learned some awful lessons early in life, making mistakes that threatened to turn him into just another statistic. Before he married his wife, he had gotten her pregnant and asked her to get an abortion. Even though he went to college, he initially failed to take advantage of it. After college, he got a job in a factory, but the position was cut after the factory moved to Mexico.[5]

He also believed common stereotypes about certain ethnic groups that threatened to hold back his social advancement. "I saw there was always this aura of suspicion [around Asian people], always this thing where people would say, 'Oh, he's an Asian kid, so he's always going to get valedictorian in the class,'" he recalled in an interview with me.

Critical Race Theory—the relentless pounding of the racism narrative, with its emphasis on oppression by white people and other races, into the heads of young Black men—pervaded this poor part of East Greensboro, in this poor part of the South, in this poor part of the country. It certainly stuck with an impressionable Mark, who spun his wheels for many years. "One of the things we [as Black folk] deal with is jealousy and suspicion," he said. Even in college, he was told that Republicans, conservatives, and "the system" were out to get him, specifically because he was Black. This was a bad thing, because the majority of people around him were self-described conservatives. If this wasn't Harvard Law School's version of CRT, this was certainly its working-class iteration. Mark constantly dealt with words intended to denigrate, words that made him feel like a useless laborer in a machine designed to flatten him.

But the systemic-racism narrative worming its way between Mark's ears had not yet fully taken hold of his brain. During late childhood, Mark felt the divine presence of words from God, and his Christian faith became a big factor in his life. At his church, he learned words that helped build him up and restore him. He learned that God does not make racial distinctions; that God views all humans as His children.

He also had a few friends who nurtured him out of the vicious cycle of endless racial grievance. When he was in college, Mark was watching television with one of these friends when the screen cut to one of the most famous talk-show hosts of his time, a man named Rush Limbaugh, who was gearing up to host his daily program.

"I cannot stand that guy," Mark muttered to his friend, Wayne.

"Why?" Wayne asked.

"Cuz he's a racist," Mark Robinson, a Black college student out of East Greensboro, said about the red-faced man on the television. He gestured toward the set, as if it were self-evident. But Wayne, surprisingly, did not play along.

"Well, do ya know him?" Wayne asked Mark with bemusement.

"No," Mark replied.

"Have ya ever read any of his books?"

"I dunno," Mark said, a bit taken aback by his friend's sudden lack of compliance with the turn of the conversation.

"Don't ya think that's a bit of a *high* charge to say this man's a racist, and ya don't know him?" Wayne asked.

And Mark said no.

Wayne said: "Ya know, one time ya told me, when it came to television, ya said television misrepresented what Black people are like. Ya told me television said that Black people are thieves and they don't take care of their families and they're criminals. Ya said the TV could be lyin' about Black people. How do you know the TV ain't lyin' about Rush Limbaugh?"

Mark got angry at Wayne. Wayne had circumambulated his stick-in-the-mud worldview, turned it on its head, and left him without a response.

The next day, rattled, Mark went to a bookstore and picked up Rush's book *The Way Things Ought to Be*. He read through it, scanning for racist material.

He left realizing that he, like Rush, was a conservative.

You see, the young Mark *had* learned some things, things that Rush simply reminded him of, things that taught him something else besides the idea that there are ingrained caustic differences between him and white people.

He was led to recall a time in high school when a teacher used a language of common humanity that humbled him and diminished his anger at the world.

"I can remember back in the eighties, when I was first learning in school about the Civil War, and I had a very good teacher, an individual named Mr. Richard Sisk, and I distinctly remember him saying in class one day that slavery wasn't a white issue or Black issue. It was a human issue, and slavery needed to be solved by good people of all colors," Mark recalled.[6]

Mr. Sisk framed the issues leading up to the Civil War as issues of the heart, as issues we as humans can work together to solve. Mark realized that domination, racism, prejudice, the emotions that lead to the enslavement of others—these are conditions of the human heart (and of sin, he would later read in Scripture). The reason why the young Black boy's teacher said the Civil War was neither a white nor a Black issue was not because he didn't believe the fact that white people in America were largely the perpetrators of the enslavement of Blacks but because he believed that all people carry the sickness of the human heart inside them—white *and* Black (and Asian and Hispanic and everything else). Although it was mostly whites who perpetuated and protected slavery in the United States, the condition of prejudice is not *unique* to whites. Rather, any race is capable of such hatred—and acknowledgment of that fact can lead one to empathize and even forgive the other race in the interest of the greater cause of true racial unity.

There are two approaches to seeing race in America: seeing the humanity in an enemy or seeing an enemy in another human. Mark Robinson transitioned his perspective from the latter to the former through a language that disrupted his oppositional worldview. I will now describe how CRT transitions children's perspectives from the former to the latter.

Seeing Racism in Everyone

Carin Bail saw firsthand what CRT "pioneers," expanding CRT from sea to shining sea, ultimately wanted to do with children. The elementary school teacher in New York City's School District 28 was in charge of a mostly Bangladeshi group of first graders. One day, a CRT trainer under the umbrella of an "inclusiveness" group came in to do a workshop with her kids. "There was a 'Wheels on the Bus' video shown on the screen," she recalled in an interview with me. "A Black woman [CRT] trainer comes in and…asked the class, 'Do you know what was different [in this video]?' "

"They all had yellow hats!" screamed the children.

"No." The trainer frowned. "Try again."

"They were all working together!" screamed the children.

"No." And Carin, sitting in the back of the room, wondered, *What is this trainer up to?*

Finally, a little boy in the front of the room named Mohammed said, "They all have dark-colored skin!"

"Yes!" The trainer jumped for joy. "That's it!" And she proceeded to lecture the students, telling them that the dark-skinned kids on the bus had less privilege than they would have had if they were white.

Carin couldn't believe it. The whole exercise was designed to push the students to see race. It was designed to foster hatred based on skin color. "I confronted her," Carin said. "And she just said, looking at me like I was the scum of the earth, 'Wow, you seem angry about this!' "

Carin's experience seeing CRT trainers indoctrinate little children with racial consciousness is hardly unique. In the Burlington Area School District, in Wisconsin, a teacher named Melissa Statz passed out a worksheet to her fourth graders called "The Black Lives Matter Movement."[7] On the front cover was a gingerbread-like illustration of two brown children frowning and holding up signs that said JUSTICE and EQUALITY in big bold letters. Their faces were unhappy. Their mouths were turned down. Everything about the illustration radiated discontent.

Inside the worksheet was a list of words such as "protesting" and "racism"; kids were instructed to choose words from this list and fit them into the blanks in a series of sentences. Elsewhere on the worksheet, they could read the story of George Floyd's death at the hands of a police officer. They could read that "systemic racism happens" because the "people who make the rules are usually not people of color" and "people of color do not benefit in the same ways that white people do." Melissa Statz led kids to believe that the central reason why systemic racism in America resulted in the killing of George Floyd was because there are too many white people at the top giving orders. In other words: racism is around, racism is everywhere, and young minority kids should be cognizant of it wherever they go. This is CRT in action within the schools.

When questioned about her worksheet, Melissa Statz said, "I need to fight for all children of color," NBC News reported.[8] And in her eyes, she is. *She's* telling the "dark truth"—white people own the machinery of America to keep Black people down. *She's* explaining to these kids the harsh reality that no matter what they do with their lives, they will be subjugated because of something they can't control.

But does Melissa Statz think about the harmful effect that constant exposure to words such as "protesting," "racism," and the like can have on a young, vulnerable minority child? Does she think about the *damage* she could do to a child by pointing him in the direction of fear and suspicion of other people—especially when new research suggests that Black people in general are more sensitive to these downward-spiral narratives than other races?

In 2021, Eric Kaufmann, a professor of politics at Birkbeck, University of London, surveyed Black adults about whether they would say yes to the statement "When I make plans, I am almost certain I can make them work out."[9] Ordinarily, 83 percent said they would answer affirmatively, but when a subset of them read a passage from Black writer Ta-Nehisi Coates's book *Between the World and Me* that states, "In America, it is traditional to destroy the Black body," the percentage went down to 68 percent. The drop points not only to the depressiveness of the passage but also to Black people's susceptibility to it.

Discrimination and racism are stressful narratives that weigh down on a person. Studies conducted by the American Psychological Association found that nearly one quarter of adults say that discrimination is a major stress factor in their lives. That number increases to around 40 percent among African Americans and Hispanic Americans. Now imagine how much the percentage would increase among minority teenagers. Teachers need to be careful about the ways in which they teach racial justice, even to whites—14 percent of white Americans also state that discrimination is a stress factor in their lives.[10] It's extremely difficult to teach such heavy topics without putting additional stress on young minds.

And yet Black Lives Matter curricula are popping up all over the nation, turning children into resentful, indignant individuals. Take a look at Melissa Statz's worksheet: the cartoon kids on the cover aren't smiling. They're angry. Should all kids be angry, too?

Alternatives to CRT Curricula

Shouldn't kids learn to forgive? To empathize? These virtues are absent from CRT, which positions the races in eternal, perpetual conflict. But the virtues of forgiveness and empathy are remarkably closer to our discourse than anyone watching today's media would think.

Go outside the blogospheres and the media-saturated educational schemas and you discover something—people generally get along. Even people of such radically different orientations as a Black man and a KKK member can come to understand each other. In contrast to CRT's view that the two sides will always be tussling, we have stories in America that show this isn't true—stories we can teach our children as a way to model the kinds of values that *truly* advance the cause of racial harmony.

Daryl Davis is the hero of one of these stories. One of the top blues and boogie-woogie musicians in the nation, he spent the latter part of his career touring and performing—and winning the hearts of the Ku Klux Klan.

As a multi-instrumentalist playing in smoky bars across the United States, Daryl encountered a wide variety of people in his young adult days. One time, at a country-and-western bar in rural Maryland, Daryl performed a rollicking set, a real barn burner. After entertaining the crowd, he sat down at a table to catch his breath. And a white gentleman walked over and put his hand on the Black man's shoulder. "This is the first time I've ever heard a Black man play as well as Jerry Lee Lewis!" he said enthusiastically.

"I wasn't offended," Daryl said, recounting the story, "but I was surprised." The man's overt racism caught him off guard. But the fact that it was *combined* with a strangely gregarious spirit really threw him off. So he didn't call the man a racist immediately. Rather, he asked sincere questions in a lighthearted way.

"Where do you think Jerry Lee Lewis learned how to play?" he asked the man.

"What are you talking about?" The man cocked his head.

"Jerry Lee learned that style in the same place I did—from Black blues [and] boogie-woogie piano." And Daryl smiled and turned away.

But the man persisted, refusing to buy it. He thought Jerry Lee Lewis, a white rockabilly performer, invented the genre. He wouldn't believe Daryl, even when he explained that he personally knew Jerry Lee Lewis.

Yet the man was fascinated by Daryl and offered to buy him a drink. Daryl shrugged and took the offer. "I don't drink . . . but I had a cranberry juice," he said. It was at that bar table where the man revealed to him that he was a member of the Ku Klux Klan. In other words, he was an *actual* racist...and he just had a relatively pleasant conversation about music with a Black man!

Now, that *really* took Daryl for a whirl. He, like most people, thought KKK members were disgusting human beings who wouldn't approach a man like him with a ten-foot pole. But the man *wrapped his arm around him.* Daryl thought, *If he can do that, surely he can't be that bad.*

Eventually, the Black musician and the white KKK member struck up a friendship. That same white KKK member eventually renounced his robes, as did some of his KKK friends. Daryl went on a spiritual and activist journey, persuading more than twenty other KKK members to give up their robes. He became friends with many of them, and they counted Daryl's company as a privilege.

"How can you hate me," Davis said, echoing Wayne's words to Mark Robinson when the young Mark accused Rush Limbaugh of being a racist, "when you don't even know me?"[11]

Disagree with me if you want, but *this* is racial progress. Talking KKK members out of their deep-seated racial prejudice? Having wizard hoods in your closet as the trophies to prove it? It appears as if people like Daryl are the keys to ending racism in America. What his story shows is that if racism can be deprogrammed out of KKK members who were nourished on it their whole lives, then maybe the people we call racists on the internet are in fact humans capable of understanding rather than obelisks of white supremacy we should throw stones at.

But in order to gain that understanding, Daryl did not try to indoctrinate. He did not heckle these white racists. He did not protest against them. He listened to them—and corrected them when necessary. His method of eliminating racial prejudice started with revealing the human heart within himself to other people—and only confronting strangers about their views after he had earned their trust.

When CRT began to percolate in the nation's educational discourse, in 2015, Daryl disapproved. CRT was not consistent with his experience, and it was not consistent with the way he wanted to teach his progeny. "Science has shown there's only one human race, and that is what we should teach our kids," he said.[12] We should be teaching mutual under-standing and compassion, he says, not enmity.

Daryl Davis has partnered with nonprofit organizations that present better and more humane curricula for children, addressing the realities of race without emphasizing its divisions. One such organization is called the Foundation Against Intolerance and Racism (FAIR), which recently cre-ated the FAIR Pro-Human Learning Standards, based on the premise that *all parties* are capable of racism as well as shared humanity. Look them up. They're good.

In another book that should get more attention from schools, *Man's Search for Meaning*, Holocaust survivor Viktor Frankl writes, "There are two races of men in this world, but only these two—the 'race' of the decent man and the 'race' of the indecent man. Both are found every-where; they penetrate into all groups of society. No group consists entirely of decent or indecent people."[13] These are the words we should be getting across to children, carrying the same message that's present in the Decla-ration of Independence: "We hold these truths to be self-evident, that all men are created equal."

We are all equal. We are all one race. We are common humans trying to find solutions together. Teach this to your young minority child. Teach him to relinquish his anger. Teach him to see *beyond* skin color into the heart of another person.

Back to the Books

After his entanglement with a racist police officer, the lead character in the book *Dear Martin*, Justyce, finds himself in a tryst with a white girl at his school. But his mom bans the romantic relationship because of the girl's race. Justyce gets into Yale but is publicly criticized by a snarky white boy for being an affirmative action admit. A white police officer kills a Black man, and the story is all over the news. Meanwhile, Justyce gets invited to a party where everyone dresses up as a "racial stereotype." At one of the house parties he attends, he sees a framed picture of someone in blackface.

Justyce and his Black friend Manny are driving down a road playing loud music when a white police officer confronts them. Manny refuses to turn down the music, and the police officer pulls out his gun and shoots Manny. Manny dies. At the trial, Justyce is interrogated by a white woman meant as an obvious stand-in for a "Karen," slang for a white woman who feels entitled because of her race. He is unable to defend himself; the court convicts the racist police officer of mere misdemeanors. Justyce determines that he can't be like Martin Luther King Jr., and the book closes on an uncertain note.

This is how the language of racism is too often used—to depress young minority readers. And *Dear Martin* is hardly the only book that pushes this narrative on our young people. In fact, the use of the word "racism" in American books between 1990 and 2019 shot up 200 percent.[14] Relentless, without stopping to catch a breath, it sprints through our public discourse. Our young people are hearing it every day and every night.

One theme, and one theme only, runs through *Dear Martin*: the persistence of racism in a poor Black kid's life. There is no redemption arc in this book. There is only the relentless assault of scenes in which Justyce deals with racism, day after day after day. This is the book chosen by the American Library Association as a finalist for the 2018 William C. Morris YA Debut Award, given to *the* young adult book that we should be encouraging our children to read. In op-eds defending the book, the content is repeatedly construed as "hardly 'unacceptable' or 'extreme.'"[15] Phoebe Yeh, an editor at Crown Books for Young Readers, which published the book, said the book "solidifies" what happens "in the real world." She said instead of censoring *Dear Martin*, "let the students read it and decide for themselves."[16]

I am the most pro–free speech person I know. In eighth grade, I read out loud a short story I wrote about a burglar escaping from a cop—*from the burglar's perspective*—that almost landed me in school detention. Not exactly "beneficial" for children to hear. But I do wonder why Phoebe Yeh went directly from "don't censor *Dear Martin*" to "let the students read it for themselves." Should we "let the students read for themselves" the orgies in *Gender Queer*? Phoebe skipped right through the moderating force in all this: the opinion of the parents. Parents know their children better than schools or teachers do. Their opinions should be respected in this process.

For the Asian boy, there is *American Born Chinese*, by Gene Luen Yang; for the Black boy, there is *Dear Martin*, by Nic Stone; for the Indian boy, there is *The Absolutely True Diary of a Part-Time Indian*, by Sherman Alexie; and for the Latino boy, there is *The Brief Wondrous Life of Oscar Wao*, by Junot Díaz. All four of these books—and many others—place race and discrimination front and center in their characters' lives. And all four of these books were bestsellers.

I read all four of these books as a teenager. As an adult, I can handle their content. But now I wish I had had an adult at least guide me through the reading. When I read *American Born Chinese*, I wondered about the way I was looked at for years afterward. There were days when I looked in the mirror and reminded myself that I wasn't handsome because I had slanty eyes and coarse, jet-black hair. And I wasn't the only one who thought this way. The young adult author Raquel Rivera wrote about her Native American son reading *The Absolutely True Diary of a Part-Time Indian*:

> It is an excellent book and happens to have much useful material for a boy entering his teens . . . But there is a scene in *Part-Time Indian* in which a racist joke is told, and the protagonist is compelled to fight. For me, the joke was nothing more than a tool to propel the plot. In the story it is duly vanquished and forgotten. But the joke stayed with my son, and he continued to be bothered by it.[17]

Books that deal with race are not to be taken lightly. They attack a child to his core—based on something *he cannot change*. If a child is rattled by something he *can* change, we can inspire and motivate him to take action. If, however, he believes early on that he is at a disadvantage because of something he can't change, then there is nothing for him to do but despair.

It is up to the parents to provide supervision over the reading of these books—supervision that affirms a child's agency and builds him up into a self-confident human being. Books like *Dear Martin* do not reflect the "reality" of a Black kid but simply one fictional experience, which is something parents should remind their children of as they read these books with them. So long as there are ideologically possessed teachers out there who present these books as unquestioned truth, there will be kids who get the wrong message: that racism is the norm and that minority kids should expect to face it daily for the rest of their lives.

What's the conclusion regarding the books and other media being presented to children in the name of CRT and gender ideology? On balance, the injection of these ideologies into the veins of children can't be seen as anything other than bad. Sure, there are some legitimate instances of discrimination and racism that these books can explore. But too often, books like *Dear Martin* and *Gender Queer*—and even some of our core history textbooks—emphasize the idea that society is built on binary privilege and oppression. Reading these books makes me increasingly concerned about Black people, society, and the world.

My conclusion about the books is this: don't ban them (except *Gender Queer*, which is patently and graphically obscene and shouldn't be placed anywhere near children). But don't install them in the curriculum, either, in the name of social justice. There's social justice—and then there are violent, pornographic, and racially depressive fantasies masquerading as "diverse" children's literature. Let caring and kindhearted librarians decide by *reading* these books if they're good for our children. And respect the parents who vet these books and determine that they aren't suitable for their children, especially minority children susceptible to these ideas. Our minority children deserve better. Our minority children deserve to read truly empowering books that don't make them think about how hateful this country is to people like them.

CHAPTER 7

Critical Race Theory's Assault on Merit

Seeing Ann Hsu, newly appointed member of the board of the San Francisco Unified School District, hang her head in shame as the jeers came for her felt like something awful. Dressed in all black, the candidate who had successfully won an appointment to the San Francisco School Board on a platform of merit-based admissions and the elimination of distractions to achievement in the public school system was facing an even tougher test—holding her head high in the face of woke anger.

Days earlier, a candidate questionnaire had presented the following question to Hsu: "How can [the district] increase academic outcomes for the most marginalized students? How can [the district] challenge and create learning opportunities for higher achieving students?"[1]

Hsu replied, in part:

From my very limited exposure in the past four months to the challenges of educating marginalized students especially in the black and brown community, I see one of the biggest challenges as being the lack of family support for those students. Unstable family environments caused by housing and food insecurity along with lack of parental encouragement to focus on learning cause children to not be able to focus on or value learning. That makes teachers' work harder because they have to take care of emotional and behavioral issues of students before they can teach them. That is not fair to the teachers.[2]

No part of this statement is untrue. There *is* a lack of family support for many Black children across the United States. A 75 percent out-of-wedlock birth rate tends to foster that lack of support. But this isn't the only issue facing Black children in the United States. Many Black single parents give their all to help their children succeed, working two jobs to make ends meet. And even when they do, sometimes the community or the school system falters.

But this is not to say that Hsu was wrong. In fact, she was more on target with her point than the others around her who attempted to blame the district's real inequalities—inequalities that were sparked in part by the city's progressive policies—on "systemic racism" in order to cover for their own failures, failures that, as I pointed out in chapter 4, are endemic to the most progressive school districts in America.

What could possibly be going on that could cause these inequalities? Let's start here: in American high schools, Asian students, the children whom Hsu observed in Chinatown, study an average of 110 minutes per day. White children study an average of fifty-five minutes per day. Black children study an average of thirty-five minutes per day.[3]

Many of the reasons why Asian kids can study for such relatively long lengths of time are because their family members take care of their other needs so that they are able to come home to a sheltered environment where they can focus on schoolwork. In my book *An Inconvenient Minority*, I highlighted the experience of Royce Chen, a child of Taiwanese immigrants who grew up near San Francisco. Royce recalled that the family structure in his Bay Area Taiwanese household was basically designed to support the children's learning. The parents would do the various household tasks; the children would study. Royce said, specifically, "Family culture was defined by each person having a certain task to do...the tasks were built to complement each other. Mom would do the dishes and I would do the homework."[4]

Royce's anecdote is supported by institutional research into this subject. The Brookings Institution conducted a study of this so-called homework gap and found that other variables, such as parental education levels, income, and time spent caring for family members, could not fully explain the large differences in study time.[5] Even when the researchers controlled for all these variables, Asian families still came in first in homework time, while Black families still came in last.

The Brookings researchers then began to speculate on the reasons why certain racial groups do less homework than others. One of their conclusions was that "teachers perceive students of color as academically inferior to their white peers." But how does this lead to the *students* doing less homework? If anything, a properly motivated student aware of discrimination would be inclined to work harder to prove a racist teacher wrong. Brookings researchers then argued that students of color are "less likely to attend high schools that offer advanced courses (including Advanced Placement courses) that would likely assign more homework."[6] The researchers continued to throw out various explanations that pin the blame for the homework gap on the school system, particularly on the racial biases of the teachers. But they also refused to consider any explanations that suggested that Black families simply need to *put more effort into helping their children study.* They even said directly that "we should be wary of blaming disadvantaged groups."

No one is blaming disadvantaged parents. We all know many of these parents are trying their best. But the fact remains: you can try and not succeed, but wouldn't it be so much better to try *and* succeed?

At what point in this discourse do we stop making excuses in the name of racism and ask parents simply to put more effort into their children's education and rearrange their priorities so that home life is at the top?

If you ask woke progressives, the answer could be: never.

The End of Merit

Critical Race Theorists would rather get rid of the whole idea of meritocracy itself rather than impose higher standards on the people they're supposedly uplifting. Instead of "Do the push-ups," CRT's victimhood-based message is "Merit equals whiteness," and therefore merit should be avoided by Black and Latino families.

Nowhere is this made plainer than at the National Museum of African American History and Culture, in Washington, DC. It is very sad that CRT ideals have corrupted such a fine museum and institution, but the damage is unmistakable. The title above a section of the Smithsonian-sponsored online portal about race and racism in America reads in big bold letters: WHITENESS. The full title was "Aspects and Assumptions of White Culture in the United States."[7]

The aspects of "white culture" highlighted include "rugged individualism"—that is, the idea that "you get what you deserve," or treatment according to individual merit. "Hard work is the key to success" and "objective and rational thinking" are other things the museum describes as characteristic of whiteness—which it views with obvious derision.

A public outcry led to the excision of that message from the online portal, but the damage was done: we got incontrovertible evidence of how these wokesters really think.

Suzanne Kim, a sociologist and scholar who studies Asian Americans, attempted to argue that the United States' "merit-based" immigration and naturalization system, for example, is in fact simply a test for conformity to whiteness and white values. She advocated interpreting the Supreme Court cases *Ozawa v. United States* and *United States v. Bhagat Singh Thind*, both of which deal with the legal status of immigrants to the United States, as tests of the "division between 'white' (fit for naturalization) and 'non-white' (unfit for naturalization)" and "as invoking connotations regarding 'agency, will, moral authority, intelligence, and belonging.'"[8]

Remember this line of argument? It is the Critical Race Theory idea that all these positive character traits—agency, will, moral authority, and so on—are really constructs that white people made up to justify their positions of power.

There is definitely truth to the idea that some white people in the United States historically justified their superiority over Black people with presumptions of the latter's low intelligence, low sense of individual responsibility, and low moral character.

Still, Critical Race Theorists have taken their notion that certain characteristics are exclusive to white people way too far. They have even described some of the core subjects essential for academic achievement as white supremacist constructs. How far did they go? They went after *math*.

It goes without saying that math is not a subject universally loved. But math causes particular ire among Critical Race Theorists, who hate the fact that math problems have one right answer and that all the other answers are wrong. In fact, Harvard University accepted and even promoted a statistics PhD candidate named Kareem Carr, who argued that 2 + 2 = 5, presumably because 2 + 2 = 4 is a construct based on one's subjective reality—quite like the differentiated experiences that separate white and Black people according to Critical Race Theory. In 2021, the state of California adopted the Dismantling Racism in Mathematics Instruction program, which argued that correcting students' mistakes in math class is a form of white supremacy.[9]

If you thought math was a subject that Critical Race Theorists left to the mathematicians, you would be wrong. Jian Chen witnessed firsthand the unfortunate reality of CRT infecting the field of mathematics. In 2021, he walked into a Princeton Public Schools board meeting in Princeton, New Jersey, and heard the school board discussing the replacement of middle school and high school algebra and geometry with "real-life math." *What is real-life math?* Jian wondered as he sat in the back row of the auditorium. He started to listen. Evidently, the largely Black and Hispanic low-income students in the Princeton public school system, which had been considered one of the best in the state of New Jersey, were not doing too well in math. "It was pretty discouraging to look at the results," Jian said in an interview with me. "[But then board members] started saying they needed to interpret these data with a particular lens of socioeconomic factors."

If any district should be able to make up for the effects of poverty, it's Princeton, a district rolling in property-tax wealth. It's home to the world-renowned Princeton University and populated by affluent bankers and other professionals. In this district, money wasn't the issue.

Finally, a board member went up to say, "We know that some of the kids are really struggling with math, with geometry." It was a good opener, Jian thought. He felt sympathy for the less fortunate in his community. The former financier and consultant knew the importance of understanding basic math. Math skills are a social lubricant, helping one find good work nearly anywhere. He hoped that the low-income students could get the improvement in results they desperately needed.

But then the conversation soured. The board member went on, saying, "We are actually learning something from the New York City public schools."

Jian was uneasy. "We are one of the best public-school districts in the country, and we are learning from the *New York City* public schools?" Former New York City mayor Bill de Blasio unabashedly presided over a public education system that had one of the worst records for low-income Black and Latino students in the nation.[10] New York City is a place where only a quarter of Black students pass basic math aptitude tests.[11] In New York City, high school principals are alleged to have run a cheating ring that passed minority kids who failed to show up for class. They called their scheme the "Maspeth Minimum," after Maspeth High School, a blue-ribbon school that boasted a 99 percent graduation rate—achieved only by excusing extended student absences and making up "ghost classes" for kids to pass.[12]

"So what did [the Board members] learn from New York City?" Jian said. "Instead of teaching algebra and geometry, the board members say, they are going to test the [kids] on *real-life math*." In other words, they planned to change math to fit the lower expectations they placed on Black and Latino kids, Jian realized with horrifying clarity.

For answers as to the origin of "real-life math," one should read an article in the spring 2016 issue of the *Journal of Mathematics Education at Teachers College* (published by Columbia University, the nation's most prestigious institution for training educational leaders) entitled "Teaching Mathematics for Social Justice: Examining Preservice Teachers' Conceptions." Using "critical pedagogy," the article is a study of "preservice teachers' conceptions of teaching mathematics for social justice," which it then asserts is "crucial for teacher education programs." Teaching math for social justice includes the idea that students should have "instruction that is equitable and connects to their lives."[13]

The racial achievement gap between Black and white children has been inequitable for a generation plus. In 1996, Black children scored an average of one hundred points below white children on the math SAT; in 2016, Black children scored 110 points below.[14] In progressive districts, as I have shown, the gap is wider and yet more skewed.

But Critical Race Theory activists in the math sphere blame the lack of math competencies among Black and Latino children on the strange idea that math lacks "connection to their lives" instead of on the methods of teaching and learning—and parenting—that are hamstringing these students. As usual with CRT, there is a kernel of truth in this "real-life connection" idea. Marcus Spratley, a Black graduate of the Baltimore City Public Schools, explained in an interview with me his inherent lack of interest in a subject like calculus, what with everything going on in his life—including work and family. "Every time in school, [calculus has] always been about memorization. School isn't built the way it needs to. I don't need no calculus. I have to go home and help my family with the house," he said. To Marcus, calculus is an extraneous subject in which little "real-life" material is gleaned.

Perhaps it is in stories like Marcus's where the roots of "real-life math" lie. But the pedagogy was conceived in an idealistic bubble in which the problem is math itself, not the effort the students put into it. Therefore, math had to be made "relevant" to them through "real-life" connections that "inspire" them. Get what this is starting to sound like? That's right— the bushy beard of the Brazilian critical pedagogist Paulo Freire is peeking out from behind the corner. "Teaching Mathematics for Social Justice" blatantly says, "Teaching for social justice is a critical pedagogy used to empower students to be social agents in the world they live [in]."[15]

Real-life math, a CRT-infused curriculum predicated on the assumption of a racist society, assigns no responsibility to the student or his family to meet a certain math standard and instead allows the inferiority of the student's initial achievement to dictate the expectations levied upon him. Because of society's repressive racist burden on minorities, these fragile kids cannot be expected to individually perform to the white man's standard, or so the theory goes. In the name of diversity and inclusion, these standards must be done away with so that students can learn at their own liberated pace.

The University of North Carolina–Chapel Hill, one of America's flagship public universities, recently moved ahead with a real-life-math policy recommendation: scrap the current math approach and replace it with a program called Math Pathways. Shannon Watkins, who works for an education advocacy group in North Carolina called the Martin Center, said in an interview with me that the university is "looking to design alternative math gateway courses, because college algebra is considered 'a stumbling block' for these students." The same attitudes that undergird Critical Race Theory's contempt for absolute math standards undergird this curriculum. "Why, for example, should drama or history students have to grapple with something as 'irrelevant' as algebra?" Watkins sardonically quipped.

Under this Math Pathways program, college freshmen can choose one of six "meta-majors," divvied up into "algebraically-intensive" and "non-algebraically-intensive" subgroups, and only one of these meta-majors leads to calculus in college (the STEM Pathways).[16]

Other students—accustomed to, say, learning about racism—can take Math 1332, Introduction to Mathematics. Introduction to Mathematics uses a textbook called *The Heart of Mathematics: An Invitation to Effective Thinking*, which proudly asserts that it will teach mathematics in a "*non-computational style*" (emphasis added). *The Heart of Mathematics* is an okay introduction to some of the concepts of high-level math, and it does a lot to try to make math seem fun and "relevant." However, the concepts taught in the book simply do not contain the prerequisites for high-level math that rigorous college algebra does. In *The Heart of Mathematics*, we learn about fun ways to count, math applications in voting (harking back to the "Teaching Math for Social Justice" article), and the beauty of fractals. We learn about the various ways people have historically used math to speculate on land or build ships. We do not learn calculus or even pre-calculus. Teaching in this kind of nonrigorous way immediately sets up an artificial barrier for students that reads: "You shall not pass."

It is abundantly clear that educational activists have been promoting "real-life math" as a direct result of Critical Race Theory and its view of societal standards as inherently oppressive and constraining. It is a depressing unraveling of the standards we have fought so hard to uphold. It is depressing because our education system, by caving to the woke, is denying even the possibility of bright mathematical futures for our young children and minorities.

I talked with Allison Coates, the founder of the Middle School Mathematics Institute and BRIGHTLinks, an organization whose mission is to "create opportunities for emotional, social, and intellectual growth of profoundly gifted children." She has more than ten years' experience in teaching math in a way designed to accelerate student learning in the subject—which of course should be the goal of any math teacher. "Unlike other subjects, math has a strict linearity of learning," she explained to me. "You can't progress in math unless you learn algebra and geometry, then calculus. Your mind is not equipped to move forward without these prerequisites." This means, of course, that kids who spend too much time fiddling around with slow-paced math are bound to fall behind—and stay behind—the students who take private advanced classes.

Unfortunately, real-life math dooms children to this fall-behind fate. It means, according to new textbooks and educational guidance written in the name of social justice, learning multiplication by counting beads and odd formulas rather than by memorizing multiplication tables. Real-life math means making excuses for students' lack of abstract reasoning ability—and holding them back for the rest of their lives because of it.

Although UNC chief academic officer Kimberly van Noort stated that "this work [on Math Pathways] reflects our ongoing commitment to improve student success and support equitable access to education," the reality is that allowing low-performing students to opt out of the wretched challenge of completing a rigorous course in algebra or even calculus—and thus denying them the immense personal reward such an achievement confers—only serves to produce a less well-rounded liberal arts student and therefore lowers that student's confidence in his own ability to think critically. It also lowers his ability to secure a high-paying job that uses those skills.[17] Ironically, the dysfunctional real-life math curriculum will only increase inequity based on race and social class. "Now those who have the luxury of time after school, those who are in two-parent families—they're the ones who can excel at math," Allison Coates said.

This of course falls directly in line with what Ann Hsu suggested in the questionnaire. If the public schools won't teach a rigorous math curriculum, the only people who will get that education are those kids whose parents are educated and resourceful enough to help them. The kids with uneducated parents will be left in the dust.

We are actively choosing to dumb down our children instead of holding parents to a higher standard of effort—all in the name of fighting racism. Isn't that ironic? We are using the language of fighting racism to keep racial inequities where they are, presumably so we can enrich the people fighting racism by keeping the narrative alive. As the economist Thomas Sowell said, "Much of the social history of the Western world...has been a history of replacing what worked with what sounded good."[18] This is definitely the case with Critical Race Theory's assault on merit.

How to Really Reverse Declining Math Performance

In some ways, the willingness of critical pedagogists to take a stand on this issue—yelling their Critical Race Theory perspective about math standards being "racist"—is truly amazing. Gloria Ladson-Billings, the premier Critical Race Theorist in the education sphere, wrote in a 1998 journal article that "CRT suggests that current instructional strategies presume that African American students are deficient."[19] That's right—our educational techniques, developed from the time of Plato and reinforced by centuries of science and innovation—are outright racist. Teaching kids to value hard work, rewarding kids for performance, standardizing tests to determine intelligence, and disciplining children for misbehavior—these are all emblems of a racist educational society.

One almost has to appreciate how Critical Race Theorists like Ladson-Billings, who holds numerous titles, including former president of the American Educational Research Association, could state with such clear conviction that the judgments of teachers, of standardized tests, of the entire educational system are racist and wrong and that there is nothing wrong with the students or their families; rather, it is the biases of these instruments of white supremacy that are at fault.

But Ladson-Billings made a critical blunder. The blunder is nearly imperceptible except to discerning eyes, but it says all you need to know about the people who are advancing these kinds of arguments. In a paragraph about Critical Race Theory's view of instruction, she suggests a "counterpedagogy" based, of course, on Paulo Freire and critical consciousness. But as an example of this counter-pedagogical strategy, which inspires revolutionary critical consciousness among students, she brought up the educator Jaime Escalante, calling his teaching style a "counterinsurgency." Ladson-Billings wrote:

> Examples of counterpedagogical moves are found in the work of both Chicago elementary teacher Marva Collins and Los Angeles high school mathematics teacher Jaime Escalante. While neither Collins nor Escalante is acclaimed as a "progressive" teacher, both are recognized for their persistence in believing in the educability of all students. Both remind students that mainstream society expects them to be failures and prod the students to succeed as a form of counterinsurgency. Their insistence on helping students achieve in the "traditional" curriculum represents a twist on Audre Lorde's notion that one cannot dismantle the master's house with the master's tools. Instead, they believe one can only dismantle the master's house with the master's tools.[20]

Jaime Escalante is one of the most famous high school math teachers ever. During his tenure at Garfield High School, in East Los Angeles, a gang-ridden school primarily attended by low-income Latinos, he had twelve seniors pass the AP calculus exam in 1982. The next year, thirty seniors passed, and by 1987, an astounding ninety-five students at Garfield High School passed the exam under Escalante's tutelage. Even the twelve students who passed AP calculus in 1982 were more than the number of students who passed the exam in the rest of East Los Angeles that year.[21]

Jaime Escalante's teaching is storied, but if it is a counterinsurgency against anything, it is against CRT—all the lies promulgated by Ladson-Billings and her ilk. Escalante believed so strongly in the power of the individual to transcend his or her circumstances that he started Garfield's first calculus class—at a time when barely any student in that high school could pass algebra. He kept his students for summer school and past 5:00 p.m., relentlessly impressing upon them that their success was up to *them* and was *their* responsibility. Rather than denigrate the standardized AP exam as racist, as many Critical Race Theorists do, Escalante used it to motivate his students to succeed. Sure, he also used the "society is against you" trope to motivate his kids, but such tropes are hardly limited to a particular race or a CRT point of view. Look at football star Tom Brady: the six-foot-four millionaire white guy still believes that society is against him. As Brady said in 2020, "There's always been doubt around what I could achieve." Yes, he said that in 2020.[22]

Escalante assumed the best of his students, not the worst, and rather than try to trap his students in a mindset in which the system is stacked against them, he called for the individual transformation of each person through hard work and personal sacrifice. In the film *Stand and Deliver*, a fictionalized account of Escalante's teaching career that Escalante himself called "90 percent truth," he is portrayed as an empathetic presence who would go to his students' houses in an effort to convince *the parents* that their kids could and should study calculus.[23] One moving scene showed Escalante confronting a father who wanted his daughter to wait tables instead of take calculus.

"She's just going to get pregnant anyways!" he shouted at Escalante.

That's all that happens in this barrio, the father observed. He had bought into the self-fulfilling prophecy of Latino failure. But Jaime Escalante resisted such a notion. He would not stop fighting for the girl until the father relented and allowed her to take calculus. And that girl passed the AP calculus exam.

To Jaime Escalante, the truth was evident: these students' issues with math were not about *racism* but rather about their culture and families—and their excessive fixation on race only seemed to make matters worse.

By calling Escalante a counterinsurgent, depicting him as a figure who would "dismantle the master's house," Gloria Ladson-Billings was trying to cast Escalante as a kind of Critical Race Theory figure, but that is a label Escalante himself would forcefully have rejected, both in his life and his work. For example, he came out in support of conservative Ron Unz's campaign for "English-only" curricula in California's public schools. To shoehorn one of America's most beloved educators into a CRT framework in which he clearly does not belong exemplifies the worst of CRT's parasitic practices. It shows Ladson-Billings's willingness to compromise any truth, ignore any inconvenient fact, mangle any narrative to get what she and her allies all want—critical pedagogy in schools and a promotion.

Jian Chen, who went to the Princeton Public Schools board meeting and heard the proposal for "real-life math," reflected, "Even Kobe Bryant said, 'Do you know what Los Angeles looks like at four o'clock in the morning?' Because he knew," Jian said. "That message got lost in academics. I find it really, really strange. Really strange."

No matter how you slice it, the "reforms" in math education handed down from America's CRT intelligentsia show a lack of regard for both the practice of math and the students who need a kick in the rear. Instead, they reflect the enforced averageness that "equity"-based ideologies inevitably bring to the table. They reflect a lack of respect for the value of hard work.

Jian Chen made his decision. Instead of enrolling both his children in the Princeton public school system, he decided to send them to the charter school down the street. His attitude became very simple: he wasn't going to put up with mediocrity and excuse making. "Our public educational system gives up on kids too easily," he said.

Let the critical race extremists whine about racist math and the need to foster more inclusive math-education strategies that lower standards for Black, Hispanic, and other populations. Parents like Jian will continue chugging along until the educational establishment will have no choice but to admit what is inconvenient for them to say: there is no educational innovation, no racial theory, no paradigm shift that can effectively substitute for hard work. Until the intelligentsia acknowledge this cold, hard truth, however, our nation's low-income Black and Hispanic students will continue to face untruthful imitations of solutions in communities that desperately need real answers.

Competent math education cannot be found in CRT. It must be found in its opposite: a liberating, individualistic education system based on achievement through hard work.

Back to Ann

Ann Hsu wasn't always an activist for school excellence. After she had, amazingly, recalled three woke San Francisco School Board members on February 16, 2022, during happier times, I had a conversation with her about her win and her life story. Ann Hsu, born in 1967, has lived the life of three women. The first was as a girl growing up in China. The second was as a skilled immigrant with a degree in electrical engineering who founded a start-up in America. And the third is as a fully assimilated member of the San Francisco, California, community.

"Best thing to have in life is an interesting life," she said, laughing. She was in a jovial mood after emerging victorious over three woke school board members in an election that Chinese Americans turned out in unprecedented numbers for (Chinese Americans make up 22 percent of the city).[24]

A transplant from Beijing, China, Ann first came to America on a student visa. After graduating from Penn State, she lived and worked in Erie, Pennsylvania, a town she describes as "the quintessential Middle American city."

"It had 250,000 people. Forty [of them] Chinese," she said. There wasn't even a Chinese restaurant in Erie in the 1990s. For years, Ann experienced the feeling of being the only person around with Asian features. But she didn't hesitate when I asked her, "Would you say there is racism there?"

"No. I did not experience it," she answered flatly. "And I was kind of bullied when I first got there, in middle school, but it was not because of my race. It was because [one kid] was a bully. And I was a small girl...he pushed me against the wall, and I kicked his shin. And then another boy came over and defended me. And they were all white."

That was the kind of girl Ann Hsu was, a feisty one. And feisty girls don't let victim narratives define them.

The immigrant, wife, and businesswoman brought that same canny disposition to her Silicon Valley career, becoming one of the most successful electrical engineers in the Bay Area and subsequently an angel investor for others. Then, later in her life, Ann became a plugged-in member of her Chinese American community in San Francisco.

In her view, the San Francisco school board was just raking local kids over the coals. First, during the COVID-19 pandemic, the board refused to come up with a plan to reopen schools. Then, while students were rotting their brains on virtual learning (read: no learning), the board members insisted on renaming some of the schools—including *Abraham Lincoln* High School. "I was like, what the hell are you doing?" Ann recalled. "And they refused to acknowledge it. That's when I got really mad. Our kids were wasting their lives away."

Ann made a decision. She was going to get these hucksters out. She pushed her Chinese American community to start a massive recall campaign, gathering the signatures necessary to initiate a recall with the Department of Elections. As it turned out, the other community members were just as pissed off as she was about the lack of urgency to reopen schools. Using grassroots social media campaigns, she communicated a single message, over and over again, to her neighborhood and her community—the school board is focusing on everything except educating students. It's going woke and destroying the foundations of our children's education. There was no alleyway, no Chinatown tea shop, where the school board recall election was not a topic of discussion.

And Ann got results. More than 37 percent of the city's Chinese-speaking voters voted in the election, which recalled all three of the wokest school board members: Alison Collins, Gabriela López, and Faauuga Moliga.[25] The turnout of previously untapped Chinese Americans significantly outpaced that of the rest of the city, where there was an approximately 25 percent turnout. The results were decisive: 79 percent of San Francisco voters voted to fire those three wokest school board members in one fell swoop—which is remarkable in any county but especially in one as progressive as San Francisco.

Yes, the COVID-19 lockdowns were an issue. So was some of the woke posturing regarding the renaming of schools. But what really got Ann and her first-time voter friends fired up was an issue that may seem irrelevant to the majority of the voting public but was decisive among the striving immigrant population of Chinatown. It was the matter of the school board's intent to dismantle the merit-based admissions program at the most selective public school in the city, Lowell High School.

A former Supreme Court justice, Stephen Breyer, and many other luminaries had attended the prestigious school, in the heart of San Francisco. For a period of time, it had an admissions system that was basically blind to race, one in which students were admitted based on grades and test scores. It also boasted a historically high Asian student population—70 percent in 2002. Then racial ideologues began slowly chipping away at its merit-based infrastructure, asserting that in the interest of "racial diversity," the school should make admissions decisions in part based on race. Thus began a steady decline in Asian American admissions over the following eighteen years. By 2020, the Asian population at the school reached a low of 49 percent.

Still unsatisfied, the woke board continued to push for a further reduction in Asian admissions by making the process a lottery, without any consideration of merit at all. They did this in the name of racial "equity"—ensuring equal outcomes between the races in San Francisco. They did not even consider the idea that many Asian students at Lowell come from low-income families and reside in Chinatown or that maybe some Lowell High School parents could *learn* from the high-achieving Asian American community rather than exclude them.

When Ann and her fellow Chinese Americans complained about the precipitous drop in the number of hardworking Asian students because of the lottery admissions system, ultraprogressive school board member Alison Collins responded by tweeting out one of the nastiest tweets you'll ever see about Asian Americans.

"[Asians] use white supremacist thinking to get ahead," Collins wrote, citing her time "[growing up] in mostly As Am middle schools" as evidence to support her characterization of Asians as abettors of white supremacy.[26] "Being a house n***ger is still being a n***er," she wrote. "You are still considered 'the help.' "

The school board member was not shy about divulging the source of her thinking toward the Asian Americans she supposedly served. "Many Asian [students] and [teachers] won't engage in critical race convos unless they see how they are impacted by white supremacy," she tweeted. It was from Critical Race Theory that Collins got the idea that Asian Americans are white-supremacy allies, that they are "white-adjacent." She was saying that Asians, *by performing well on merit-based exams and earning top grades*, thereby gaining admission to the top public high school in San Francisco in large numbers, were abetting "white supremacist thinking" and are in fact coconspirators in white supremacy.

This was the turn that Ann Hsu was fighting: the pronouncement that Asians are "white-adjacent," shoehorning them into the CRT narrative. For woke school board members, whites—and now Asians—are the oppressor population, racist toward Blacks.

Once this narrative is established, these ideologues can push through any policy that lowers the percentages of Asians in top schools—and how righteous are they! How righteous are they for discriminating against Asian Americans.

The Uphill Climb

The master's house *is* being dismantled. All our structures of merit, of achievement, and of individual excellence in this country are targets for the woke.

Ann Hsu learned all this the hard way. Cruising off a victory high after the recall election and running the gamut of *New York Times* interviews and interviews with other journalists, including me, could only last so long. Her campaign to topple the establishment made her some enemies among the woke. Her calls for moderation and merit-based standards engendered skepticism among the CRT crowd, and she felt it in the months after the San Francisco mayor, London Breed, appointed her to the school board in place of one of the members who had just been fired.

The new appointee faced enemies who seized on her the instant she made one mistake (and it is debatable whether it was actually a mistake). She dared to challenge Black and brown communities in a critical manner. She dared to say that lack of family responsibility for children's education was an issue in many African American communities in San Francisco. And she dared to correlate that issue with disparities in academic performance. She violated the tenets of woke mob rule number 1: don't blame the victims of oppression, ever, at all, for anything.

The result was predictable and predictably Communist and Cultural Revolution–esque. Progressives gaslighted her regarding the scale of the offense. Fellow school board members coaxed a public apology from her, admonishing and roasting her. And then these ideologues reprogrammed her into a tool of the woke mob, much the same way they did former governor Ralph Northam of Virginia in the wake of his blackface scandal (a much greater sin, in my opinion, than Hsu's comments). So Ann Hsu went back and edited her own comments in the transcript of that town hall meeting, particularly the language: she changed "family support" to "historical inequities." In the language of wokism, there's a script to which you must conform. And Ann meekly did so.

I would say I have sympathy for Ann Hsu, but I temper that sympathy with disappointment. You don't know a statesman or stateswoman until he or she is dragged through the mud. And Ann completely caved. I doubt she will recover, and if she does, she will be "rehabilitated" into using the progressive-speak that she once fought righteously against.

Trying to strike a weak middle ground between bowing to the Democratic Party establishment, who hated her, and the constituents who initially rallied behind her, Hsu officially lost her special-election seat to challenger Alida Fisher in the general election on November 17, 2022.[27] Hsu had 17.14 percent of the vote for the third school board seat, but Fisher surpassed her at 17.75 percent. That margin of victory could have been closed by the Chinese American voters who turned out for Hsu in droves based on the initial purity of her message. Instead, many stayed home in the general election after she caved to the woke establishment.[28]

Never mind about Ann Hsu. The people I really feel sorry for are the Black and Hispanic kids watching these town hall meetings. Their minds are poisoned yet again with the cruel contention that society hates them and that they should blame "racism" for their plight rather than work to improve themselves.

The assault on merit is the assault on the values of personal responsibility that made this country excellent. These progressive ideologues are leading hopeful young Black and Latino children astray. They are exploiting their desire for guidance from members of their own race and creating a destructive narrative that denigrates individual achievement and sets low expectations for them. It truly shows that Critical Race Theorists would prefer a society where all are mediocre rather than a society where some are excellent.

CHAPTER 8

Critical Race Theory's Assault on Identity

The Gevirtz Graduate School of Education sits on a pristine piece of sun-kissed rock jutting out toward the Pacific Ocean. Its location on a prime piece of real estate at the University of California–Santa Barbara carries with it an aura of triumph. Like the explorer Juan Rodríguez Cabrillo planting his flag on the California shores, the Gevirtz School signals to the world that it stands as the conqueror of the modern-day city of Santa Barbara. It occupies the most valuable stretch of land in the highest and most gorgeous place in the county, on rocks so high that the town—and even the other schools—seem to bow down before it. UCSB is the ruler of this fiefdom.

Go into the Gevirtz School building, and you are instantly greeted with some of the most palatial contemporary architecture you've ever seen. Floor-to-ceiling windows tower over a magnificent sheet-white interior that would feel right at home in the Cyclades, the historic islands off the shore of Greece. The ceilings, twenty feet high, and open-air foyer allow a tourist to see three stories above him upon entering the grand facility. There's nothing more that could be said except that it is a temple. It is a secular cathedral.

It's easy to see why undergraduate students would visit UCSB's Gevirtz School and feel like it is a place where they could go on to do great things. Coming into this building, you could potentially be convinced it has all the answers to the educational problems on campuses across the United States. At the very least, you would feel like this is where the university's institutional priorities lie (and you wouldn't be wrong—the physics department sometimes meets in trailers). So large and imposing is the education school that it retains a staff of four full-time development officers just to raise the money to pay for it.

Yet when I sneaked inside the Gevirtz School building in the fall of 2021 by following a student who had a key card, I saw a mostly empty school except for a few students chatting in a corridor. I approached them and asked where everyone else was. "Oh," they replied, a little surprised. "No one comes into this building anymore. Everything is virtual."

I was disappointed, because I was hoping to interview a few education professors, and I figured it would be harder for them to turn down an interview if I could catch them in their offices. Nevertheless, I began to roam around the building, exploring the literature and posters the school faculty and administration had left up before they all bolted from this temple.

I took a self-guided tour through the teachers' offices. I knocked on a few doors, particularly those of the teachers I wanted to interview. The students were right: no one was there. Frustrated, I began to second-guess my decision to visit. That was when I noticed the research papers that had been taped onto the walls by former dwellers of this modern temple—the lone artifacts left behind during the Great COVID-19 Abandonment. I began to read the "etchings." Then the true "religion" of the shrine began to reveal itself to me.

Nearly all of them—*every single research paper* posted in the Gevirtz Graduate School of Education—had something to do with race or gender. One of the titles was "The Influence of Teacher Gender on Female Students' Math Self-Efficacy." Another one was "Engaging Latino Middle-School Students in Literacy-Based MakerSpace Activities to Enhance STEM Practices and Engagement." What intrigued me was just how many of these research projects seemed to line up with common negative stereotypes of the various groups studied. For example, girls were assumed to be in need of "female support" in math, while Latino middle school students were assumed to be illiterate and, according to the paper, "historically underrepresented." Although one certainly can't be blamed for caring about Latino literacy, the fact that all the highlighted research seemed to conform to common stereotypes suggested that the researchers believed that they and certain people were assumed to be inferior because of the color of their skin or because of their gender. This was a symptom that diagnosed the CRT disease in their systems.

Some of the research papers were written in jargon, and breaking down the nearly incomprehensible education-speak was a laborious task. But one flyer left on the door of a professor's office provided a cipher. It featured a collage of obviously Latino faces staring into the camera, above and below which was a statement in large print: MY APPEARANCE DOES NOT DEFINE WHO I AM.

Oh, okay, I thought. *So this is another one of those identity-affirmation posters I often see in colleges and counseling offices.* I was going to move on, but a line at the bottom of the poster caught my attention: MY LANGUAGE DEFINES ME.

My language defines me. *My language defines me.* Why would someone make a flyer attributing a person's *language* to identity formation? And why specifically for Latino people? The language referred to in this poster, obviously, was Spanish. Yet English was mandatory in every school in California. Surely this poster was not referring to *English* as the language that defines these Latinos—weren't they taught to think that English was the language of the oppressor? Then I looked at the bottom of the page and saw the name of the organization that the flyer was promoting. The words RESPETA MI IDIOMA beamed out at me. *Respeta mi idioma*—respect my language—is a slogan for a UCSB-sponsored Spanish-language advocacy organization called SKILLS. What is unclear is why Spanish speakers feel the need to demand respect, as if they were disrespected in the first place. I scrutinized the poster for a second. Then it dawned on me.

The students and professors at the Gevirtz School of Education couldn't care less about Spanish. It was *English* acquisition that truly bothered these people at a visceral level. It was the obsession with doing away with English, which they viewed as the language of the oppressor, that motivated them.

As I mentioned at the beginning of this book, CRT is a *reactive* paradigm. Its objective is to locate the greatest source of tension in the racial dialogue in America and exploit it, thereby constructing a privileged-oppressed dichotomy. For Blacks, the tension is in our history of real racial discrimination. For gays, there's certainly been some history of discrimination. But for the Latino case, there is much less history of discrimination—and it simply resonates much less for them than it does for Black people. I give Gloria Ladson-Billings an iota of credit, at least, for this idea: "Citizens of Mexican descent were considered White, though over time, political, economic, social, and cultural shifts have forced Mexican Americans out of the White category."[1] Mexicans did not largely face systemic oppression in America, so they couldn't be radicalized based on this lack of history. Therefore, CRT ideologues found a new way to insert their bitterness into Latinos—anxiety about their lack of assimilation. And that lack of assimilation is embodied in the language divide.

The Gevirtz Graduate School of Education was creating artificial ghettos based on language—separate and unequal, built into the *foundation* of Hispanic education, according to progressive Critical Race Theory. The school was trying to separate Latino kids from white kids based on their lack of English acquisition. That was the agenda, I realized with horror.

It's Hilda Time

In the summer of 2020, the Santa Barbara Unified School District, in a Southern California county where Joe Biden got 32 percent more votes than Donald Trump, introduced its next superintendent of schools, Hilda Maldonado.[2] The Mexican American woman came from the struggling Los Angeles Unified School District to take over for the freshly fired Cary Matsuoka, who was deemed by the Santa Barbara school board to be incapable of doing the job the board wanted him to do. Cary was too professional, too methodical—not truly one of them. So the board had to make a change.

Hilda's career was basically nurtured by the Diversity, Equity, and

Inclusion department at LA Unified. She was the "senior executive director of diversity, learning and instruction" in her last two years there. Before that she was the "executive director of multilingual and multicultural education." There's no beating around the bush. She was a creature of the woke establishment.[3]

Hilda came to Santa Barbara riding a wave of praise from the all-female school board that appointed her. "She is clearly a courageous, inspiring, tireless leader whom we can lift up, look up to, and learn from," said the board president, Kate Ford.[4] "Our appointment of Ms. Hilda Maldonado gets a Triple 'R' rating: Right Person, Right Place, Right Time," said board member Wendy Sims-Moten.

Maldonado was hired on May 26, 2020—the day after the killing of George Floyd. In fact, she was hired in that small, liminal bubble of time between the day that George Floyd was actually *killed* and the day that his killing became an international sensation—sparking the resurgence of Black Lives Matter and forcing the world to grapple with a powerful "systemic racism" narrative that extended way beyond policing into schools, health care, and even sports.

Ingurgitated by the flooding strand of racial sentiment, Maldonado instantly became one of the most powerful superintendents the district had ever seen, and her arrival signaled a new era of woke CRT ideology in Santa Barbara schools—abetted by the highly progressive Santa Barbara school board. "Philosophically they are in the same circle . . . they actually partied together," said Rosanne Crawford, a former educator and candidate for the board, about the board's relationship with Maldonado. "They would refer to each other as sisters," Crawford recalled in an interview with me.

The fact hadn't gone unnoticed among the city's residents. "Our school board, which was historically balanced and had debate, dialogue and diversity of opinion, became 5–0 of one political viewpoint, and it's not a moderate or centrist viewpoint," wrote Alice Post, a member of the Coalition for Neighborhood Schools, in the *Santa Barbara News-Press*.[5] Members of the city's progressive wing were already entrenched—and now that they had a "sister" to lead them, there was no limit to the extremes they could go to with their new agenda. Cage Englander, a former candidate for the Santa Barbara school board, told me that "since the time of Reagan, there was nobody who got elected to the board; it was all people retiring halfway through their terms, nominating someone new and nobody [ever running] against them." The board members in this district consistently voted with one another; "95 percent" of the votes were entirely unanimous.[6]

With all this open praise and a board mandate, you could imagine even my surprise when I saw the classified first-year report on Hilda Maldonado's tenure as evaluated by the Santa Barbara district's teachers and paid staff.[7]

> Hilda = Mussolini. The only difference is Mussolini was more empathetic.

> I do not feel that Superintendent Maldonado listens to the teachers of her district. We do not feel supported by her, and she treats us as though we are dispensable.

> The policies she presents to the public is not what is actually happening in the schools. The public needs to know this.

> A school district leader should serve ALL students. Current leader seems to only speak and work for the progress of one group. While others are expected to have a lens that encompasses all students, her speeches and most of communication with staff is about only one group.

> Go back to Los Angeles, please.

These were *teachers* in Santa Barbara who said this—not the type of people you'd think would complain so vehemently unless things were truly out of hand. In a survey about Maldonado's performance, this same cohort was asked how much they agree or disagree with the following statement: "The superintendent provides leadership to the district to improve outcomes to the district." Answers were given on a scale of 1 to 5—1 meant "strongly disagree" and 5 meant "strongly agree." A full 40 percent of SBUSD teachers answered with a 1, the lowest evaluation, while 26 percent answered with a 2. A mere 1.9 percent answered with a 5.

The primary issue that teachers raised with Maldonado was that she was "adding too many new programs" instead of just letting teachers do their jobs (58.5 percent of teachers viewed this as one of their top three concerns). The other big issue teachers raised was the need for "small class sizes."

Maldonado responded with predictable arrogance and self-victimization, even playing the race card: "Some of our parents from the Latino community...came to me and said, 'if people say these things about you... how do we know teachers are going to treat our kids fair if they treat the Superintendent this way?'" she said.[8]

Roll your eyes.

What happened? In a majority-Latino district, how could this highly touted, board-approved Latina have fallen so far over the course of just one year?

What exactly did she do?

Maldonado's Pet Project

When she arrived, Hilda Maldonado's top priority was to entrench bilingual learning in the county's curriculum, a program she had spent most of her career advocating for as part of her woke agenda. On March 22, 2021, she introduced the first of many proposed "dual language immersion" programs she would institute, starting in McKinley Elementary School. This program follows a "90:10 model," in which kindergarteners are instructed 90 percent in Spanish and 10 percent in English; first graders are instructed 80 percent in Spanish and 20 percent in English; second graders are instructed 70 percent in Spanish and 30 percent in English; and so on.[9] The slogan unveiled was: "Go slow to go fast."[10]

The slogan should have been: "Go slow to go even slower." In a longitudinal study of the value of bilingual language education to preschoolers, researchers found that kids randomly assigned to a TBE (transitional bilingual education) program, in which they were instructed in Spanish more than 70 percent of the time, produced overall English-language learning results significantly lower than kids randomly assigned to an EO (English only) teacher.[11] Although the sample used in the study is too small to be statistically significant (only thirty-two kids), it reflects the experiences of teachers who have taught bilingually in the past, including Karen Lithgow, the northern Virginia teacher whom I interviewed in chapter 2. Lithgow said skeptically that "it depends on the kid" whether bilingual education really helps, adding that while it could help kids who had "just come from Mexico" (mostly children of illegal immigrants) feel more comfortable in the classroom environment, it ends up being unhelpful to kids who want to raise their English skills to the level of their American-born peers.

Hilda and her allies justified her bilingual education program in the language of cultural exchange: "We're providing a gift to students to connect with cultures that they might have not connected to before," said the McKinley principal, Elena Garcia-Yoshitomi.[12] But others framed it more specifically in terms of race: Maria Larios-Horton, the director of diversity, equity, and family engagement at Santa Barbara Unified, said, "Let's say I don't look like some of our other families; maybe my child has blonde hair and blue eyes." She continued, "By the end of kindergarten, you'll be able to see the children talking to one another in Spanish, singing together, talking together. It will bring tears to your eyes."[13]

The district's wealthy white liberals cried with joy. I'm sure the picture of diverse kids speaking more than one language played well with the champagne-and-caviar crowd that populates Santa Barbara's rolling hills. Maldonado advanced, triumphant, a wide grin on her face—the face of the new education program imprinted upon the heavily Hispanic McKinley Elementary School and soon to be exported to schools across the county.

Only one educator seemed publicly skeptical that day, and she was out of power, disgruntled, and forced to air her opinions in the back page of the *Santa Barbara News-Press*. "How are they going to compete [in

English]? They're going to be so far behind," an elderly Rosanne Crawford grumbled.[14] The silver-haired lady, a Hispanic mother of two, wore a pompadour and the haughty look of a proud woman. A former educator, she saw only bad things in the new push to make low-income Hispanic children learn via multilingual education. Why? Because she had seen the effects firsthand.

Rosanne recounted in an interview with me the story of a young girl whom she tutored in Santa Barbara, a child of immigrants from Mexico. With help from an elementary school teacher—Rosanne herself—the girl worked hard to get to grade level in English, but when she left for junior high, she lost that English-language support. That's because her parents had checked a box labeled BORN IN MEXICO when she was younger—likely thinking it would have no effect on their child's life. They were wrong. Because of her country-of-origin designation, this girl was automatically sent to a junior high class where she was with "these students that were basically English as a second language students; she was up to grade level, these guys weren't... She sat there and she didn't learn anything," Rosanne said, sighing at the misfortune of the girl she had known and tried to help. "She's homeschooling now," Rosanne said, because the Santa Barbara English-learning system failed her. Her immigrant parents had had no idea that assignment to "bilingual education," in which English is taught as little as 10 percent of the time in the classroom, would be the consequence of checking a box.

Armed with knowledge and a certainty that bilingual education programs were exacerbating the literacy problems of the low-income Hispanic community in Santa Barbara and preventing kids from moving forward, Rosanne sought to confront the new superintendent, Hilda Maldonado, about the issue. After seeing that Maldonado had been checking her profile on LinkedIn (probably because she'd heard about Rosanne's opinion on the issue), Rosanne had the stones to reach out over the platform. "Hi, Dr. Maldonado. I saw you checked out my profile on LinkedIn. Are you interesting in talking?" Then Rosanne waited.

A couple of hours passed. Then Hilda Maldonado replied, "Of course I'd like to meet!"

At the superintendent's office, Rosanne met Hilda. The gregarious Latina strolled out, charming and imposing. She was a disarming character. Her smile could convince you that she had your best interests at heart. Still, Rosanne didn't let Hilda's personality fool her. She was a woman on a mission.

"So how can I help you?" Maldonado asked.

"I just want to ask, Hilda," Rosanne said, clearing her throat, "why you are so high on this bilingual-education stuff when you, a first-generation immigrant yourself, are able to speak fine English and Spanish as the product of a monolingual program?"

"The reason I did so well [at English]," Hilda responded, "is because I had a teacher, and I had after-school help."

Rosanne stiffened as she began to recognize Hilda's strategy of evasion, her effort to frame the discussion as a matter of privilege and oppression instead of technique. But she decided to play Hilda's game.

"Well, that's interesting, Hilda, because in a lot of the schools now, students are not getting that," she said. "[These Latino students] are being taught English, but when they go home, they don't get the support. That's where it needs to be shored up. You need to support the teachers with people who will help in this regard."

Later, Rosanne told me, "And she absolutely agreed. So I asked her, 'Can we at least have one track left at McKinley that's all English, and then you can institute your META [Multilingual Excellence Transforming Achievement, a bilingual program], and we can run the [programs] side by side and you can see firsthand if this really works?'" A reasonable request: just run a side-by-side experiment before putting all your chips in.

"And she said, 'No, and I'll tell you why... When I was down there [in Los Angeles], we got investigated by the State Department'—no, I think she said the Department of Justice, if I recall correctly. I'm not sure which one. 'We really got in trouble because they found that... there was a lawsuit. I remember there was a big lawsuit. They found that forty thousand minority students were passed along to the next grade... who had no comprehension [of English]. Their comprehension was so low that they could read something and then they'd be asked, "What did you just read?" and they wouldn't know. It was a disaster.' So they got in really, really bad trouble, and that's what the lawsuit was about. That's why they investigated."

Unsurprising: an Obama-era Department of Justice filing racial-discrimination lawsuits to get school districts to fall in line. Where have we seen this before?

So Hilda said, according to Rosanne, "Had I not seen that, I would be totally on the same page with you. But there are new studies…"

Which new studies?

"She cited none," Rosanne said. "[It was] such a political kicking the can down the road—[the idea that] if they're taught in their own language, they'll do better later. And I thought, 'Yeah, but then you miss the boat on getting kids into these classes that in fact set them up for their [standard-ized tests] at the end of high school.' So she had nothing to say about that."

Rosanne was frustrated by Hilda's refusal to help. But the veteran edu-cator and mother, still a bleeding-heart liberal cursed with naivete, was missing the bigger picture. Whatever the initial purpose bilingual educa-tion was created to have, it had departed from it to the point where its purpose was not to build up a student's ability in either Spanish *or* En-glish. Rather, its new purpose had become to create government-sponsored language barriers that instill Critical Race Theory narratives of Hispanic failure and victimhood in Hispanic children.

Hilda's conversation with Rosanne illustrated the fact that her main motivations for mandating bilingual education were to (1) avoid a DOJ lawsuit for "discrimination" against Latino kids by daring to teach them in English only and (2) frame English-only versus Spanish-language edu-cation as a matter of privilege and oppression. In Hilda's mind, learning English correctly was a skill only attainable by the "privileged," so she had to lower the standard for the sake of "inclusion." She cited no studies to justify this. She ran no tests to justify this. In fact, she refused to run one. Her mind was filled only with the political garbage taught by schools like the Gevirtz Graduate School of Education.

Critical Race Theory narratives of "oppression" against Latinos merely by means of the enforcement of English-language learning fall into the early Critical Race Theorists' paradigms of the dominant culture's "hegemony" against minorities. They also provide convenient ways for compromised people in authority to exploit the ensuing failures in education for their own personal gain. State that the failure is because of "racism" and "white privilege." Anoint yourself as its savior. Get a promotion. Rinse, repeat. What a strategy in the woke world we live in.

All the while, the Latino kids don't learn, the good teachers get fed up with the leadership and leave, and the public school systems in these highly progressive school districts descend further into pits of wokeness and insanity whose effects we thought were reserved only for leftist radicals in the academy.

Radicals, Reeducation, and Revolution

Hilda didn't stop there. At her first opportunity, when schools were reopening for the 2021–22 school year, the woke superintendent sought to ensure swift implementation of her equity agenda. I'm not exaggerating. That's word for word what Jerry Roberts of *Newsmakers with Jerry Roberts* characterized Hilda as doing over the course of the 2021–22 school year— "pushing hard to implement previously delayed policies of her 'equity' agenda, while also moving to change several existing administrative and financial processes and systems."[15]

Phase 2 of Hilda's woke agenda was to strip protections from teachers who discipline children, making it much more difficult for teachers to achieve order in their classrooms.

Instead, in the name of lowering the suspension rates for Latino kids, Hilda announced a tiered discipline system that teachers had to follow to a T or face punishment. A "tier 1" offense included insubordination, cursing, defacement of public property, "minor" physical contact with other students, and smoking marijuana in class; a student *could not* be suspended for any of these behaviors. Only if he was caught selling marijuana could he face a tier 2 "possible" suspension (although teachers were "strongly encouraged" to pursue counseling and other time-intensive measures first). Teachers had to put *all* infractions on a database called Aeries, which greatly increased their workload. Doesn't a teacher know how to get a child to behave? Not according to the new system. Hilda, the woke superintendent from Los Angeles, suddenly seemed to know everything one needed to know about school order—and that was to not have it.

The sick part of this very confusing "restorative justice" discipline policy is that the choking set of rules applied to teachers reflects a lack of trust in the teacher. She is made to feel blameworthy for a *student's* insubordination. The kid smoked marijuana in class—*you* need to sit down with him and counsel him. It's *not* his fault. But it could be yours if you discipline him too harshly. And when the teacher can't handle this mess? Then what happens?

Christy Lozano, a physical education teacher at Dos Pueblos High School, northwest of Santa Barbara, broke it down: "They proposed that teachers could use swear words along with students rather than telling them not to swear," she said glumly in an interview with me.

Hilda Maldonado's new initiatives distressed teachers like Christy, who had been teaching in the Santa Barbara public schools for most of her adult life. But worse than Hilda's new initiatives might possibly be the continuation of woke efforts that started under her predecessor but went into high gear once she took office.

One day, on a break between classes, Christy decided to meander into a workshop session conducted by a twenty-year-old Santa Barbara nonprofit organization called AHA!, which stands for attitudes, harmony, and achievement. AHA! was started by the social psychologist and astrologer Jennifer Freed. It employed more than twenty adult "peace builders" who fostered "essential connections between social groups."[16] It sounded nice, so Christy tolerated the intrusion into the lives of teenagers of what looked like twenty-four-year-old or twenty-five-year-old fully grown adults with no teaching credentials.

The memorandum of understanding signed between AHA! and its

middle school partner, Goleta Valley Junior High School, in 2021 called for students to attend a series of workshops conducted by AHA! trainers that would "[inspire them] to find the power within themselves to make a true contribution to our school community." Students "were able to go into breakout rooms and talk about what it means to be emotionally brave and join with others to create a culture of caring, respect, and empathy," the information packet said. The students would go into closed-door sessions with AHA! mentors and talk and dissect their experiences with them. To an educator who recognized the value of holistic health to a student's academic well-being, social-emotional learning seemed like it would help Christy's kids. The list of studies AHA! wheeled out to show the workshops' usefulness also helped: the organization claimed a 19.2 percent increase in respondents' feelings of self-awareness and a 20.18 percent increase in respondents' feelings of social awareness.[17]

When the longtime PE teacher walked into an AHA! session, however, she heard swearing and negative words flying around. The trainers were grilling the students, "letting the kids know that they were open to cussing and talking about whatever." Children were crying. *Something's not right*, Christy thought. This did not seem like students were experiencing a 19.2 increase in feelings of self-awareness. In fact, where the heck did AHA! get those numbers anyway? A 19.2 percent increase in "positive emotion"?

Initially, Christy thought the trainers may have been discussing a particularly sensitive subject, or she had just come to the workshop on a particularly bad day. But then she attended one of the school's professional development seminars, which were like AHA! seminars for adults. These were weeklong excursions paid for by the school district that trained teachers in a variety of techniques. They were twelve-hour-a-day affairs, Christy recalled. They were the equivalent of teacher boot camps.

At one of the sessions, a trainer named Artnelson Concordia appeared in front of the teachers. In a professorial manner, he asked for the teachers of color to sort themselves into a group and the white teachers to gather outside this group. He pointed at Christy and instructed her to go to the perimeter of what was becoming a human fishbowl, with the nonwhite teachers on the inside and the white teachers surrounding them.

Artnelson instructed the nonwhites to write every bad thing a white person had said to them on a whiteboard. The nonwhites got up; some looked confused, but others looked mirthful. Perhaps this was the time to unleash their long-held grievances. A steady stream of words appeared on the whiteboard with increasing velocity as the white teachers remained seated, some trying their best to look polite, others scowling. Christy had to just sit and watch.

At the end of the session, Artnelson instructed the white teachers and the teachers of color to retreat to separate rooms to discuss the exercise. He asked them "How did that make you feel?" and "How do you think they were feeling?"

Christy felt embarrassed more than anything.

This series of events awakened the political consciousness of the otherwise apolitical Christy. Before becoming a physical education teacher at Dos Pueblos, she had served in the National Guard and worked as a gas company meter reader, preparing herself through mental and physical toil to be a productive member of society. One picture Christy showed me depicted her surrounded by a group of Latino children doing leg stretches before a rowdy game of dodgeball. The children were grinning, wantonly carefree, tugging at the gloriously overwhelmed PE teacher. She smiled as she scrolled through her Facebook feed, filled with photos of her and these children. "We are a color-blind community," she said. "That's all I want with these kids."

Christy had been deployed to Iraq and Afghanistan as an aeromedical evacuation specialist. She earned her Christian ministry license in 2017. But even the wealth of experience she gained and the principles she developed as a result of her various activities could not have prepared her for the shocking changes she witnessed as a result of the Diversity, Equity, and Inclusion reforms that were happening in and around her school district— the fishbowl exercise chief among them.

She began to notice things she previously hadn't—things both done to her and done to the kids she was teaching. "They asked eight-year-olds to write essays answering the question, What is activism?" Christy said. "One of the kids wrote: to get me or someone I know to think like an activist."

All this had been around before Hilda Maldonado—but under the new superintendent's tenure, it had greatly increased in scope and ruthlessness. Hilda removed and retaliated against teachers who didn't buy into her domineering agenda. Sheridan Rosenberg, a parent living in the district, said in an interview with me that as much as 90 percent of the old staff at McKinley Elementary School left when the bilingual program was introduced. All the while, Hilda started importing lackeys from LA Unified and other hotbeds of wokeness to teach bilingual education instead. "Why are you going out of our county to recruit district personnel when there are so many teachers in our own district who hold the administrative credentials?" read the complaint written by a host of teachers representing Santa Barbara High School. If I could speak directly to these teachers asking pointed questions, I would say: Don't you know that woke people can't tolerate any opinions besides their own? That's just the way they operate. You disagree with Hilda, you get reassigned.[18]

It was very clear that instead of mandating that these students learn real skills, such as the English language and math, Hilda was quickly repopulating the district with teachers who had activist and indoctrination agendas. In a way, we shouldn't be surprised. These were the people who went to graduate schools of education that we funded twenty years before in the name of social justice. Now those graduates are teaching public school kids, even holding leadership positions. The chickens have come home to roost.

Ethnic Studies and Critical Race Theory Internalized

Emblazoned on a shirt that Matef Harmachis wears to Santa Barbara High School events is a drawing of a raised fist. It's a clenched scarlet-red fist on a black background. His students largely do not know that this is the Black

Power fist previously adopted as a symbol by the Black Panther Party, a militant group in America prominent in the 1960s founded to bring about a "Black revolution." But Matef Harmachis knows.

It is no accident that the Black Power fist is on his shirt. "I'm going to tell you what leadership means to African people...you must, you must, you must, love your people, unfortunately sometimes to death so your people can live...We take orders, and we follow them to the letter on behalf of our people," Harmachis said before a captive student audience at a nonprofit youth seminar in 2018.[19] He was street-preaching a message of Black solidarity that the Black Panther Party did more militantly in the 1960s. "We, the Black Panther Party, see ourselves as a nation within a nation, but not for any racist reasons," wrote Bobby Seale, the cofounder of the Black Panther Party, in 1970. "We do not fight racism with racism. We fight racism with solidarity. We do not fight exploitative capitalism with black capitalism. We fight capitalism with basic socialism."[20] Matef did not say at the public seminar with high schoolers that he wanted to incite a racial revolution, but he was veering as close to it as he could get away with.

The charismatic Matef Harmachis, who was born Leigh Barker in California, was practically a staple in Santa Barbara Unified, and his legacy was a core part of Santa Barbara's woke agenda and the agenda of California progressives at large. In particular, he was the key organizer of a student-and-teacher group called the Ethnic Studies Now Coalition, which was supported by the school board and which advocated for ethnic studies to be a state-mandated course in California.

Ethnic studies is a classroom curriculum that analyzes "systems of oppression" of minorities, particularly Black, Latino, and Asian minorities, in America.[21] It is Critical Race Theory internalized. Explicitly put forth in the Overview of the ESMC—the ethnic studies model curriculum—is the term "critical consciousness."[22]

The ESMC has a "Black and African American Studies" section that fails to even mention the Civil War—including Black participation in it— even once.[23] Instead, the focus is on slavery. Then the curriculum moves right ahead to Jim Crow before paying lip service to the civil rights movement and spending the majority of the time addressing what the CRT ideologues really want to talk about: their view that America is still a racist country with a "prison-industrial complex" that practices "modern day redlining." The curriculum also includes other topics that relate to America's current systemic racism. Similarly one-sided accounts abound in the "Latino History" and "Asian American History" sections.

Ideologues and woke bureaucrats within the district were counting on Matef and his allies to establish a Critical Race Theory ethnic studies mandate—and he delivered the goods. "Not only is this a movement," said SB Unified board member Wendy Sims-Moten to the *Santa Barbara Independent*, "but it is a shift in culture, the way we think, and [the way we] have conversations moving forward."[24] Matef was a local star, working within and without the progressive establishment to push for Critical Race Theory in the schools. By all accounts, he was highly successful.

Coraline Crannell, a graduate of Santa Barbara High School, epitomized the kind of activist Harmachis trained and nurtured in the service of his critical-pedagogical goals. I talked to Coraline while she was studying abroad, in France. In many ways, she sounded convincing. The current history curriculum, she said, is that "of a very specific group of people who tend to have the same profiles." She believes in the importance of "bringing to light and being really willing to teach some alternate versions of what happened, or just being able to say, like, 'Look, this is not representative of the community that you're living in, of the community that you're from.'"

While at Santa Barbara High School, the French-language student helped organize meetings of Ethnic Studies Now!—as the movement was called—pushing her school board to require one semester of ethnic studies. "It was such a huge community effort, there was...so much interest backing it," she says. "Just at the meeting itself, in November of 2018...so many members of the community showed up."

Well-mannered and *white*, Coraline would convince the suburban moms in the district that Ethnic Studies Now! was an honest effort—without knowing the full context of the real purpose for which she was being used.

I'm glad that young people believe in something. I genuinely think that Coraline Crannell's passion is sincere and that having a passion for ethnic studies is better for her than having no passion at all. We stifle a young person's passion at our own peril, and Coraline has good reasons for hers. "There's value for everyone in the history that we're taught, the stories that we're taught, the stories that run rampant in all aspects of our society," she said, honestly wanting to make the experiences of her minority friends more salient in the public discourse.

But there's a dangerous idea embedded in the presence of ethnic studies in school curricula. By teaching United States history and ethnic studies separately, side by side, we create a picture that US history—the former—is not for ethnic minorities. CRT ideologues seem to want to keep America's moral progress away from the minds of ethnic minorities with a ten-foot pole, and that tradition of exclusion is continued in ethnic studies.

Not addressed in the Black and African American studies curriculum proposed by the Ethnic Studies Now! designers, which included Matef, is the fact that 60 percent of Black Americans feel that they're better off financially than their parents were, the fact that Black Americans graduate from universities at an 82 percent higher rate than they did in 1960,[25] and the fact that Black Americans have dropped their poverty rate from 40 percent to 18.8 percent during that same period.[26] In short, the Black oppression narrative is taught; the American progress narrative, unless it has to do with dismantling white supremacy, is not. This narrative estranges a population already sensitive to its skin color, a population whose future in part hinges on its ability to see society as welcoming and open rather than hateful and racist.

I am not opposed to schools teaching histories of historically marginalized populations. But I am opposed to teaching American history in a way that *excises* from the curriculum the privilege of learning about the accomplishments we've made in the effort to become the truly diverse and inclusive country that we are today. And that's what the ethnic studies curriculum and Critical Race Theory are doing. It is like the Jefferson Bible of our history: it pledges to teach only the bad about our country and line-item-veto the good. This, of course, is Critical Race Theory propaganda, and it should be viewed that way.

A Curriculum Motivated by Jealousy

There's one example from Santa Barbara's ethnic studies curriculum that I want to dig into that perhaps illustrates its propagandist nature best. It is the exclusion of Jewish Americans.

In 2016, in response to activist foment, the state of California ordered the draft of an ethnic studies model curriculum. What came out of that 2016 draft was . . . anti-Semitism. The 2016 ESMC fails to mention Jewish Americans in its list of minority groups. It portrays positively the Boycott, Divestment, and Sanctions movement, which aims to delegitimize the Israeli state, and characterizes Muslim Palestinians as "oppressed" people fighting against the Jewish "oppressors." It even fails to define anti-Semitism as a form of minority oppression.

Matef Harmachis, the Santa Barbara world history teacher who led students in a pro–ethnic studies march, was forthright in his assessment of the reasons for excluding Jewish people from the curriculum: "Adding Jewish people to the model curriculum makes no sense," he wrote in an email to the superintendent of schools. "They were never in the original areas of study and as a group did precious little to help bring ES to our university and college campuses. And now they believe they have some say in the matter? Perhaps if it was Jews making complaints I would listen, but these are zionists who are hiding behind a beautiful religion. They are charlatans at best and, in reality, outlandish racists."[27]

So offensive was the ethnic studies curriculum to many Jewish Americans that the California Legislative Jewish Caucus wrote: "We cannot support a curriculum that erases the American Jewish experience."[28]

Even Santa Barbara's notoriously progressive residents felt the curriculum was insensitive to Jews. Members of the city's famous Congregation B'nai B'rith synagogue decided to give the ethnic studies activists a chance to explain themselves. They offered to host a meeting to help "clear the air" between ethnic studies activists and the Jewish community. And the person they brought in on the ethnic studies side was none other than diversity consultant Artnelson Concordia.

Artnelson Concordia? The one whom Christy Lozano described as asking white teachers to sit in a circle and watch minority teachers write nasty things about them? Yeah, that bloke.

In addition to holding teacher trainings, Concordia happened to be a long-standing ethnic studies activist employed by the Santa Barbara Unified School District, assisting in implementing ethnic studies requirements in the classroom. He was compensated quite nicely: that position alone fetched him a six-figure salary, which was supplemented by his private ethnic-studies consulting fees. One would hope this means that Concordia knew what he was talking about and represented his position well.

There were high hopes for the meeting at B'nai B'rith—an opportunity for the Jewish community to share its feelings about being represented. Concordia started off nicely, saying that "anti-Semitism should be included in the discussions of the curriculum."[29] Maybe this would lead to greater understanding rather than division, people started hoping.

That's when B'nai B'rith member Jillian Wittman pressed Concordia on a question about Jewish ethnicity. "How is our Jewish ethnicity represented in our school district?" she asked.

"Okay, we need to focus on Jews of color," Concordia responded.

Jews *of color*? The silence from the crowd was a question in itself. The question was, *Did he really just say that?*

Concordia elaborated by saying that having an ethnic studies class focus on Jews would be like having a feminist studies course discuss the experiences of men. He would not say whether white Jews are considered oppressed, despite their experience of the Holocaust.

The air in the synagogue was immediately pervaded with "staleness," Wittman said in an interview with me. Every word Concordia spoke seemed like nails scraping down a chalkboard. Jews? Privileged? The consultant was layering it on, thick and slow. "His answer floored everybody," another attendee at the event, Clare Lopez, told me. "It's really contemptuous of the concerns of Jewish parents" who are sensitive to the history of Jewish oppression and modern anti-Semitism.

Yet Concordia *had* to preserve the distinction between white Jews and other minority groups in order for Critical Race Theory to make sense—his whole activism depended upon it. To characterize Jews as a minority group would be to concede that Critical Race Theory's construct of a privileged-oppressed dichotomy was more complex than one would initially think. On the one hand, Critical Race Theorists need white Jews to be characterized as oppressors because of their supposed outstanding wealth and social status in America. (Some also view the state of Israel, founded upon what they believe to be indigenous Palestinian territory, with disdain.) On the other hand, Jews have faced much persecution in the Western world, although less in America than in Europe. So Concordia was caught between a rock and a hard place regarding Jews—even though the answer is: let's stop labeling people as privileged and oppressed in the first place. Sadly, that thought never occurred to the professional Critical Race Theory activist. He had to find some way to shoehorn Jews into one or the other category—so he went with splitting the baby, implying that white Jews were privileged while Jews of color were oppressed.

There is a poem called "Inside Dachau," written by Native American author Sherman Alexie, whom I mentioned in chapter 6 and who wrote *The Absolutely True Diary of a Part-Time Indian*. It contains the following stanza, referencing the Dachau concentration camp and its associated memorials:

What do we indigenous people want from our country?
We are waiting for the construction of our museum.[30]

This poem isn't about Native American and Jewish friendship. This poem is about jealousy—the perception that Jews get all the museums in our country, despite the fact that the Native Americans suffered also in the West. *We are waiting for the construction of our museum.* No, American Indians are not Holocaust deniers. But some of them *are* resentful that Jews have many monuments and organizations all over the United States that memorialize their plight during the Holocaust, a *European* tragedy, even as American Blacks who were enslaved and Native Americans who were killed by *Americans* don't get nearly as much commemoration, in their eyes. The Jews get Holocaust museums and Anne Frank's diary, but Native Americans get nothing of note.

And although you could say that Native Americans are in fact directing their anger at American society's favoritism toward Jews, not at Jews themselves, you would still have to contend with the question of why American society would favor Jews in the first place if it weren't for the fact that they are closer to the power structures and have greater access to financial and cultural capital than Native Americans do. Jews are *white-adjacent*, ethnic studies activists argue.

Theodor W. Adorno opined that "to write a poem after Auschwitz is barbaric."[31] Native American ethnic studies activists would counter, "Oh, yeah? And it wasn't barbaric after the Trail of Tears?"

This makes the issues of race, diversity, and ethnicity in our country yet more complex, because we have an obligation to remember the history of the truly oppressed. For a brief moment, it makes ethnic studies activists understandable—and deathly rational. They are arguing that America has, in fact, a selective memory. And that may be true. But we shouldn't kid ourselves. Ethnic studies activists aren't motivated by some sort of high ideal of a color-blind America. They're motivated by jealousy.

On October 12, 2021, the California governor, Gavin Newsom, signed an ethnic studies mandate and the ethnic studies model curriculum into California law. Ethnic studies became a course requirement for every high schooler in California. And the activists pushing for Critical Race Theory in history class got a lot wealthier and more powerful as they flooded into the gates opened by the new mandate.

By elevating ethnic studies to the level of a mandatory class for high schoolers, California put Critical Race Theory right up on the same pedestal as math, science, and English. At an estimated cost of $73 million to the Los Angeles Unified School District alone and $40 million to the Hayward Unified School District, ethnic studies adds up to a more than $1 billion proposition injected into the state's enormous public education system.[32] Not only that, schools also have to hire a bunch of trained staff to teach ethnic studies to these children. "We figured we are going to have to add at least one teacher per school site, and that's an ongoing cost," Angel Barrett, LA Unified's executive director of curriculum and instruction, said about the new ethnic studies mandate, radio station KPCC reported.[33]

I wonder where those teachers are going to come from?

Unfortunately, they're going to come from the pipelines that Harmachis and Concordia and their ilk built for the purpose of inserting Critical Race Theory into the classroom.

Good for the activists. They worked hard to get this. Artnelson Concordia bagged a six-figure salary. All the consultants and administrators in this space are happy. Only the children suffer.

Oh, the obsession with identity. Oh, the obsession with racial dichotomization and the oppressor-oppressed narrative. This is about playing out our resentments toward one another, our hatred toward our fellow men, in the field of children's education. Ethnic studies pledged in its curriculum to focus on four main themes: "identity; history and movement; systems of power; and social movements and equity."[34] But what about love? What about brotherhood? How can you teach about identity without teaching about our relationships with other people? How can you teach about identity without showing that people can come together in times of ethnic strife to fight back and create a more beautiful country? Is history without love and friendship real history?

But this isn't about history.

CHAPTER 9

Queer Theory's Endangerment of Children

As you will recall from the previous chapter, Jennifer Freed's non-profit organization, AHA! (attitudes, harmony, and achievement), employs twenty-four-year-old and twenty-five-year-old trainers to teach public school children how to have "vulnerable" conversations about their "social-emotional health."

In 2021, Freed had just struck a six-figure deal with Santa Barbara Unified for her services as a consultant in social-emotional learning (SEL). According to the memorandum of understanding between her and the district, her job for the ensuing several years was to "build relationships with" high school age students and "help students feel connected."[1]

Social-emotional learning is a technique that first became popular among educators in the 1990s. It's based on the idea that children who are contemplating suicide and harming themselves need more attention and love and less punishment in order to become fully healthy human beings. It advocates teaching emotional and social skills to children—skills such as "respecting each other" and "managing anxiety." If this sounds like Sunday school without Jesus, it's because it *is* Sunday School without Jesus. And just as there are good Sunday schools and bad Sunday schools, this incredibly broad mission is easy to both champion and demonize. There is one unifying factor, however, that brings together SEL advocates in schools: the philosophy of "restorative approaches," which seeks to decrease the punitive nature of school policies.

A restorative approach assumes that the current state of affairs is too "punitive" to the student and encourages working "with" the student rather than "against" him. It sounds dandy. Such approaches often take on a Critical Race Theory and Queer Theory connotation as well. For example, the nonprofit organization CASEL, which advocates social-emotional learning, says that SEL can be used to address "various forms of inequity and empower young people and adults to co-create thriving schools and contribute to safe, healthy, and just communities." It later defines "inequity" as differences in "race, ethnicity, family income levels, learning abilities, home language, immigration status, gender identity, sexual orientation, and other factors."[2]

Although this all sounds nice and great, the problem is that *social-emotional learning* is such a vague, catchall term that it often is used as a Trojan horse—a way to sneak far more insidious concepts behind the walls of the public education system. Sometimes, these concepts—such as those promoted by Jennifer Freed—are in fact antithetical to the whole moral foundation of good mental health.

For example, consider AHA!'s insistence on having kids touch each other. A text message to me from a former Santa Barbara High School student, Chase Kamin, says:

> aha forces students into uncomfortable situations where they're made to spill personal experiences or feelings in front of a classroom with students they might not want to consol [*sic*] in. It's all thought to be for bonding and getting to know each other but students did not once willingly participate and constantly complained about aha...most students became uncomfortable because it involved touching other students or being put in awkward situations where you're isolated in front of the class.

Supposedly, a nonprofit organization focused on social-emotional learning should teach children how to have healthy boundaries. But AHA! was attempting to get the students to loosen their boundaries for the sake of "vulnerability." To Freed, exploring one's own vulnerabilities is the key to "emotional health." In fact, Freed makes an *astrological* connection to it on her website. "If you have a preponderance of planets in water signs, or a major Neptune aspect to your Moon or Sun, you will face lifelong challenges around dealing with your heightened sensitivity," she writes.[3] Clearly, she is wedded to a spiritual paradigm that assigns cosmic significance to the various emotional states and vulnerabilities a child exhibits.

But to people not sharing her beliefs, AHA!'s practices come off as... weird. Cage Englander, the former school board candidate and former Santa Barbara high schooler forced to participate in AHA!, said to me in an interview that "these are people coming into the classroom with biases [and] putting these biases onto the students." In a series of remarks before the Santa Barbara Unified school board, he added, "Quite frankly, from anecdotal experience...I just don't really think it helped anyone. The most it was was an awkward experience sitting inside of a circle with your friends talking about your feelings."

Sheridan Rosenberg, a parent in Santa Barbara, confided in me that her daughter was made to recall uncomfortable experiences in AHA!'s "Roses and Thorns" group circles. The game roses and thorns, which is about the highs and lows of the week, is fine. But Sheridan's daughter, Zoe, was forced to share deeply painful stories about her life and vulnerabilities. Furthermore, these were not optional classes: AHA! had effectively taken the place of a regularly scheduled health education class at least once every six weeks.

It's very apparent based on the convictions of AHA!'s founder, Jennifer Freed, and the experiences of the children and parents who have experience with its programs, that AHA! is not simply an innocent social-emotional learning nonprofit organization.

Neither are many of the nonprofit organizations that partner with schools serving predominantly poor, undocumented Latino kids in California. The *San Francisco Chronicle* reported on a camp for high schoolers called "Camp Diversity." At Camp Diversity, "Latino students will be ordered to clean up after whites and ushered into restrooms labeled 'No

Mexicans or Dogs Allowed.' Jewish students will be pinned with yellow stars and taunted about the Holocaust. Some teens will be called 'retards' and slapped on the back of the head."[4]

One high school English teacher said about Camp Diversity, "The kids are trusting us, and the parents are trusting us, and the teachers think there must be some research backing it." But how do these nonprofit organizations reward community trust?

A girl who had a problem with cutting herself found the issue resurfacing at Camp Diversity. "She cut herself as many as nine times over its four days," says the story.

There is some sick desire in these organizations to make students recount and even relive traumatic experiences. And for what purpose?

That purpose is to break down the boundaries of what is acceptable to teach children.

Listening to Jennifer Freed, a frequent guest on the popular sex podcast *Sex with Emily*, proves this. "The only irrefutable truths are our feelings and sensations. No one can tell you that your feelings and sensations are wrong," said Freed in one episode.

If the only irrefutable truths are feelings—and furthermore, if feelings, as Freed believes, reveal some sort of high, cosmic, astrological truth—then the highest purpose of any youth-oriented organization is to extract these feelings from a person in the rawest, most emotional sort of way. These camps feel like attempts to recreate emotionally charged evangelical camps for teenagers without the Jesus. These groups are *trying* to engender strong emotions in kids—without pointing them to any outlet upon which their emotions could rest.

There's only one parallel to what these organizations are doing to kids that I can think of. And that parallel is sex.

Sex is the emotional pinnacle of a person's life experience. It is an act during which men and women most often describe feeling the sublime connection to another person that's unavailable in most of daily life. But if it's engaged in with malice, or abusively, it can scar a person for life.

And yet Jennifer talks so casually about sex that she could be talking about a loaf of bread. "A lot of getting to our power [of] yes in sex is starting to extinguish the behaviors that are very based in 'victim,'" she said on *Sex with Emily*. "Instead of saying to you, I won't go down on you tonight, I just can't, that's not a power move. Be willing to say what you're willing or not willing to do."

There is a constant—and unrealistic—correlation in Jennifer Freed's eyes between sex and empowerment (which probably isn't even on the list of the top five purposes of sex). Freed seems to think that one can *will* his or her way to better sex. As anyone who's ever had sex knows, that simply isn't true.

Still, Freed's belief in this is interesting, because it points to something I mentioned at the beginning of this book: the idea that merely because a person feels a certain way, we must acknowledge it as true. This idea holds that the strongest truths are not facts but feelings—a message Freed and her fellow SEL consultants seem to be getting out on the regular. No one can deny you your feelings. Whatever you feel, you are right in feeling that. Even if that feeling is a desire to act upon your sexual attraction to children.

Sexual Abuse and Compliance

There is one thread that ties all these nonprofit organizations together, says Sheridan Rosenberg, the parent whose daughter, Zoe, was forced to undergo AHA! peace builder training under Jennifer Freed. And that thread is sex.

Sheridan Rosenberg is no ordinary parent. She grew up in a California town called Ukiah, where there was an outpost of people who followed the teachings of a cult leader named Jim Jones. Jones, head of the pseudo-Christian cult the Peoples Temple, used every abusive tactic in the book to compel his flock to obedience. "My mother saw horrible things with teenage girls who were strapped to a wheelchair and sexually abused there over and over again," Sheridan told me.

Jim Jones recognized that the abrogation of sexual boundaries was the first step in forcing compliance in any number of other ways. "One of the things that cults have in common is sexual abuse. It's almost ubiquitous.

Usually of children," Sheridan observed. And the reason is that once the walls of sexual innocence are broken down, adults who wield influence or have charisma feel like they can do whatever they want...even to children. Once parents in these cults are sufficiently traumatized, Sheridan says, they will comply with authority figures in a manner that goes against their natural instincts. "There is something that happens in this indoctrination process that triggers in a parent something that I think is biologically unnatural, where they go the opposite direction. Rather than protect their children from predators, they hand them over and they enable it, and they defend it and they excuse it away," she says.

The evidence backs her up. For years, Jim Jones and his cult leaders tortured, abused, and sexually assaulted the people of Ukiah, all in the name of religion and his vision of a free society. And when the feds started coming after him, he successfully persuaded much of his flock to move to a place he called Jonestown in Guyana, a country in South America. There he orchestrated the largest mass suicide in history—907 individuals died by cyanide poisoning under his watch.[5] "He had successfully coerced and indoctrinated these people for so long, he got them to murder their own children in their arms," Sheridan said. "Children they loved, by the way. Children they loved. By all accounts, they loved their children. And their need to prove their devotion to him was more."

Now recall AHA! and Camp Diversity. By openly pressing students to share emotional traumas and vulnerabilities, by pushing children through "conversations" about sensitive topics such as sex, these organizations are slowly but surely breaking down the barriers of innocence that discourage children from engaging in risky behavior. Freed was following the playbook in *Curiouser*, the primer on Queer Theory—questioning the whole idea of innocence in a child, having grown men introduce sexually charged topics to children as early as possible.

AHA! was bringing more than just cutesy affirmations into classrooms. It was excessively personalizing the educational experience. It was encouraging students to overshare with adults and weakening their boundaries—all in the name of social-emotional learning.

In addition, over time, the sessions were getting heavier and heavier. The emotional temperature was getting hotter and hotter.

There was only one place this could go.

Sexual Boundarylessness

The warning signs about Matef Harmachis, the unapologetically Communist world history teacher and leader of the Ethnic Studies Now Coalition, were present long before the 2016–17 school year. In 2005, he was nearly terminated by the Santa Barbara school district after allegedly physically assaulting students and making inappropriate sexual remarks. He supposedly said things such as, "Just because you're good in bed doesn't mean you can eat in class." He told one student to "rub her body all over his." Then superintendent Brian Sarvis stated publicly that Harmachis was a "detriment to students" and that the district "cannot have Matef teaching high school students."[6]

But Matef sued and ultimately retained his position. And so he was allowed to serve in a capacity in which he taught and mentored children. Neither students nor parents, unless they were particularly inquisitive, found out about his abusive history. They weren't told.

And it didn't take long for him to get out of line yet again.

"He was an attractive, charismatic man," Maria, a student in Matef's class, remembered in an interview with me. (Maria is not her real name.) "Women were really open with him and talked about birth control." He would hug girls, even kiss them. "Can I feel the fabric of what you're wearing?" he asked Maria.

"I could have sex with any of the girls here," he allegedly said during his AP world history class at Santa Barbara High School during the time that Maria was around him.[7]

After Harmachis was reinstated, he started building a network of protection in case he ever got outed again. In addition to being the leader of the Ethnic Studies Now Coalition, which kept him in contact with students, he became a noted figure in SB Unified's extensive social-justice scene, which included Just Communities and the Fund for Santa Barbara, even hanging out with its preeminent donors, including Sara Miller McCune, a leading philanthropist.

But he never changed. Over time, Maria noticed that Matef was becoming more explicit and predatory. The hugs became longer and tighter. He offered massages to female students, made sexual noises, and even asked one victim to call him Daddy. He did things that probably wouldn't be unwelcome in an AHA! seminar—attempting to cross the line from charismatic teacher to charismatic friend . . . even lover.

On May 4, 2017, Maria was heading out the door after class when the world history teacher allegedly grabbed her buttocks, bit her ear, and made explicit sexual statements. Terrified, she fled, going directly to the school administration.

This is where the accounts of the incident start to differ. Santa Barbara Unified maintains in its defense that as soon as Maria went to the administration, the officials in charge "immediately contacted law enforcement and cooperated with their investigation," according to the *Santa Barbara News-Press*.[8]

However, Maria remembers a different sequence of events. According to her, although the administration "called the police" after her report, it wouldn't keep her apprised of the situation and kept her in the dark regarding her police report. She alleges in a lawsuit she filed against the district that the school "fail[ed] to report the continuing molestations and abuse" to the appropriate child protective authority. "They didn't give me my police report for eight months," she said. Meanwhile, Matef was put on paid leave by the school district, parlaying his reputation as an activist into speaking gigs around the city, schmoozing the leafy Santa Barbara nonprofit scene, and coming into regular contact with children. He spoke at the sixteenth annual Youth Leadership Awards ceremony, sponsored by the Santa Barbara County Teen Network, on May 22, 2017—sixteen days after Maria reported his assault.

The district also engaged in some funny business to try to shut Maria up. One day, a middle-aged woman reportedly showed up at Maria's house. She identified herself as a member of law enforcement. In reality, her name was Barbara Dalton, and she was actually a private investigator hired by the defendant, the Santa Barbara Unified School District. According to the website of T9 Mastered, a training organization, Dalton is a "licensed private investigator" who conducts "third-party investigations" into "allegations of sexual misconduct and discrimination brought pursuant to Title IX."[9] The website does not specify that she often conducts these investigations *for* the institutions accused of misconduct.

Yet Barbara Dalton had a reputation in Santa Barbara for getting offending institutions, of which there were many in the moneyed California town, out of hot water. She was the private investigator hired by the Santa Barbara High School's Multimedia Arts & Design Academy to provide the school's defense with information regarding the victims of alleged sexual assault by one of its teachers, Pablo Sweeney. And this woman posed as a law enforcement officer to extract information and possibly persuade Maria to drop the case against her world history professor. "[Dalton] asked me explicit questions," Maria said. "She said I could transfer to a different high school."

But Maria refused. She was determined to report her assault and stick with her allegation. So Santa Barbara's powers that be resorted to a far more insidious tactic.

Maria was attending class, case pending, when she got a request from a middle-aged, smiling woman who offered to get coffee with her. At the time, she didn't know much about this woman other than that she was the leader of a social-emotional learning nonprofit organization, so she accepted.

That woman's name was Jennifer Freed.

Score One for the Bad Guys

What was Jennifer Freed doing leading workshops in the Santa Barbara public schools in the first place? How could an outside consultant bent on stripping children down to their most sensitive vulnerabilities get this kind of access to children—access that only vetted school officials were supposed to have?

The answer lies in the long-standing progressive economy of victimhood that pervades American schools. Jennifer Freed was an important conduit for injecting Queer Theory into the veins of the schools. She would come in, talk about sex openly with children, invite grown men to talk about sex with children, and flaunt her organization's life-changing impact to her donors—all while helping Santa Barbara and Hilda Maldonado advance their agenda of mandating Queer Theory and Critical Race Theory in district classrooms.

In one public presentation to donors, Freed told the story of a boy named Paul. She said, "[Paul] came to us at fourteen, hating, defeated," but "learned over time to be a self-expressed, confident young man, *proud of his mixed-race heritage.*"[10] She then said, almost as an afterthought, that Paul later became the deputy sheriff of Santa Barbara County. What's funny is that the thrust of her pitch to Santa Barbara donors, captured on video, was not Paul's eventual career accomplishment but his pseudo accomplishment—being proud of his mixed-race identity. Give her audience one glance and you see it—middle-aged white liberals. To these folks, a person's feelings and "pride" in "who he is," rather than his real accomplishments, are the selling points.

But these are not simply privately funded nonprofit organizations. No. AHA!'s contracts with the *publicly funded* Santa Barbara Unified School District are extraordinarily lucrative. Nowhere was that made clearer than in a school board meeting on June 11, 2019, whose purpose was supposedly to evaluate the strength and efficacy of AHA!'s measures, particularly its peer-led Peace Builders program.

The evaluator was Assistant Superintendent Frann Wageneck. In her presentation to the board, it was clear from her near-constant pauses, slipups, and general anxiety over the situation that she didn't feel good about AHA!. She presented decidedly negative results regarding its ability to get teachers to buy into the Restorative Circles and Peace Builders programs, which the board had highly touted. In fact, the results showed zero teacher buy-in, with no implementation of the circles—the same circles former Santa Barbara student Cage Englander described as "talking about your feelings"—and no acknowledgment of the student peace builders. The teachers were either not aware that these programs existed or simply did not trust the students and the staff of AHA! to teach conflict resolution in a beneficial way. And why would they? This was an outside nonprofit organization coming into teachers' own classrooms and asking kids to be "vulnerable" and touch each other. None of the board's findings—or Wageneck's recommendation, which was to cut the $30,000 in government funding AHA! received for its Peace Builders program—should have come as a surprise.

Yet something happened at this meeting that could only be described as shocking.

Wageneck, tripping over her words, continued to blubber and spurt apologies. "I thoroughly believe that [AHA!] can work," she said, even as the PowerPoint slide looming above her said the opposite. She even went so far as to blame herself for the failures of AHA!, saying, "I take personal responsibility for this."[11] Watching Wageneck blame herself for AHA!'s failures was cringeworthy.

Then board member Laura Capps stepped in to clean up Wageneck's mess and embarrassingly obvious blubbering. Capps, a prominent upperclass Santa Barbara fundraiser and school board member whose mother was a congresswoman for the district, knew everybody in the town—at least, everybody who mattered. "AHA! does raise $350,000 for Peace Builders, so I trust that you will pause this in a way that doesn't thwart any of that private funding that does come our way," she said coldly.

Unfortunately, Capps's haughty attitude may have gotten the best of her in this instance, because she inadvertently dropped a true bombshell that both signaled her out-of-touch air and reframed the entire conversation about predatory outside nonprofit organizations' presence in public schools.

Between the period of 2015 and 2019, SB Unified contributed $30,000 per year to AHA!'s Peace Builder program—which doesn't seem like a lot, but what Laura Capps shockingly admitted in that June 11, 2019, board meeting was that the district's $30,000 per year grant *leveraged* a further $350,000 per year private donation to AHA! for its services to the school district. "This evaluation is taxpayer money, but be mindful of the fact that it does leverage private donations that AHA! does bring in, and I hopefully don't want to lose that," Capps said. This means that AHA!'s provision of services to SB Unified was the selling point to a particular private donor or series of donors who contributed more than than $300,000 to enable the organization to work within the school system. What's extraordinary is that Capps *knew that* and *used that as a reason* to go easy on AHA!, even as the school district was scheduled to pull $30,000 in funding based on a lack of evidence of its efficacy with children.[12] This meant that she, a school board member, was openly mixing her role as a financial steward of SB Unified with her implied role as booster for AHA! and its founder, Jennifer Freed. Why would she express concern for AHA!'s welfare in a public school board meeting except to hint to her colleagues that AHA! is "one of us"?

What people were witnessing in that room on that day was a rare instance of a school board persuading itself out of the right decision in real time, in public, for all to see. And the results were evidence of that weakness. After a spell of just one year without the AHA! Peace Builders program, SB Unified signed a new deal with AHA! at Santa Barbara High School for the 2019–20 school year at a cost of $9,999 (likely "leveraging" hundreds of thousands of dollars more), then signed another deal in 2021–22 for $7,500 from La Colina Junior High School and another for $2,600 from Goleta Valley Junior High School.[13]

It was like an estranged boyfriend who just can't summon the courage to break up with his needy girlfriend. It was like watching a messy, half-thought-out divorce negotiation in which the initiator is having second thoughts.

This is how the game works in sunny Santa Barbara: activist organizations like Freed's take slices and slices from Santa Barbara's educational pie, using political connections to get favored access to school boards.

A little nip here: five hours of health class dedicated to AHA!'s Queer Theory–based "social-emotional learning." A tug there: $1,500 an hour for R. Tolteka Cuauhtin's activist professional training.[14] Take a look at Santa Barbara's educational system long enough and you begin to see a district hollowed out by Critical Race Theory and Queer Theory vultures fighting for the state and federal funds to implement their activist programs. The activists build their careers off money from the school district. The superintendent and the school board benefit in the lavish treatment they get from the organizations they're funding. Everyone wins... at least, everyone *involved in the transactions* wins. "What frustrates me most is that a lot of these groups...are also close friends with the boards that vote on their pay and vote on hiring them; they're groups that are entirely dependent on school districts that give them money to stay afloat," Cage Englander said to me about the nonprofit-to-school-board pipeline. And he's right. It's a closed economy facilitated in the same way Communist China was facilitated: by *guanxi*, or connections.

Englander added, "Laura Capps was a nonprofit consultant, and she was chair of SB Unified for a while," revealing the sources of the woman's supposedly independent wealth. "Anytime you have a friendly relationship with someone that you're then handing money [to] to do a superfluous task...it seems a little ridiculous to me, and I wish there was more transparency." Especially since many of those nonprofit organizations also pay *Laura Capps* money to "advise" them, which is consultant-speak for introducing them to relationships within the school system through which they will be able to strike an illicitly arranged partnership. This is wheel spinning at its worst. There's nothing about this hermetically sealed system that could possibly work to benefit the children.

But there's a lot that could hurt them.

Dark Turn

Jennifer Freed sat down with Maria, flashing a smile cultivated through years of nonprofit fundraising prowess.

Maria believed at first that she was talking to this woman to help assuage her trauma about the sexual assault. Freed seemed nice and friendly at first, Maria recounted. Then she shifted the conversation to Matef. Freed's tone changed when the victim started opening up about the alleged assault.

"I know Matef. He's a good person," Freed said to Maria. When Maria protested, Freed leaned in: "You know what the rates are for Black men in jail. You don't want to just put him in jail."

Freed asked the victim to rescind the charges against Harmachis. After Maria equivocated, Freed came in for the gut punch. "She was going to tell the principal that I was going to drop the charges," Maria told me.

In an email to me, Freed denied all affiliation with the case and ever having known Harmachis. "I didn't know him at all," she said. She specified that she was "truly not involved with this case at all" and denied asking Maria to rescind the charges against Harmachis.

But a preponderance of the evidence points to the likelihood that she not only knew Harmachis but also operated plainly in his wide professional and social circle. In a November 13, 2018, board meeting, a man named Nicolas Aguilar got up and made a case for including AHA! programs in Santa Barbara schools. On his shirt was the familiar Black Power solidarity fist, encircled by the Ethnic Studies Now! logo.[15] Aguilar, who worked for AHA!, was also heavily involved with the Ethnic Studies Now Coalition, which Harmachis led.

The significant crossover also signals the coalition's and AHA!'s mutual ties to the Fund for Santa Barbara, the city's leading activist grant-making organization. The Fund for Santa Barbara was a major donor to AHA!, giving $5,000 to its Latinx social-emotional learning program and cohosting numerous events with it.[16] The fund also cohosted an event with AHA! entitled "Hear Me Out: A Judgment-Free Space for Sharing and Listening." And by the way, guess who is on the board of directors of the Fund for Santa Barbara? None other than Diane Fujino, Matef Harmachis's wife.

Matef Harmachis, for his part, expressed no remorse for his actions at all. Calling the student who accused him of molesting her a Karen, he responded to my email inquiry as follows:

> Thank you for your invitation. But, as you know, I am in a civil case with the SBUSD. Therefore, on advice of counsel, I am unable to comment on anything involving—even tangentially—the time I spent working in ESN!SB. As you know, the karen who accused me of molesting her is under the wing of Fair Education, whose members have been attacking ES, ESN!SB and social justice in the SBUSD for several years.

One thing, based on the evidence, is beyond question: the school district was unwilling, or unable, to let one of their own go, because of political and institutional pressure to make him stay so that he can teach Critical Race Theory to children. The district's 2005 statement firing Harmachis stated, in no uncertain terms, "Mr. Harmachis is not welcome at any district function or on any district campus." Yet even after the alleged groping, even after the multitude of allegations of sexual predation made by various women and parents, even after a clearly in-name-only order to remain off campus and away from the children, the history teacher and ethnic studies activist still roamed around Santa Barbara High School, coming into contact with children in closed-door settings and activist arenas. Photos show Harmachis speaking to children at a block party hosted by the Ethnic Studies Now Coalition, documented by the *Santa Barbara Independent*.[17] Harmachis also attended an October 24, 2018, board meeting, surrounded by Ethnic Studies Now! kids, watching as the school district passed a resolution to require five credits of ethnic studies for every child passing through a Santa Barbara high school. And in the November 13, 2018, school board meeting, right in the front row for every board member and the superintendent to see, was Harmachis.

I asked Coraline Crannell, the young lady who defended ethnic studies to me, whether she was aware that Matef Harmachis, her world history teacher and ethnic studies leader, had sexual assault allegations slapped onto him during the period when she interacted with him. Coraline's face turned sheet-white. "I don't know. I can't make any more comments because it's really new to me," she said, apparently hearing for the first time about anything like this. Then, having previously praised Harmachis, she began to distance herself from him. "It's not like I know this person very well or anything."

Neither Matef Harmachis's students nor their parents had a clue that the world history teacher was accused of sexual assault, battery, harassment, and all kinds of other misbehavior. Santa Barbara Unified did not care to share this information about its prized teacher. Some students didn't know until it was too late.

It turns out that you can hide an accused sexual abuser in plain sight in a small town—if he is on your side.

The School of Woke has become more than just a factory for indoctrination. It has become a mob protecting its vilest members.

Queer Theory's Endangerment of Children

While Santa Barbara watched, Matef Harmachis roamed the school for his next victim. Meanwhile, his consultant friends broke children down by compelling them to share ugly stories about themselves. While the consultants thrived, the school board looked the other way. While the school board looked the other way, children confronted the daily reality that they were in an unsafe, predatory environment, abetted by Queer Theory and facilitated by an activist school system more interested in protecting its own instead of protecting students.

Stu Mollrich is an attorney at the firm representing Maria in her lawsuit against the Santa Barbara Unified School District for its negligent supervision of Matef Harmachis, among others. I meet Mollrich in his spacious Los Angeles office. His firm, Manly, Stewart & Finaldi, had just won an $852 million settlement against the University of Southern California on behalf of the victims of USC gynecologist George Tyndall and a $500 million settlement against USA Gymnastics for its negligent supervision

of the notorious serial abuser and doctor Larry Nassar. Yet this compara-
tively "small" case involving a victim of sexual abuse by an ethnic studies
teacher in Santa Barbara caught their attention.

"Predators go where they can be respected," Stu, an attorney at the
firm, told me in an interview. This includes public schools, where they
can teach extremely sensitive subjects such as race behind closed doors. At
Santa Barbara High School, shielded by friends and ideological activists
who needed a champion for ethnic studies, Matef, protected by a politically charged institution, happened to be in the perfect environment to
prey upon children.

Matef was respected. His ideas were revered. He was a cultural figure
in Santa Barbara, almost like a college football coach would be in an SEC
town. In a city where less than 2 percent of the residents are Black, he
was an unapologetic Black activist, the founder of the Ethnic Studies Now
Coalition, and the keynote speaker at social-justice fundraisers. He was
essential to the city's progressive establishment.

That meant the compromised school board tolerated his unacceptable
behavior and even swept it under the rug so students and parents didn't
know.

People like Stu Mollrich and his colleagues at Manly, Stewart & Finaldi may be able to win Maria millions of dollars. But even if they do,
they will have only chipped away at a broken establishment. The real
enemy is wokeness itself—the inversion of social justice for malicious
ends. This is social justice used to reify a broken system. This is an army of
ideas, businesses, schools, activists, and politicians coalescing around one
framework—the Critical Race Theory and Queer Theory dialectic of the
oppressor and the oppressed—in order to serve themselves at the expense
of everyone else. Even the children's own safety.

PART III

THE PARENT-LED REVOLT

CHAPTER 10

The Battle for the Schools

On March 29, 2021, the *Daily Mail* reported that a Facebook group called Anti-Racist Parents of Loudoun County was compiling the legal names and home addresses of parents opposed to the teaching of Critical Race Theory in Loudoun County, Virginia, schools. The list, effectively a "hit list" of people opposed to CRT and Queer Theory programs, was created by a Loudoun County mom named Jen Morse as a way to "combat the anti-CRT initiatives" of the parents on the list. She called for volunteers to "gather information," "infiltrate," and "spread information" about "these people," including their children and the schools they attended. Volunteers with "hacking experience" were specifically preferred.[1] Loudoun County school board member Beth Barts gave her implicit stamp of approval to this effort, writing, "Thank you for stepping up. Silence is complicity," CBS reported.[2]

According to the Leesburg, Virginia, *Patch*, members of the group claimed officially that the list was only going to be used for "oppositional research" and not for "intimidation," but such claims can only be seen as empirically false.[3] Why would a list need parents' legal names, their children's names, and *home addresses* if not to intimidate parents or threaten them with action against their children? (Another unfortunate source of leverage authoritarian school officials have against parents is that they often serve as teachers in their kids' classrooms, forcing parents to negotiate or risk retaliation against their children.)

"They proceeded to name sixty or seventy people, including me," Ian

Prior, the director of Fight for Schools, an advocacy group set up to oppose the teaching of Critical Race Theory, told me in an interview. Also named on the list was a school board council member, John Beatty, who was well known for being the only conservative on the board at the time. The Anti-Racist Parents of Loudoun County went after these people and others for their supposed racism, sexism, and various iterations of homophobia on a Facebook chat list—and inevitably, across the wider internet.

"I was personally attacked. My name, my first name, my last name, where my son goes to school, who my husband is, where I live and three pictures of me were all on that Facebook page," said Patti Menders, a Loudoun County mom on the list, the *Daily Mail* reported.[4]

And who was going to eventually use and wield this list? Official school board members and Loudoun County district staff. Beth Barts was on the school board. A former Loudoun County Public Schools teacher, Hilary Hultman-Lee, seconded Jen Morse's Facebook post.[5] Anti-Racist Parents of Loudoun County comprised a who's who of the county's teachers and school officials.

The names of the volunteers the group recruited were kept in store by school officials until they needed someone to do their dirty work for them—harassing parents and holding their kids for ransom. Initially, it was just a local effort by Loudoun County antiracists to subjugate parents and make them pay for speaking out.

Then, almost overnight, things exploded.

Loudoun County Presents: Cruel Summer

"My name is Xi Van Fleet," said the short Chinese woman with wise but fierce brown eyes to a throng of chagrined parents and the Loudoun County school board on June 9, 2021. Xi Van Fleet was a Loudoun County resident, but she had escaped from a country where she had personally paid the price of endless division and a system of oppressor-oppressed hatred. At the meeting, when others were scared to speak, she didn't hold back.

You are now teaching, training our children to be social justice warriors and to loathe our country and our history. Growing up in Mao's China all this seems very familiar. The Communist regime used the same critical theory to divide people. The only difference is they used class instead of race. During the Cultural Revolution I witnessed students and teachers turn against each other, change school names to be politically correct. We were taught to denounce our heritage, and Red Guards destroyed everything that is not Communist... statues, books, and anything else. We were also encouraged to report on each other, just like the student equity ambassador program and the bias reporting system. This is indeed the American version of the Chinese Cultural Revolution. The Critical Race Theory has its roots in cultural Marxism. It should have no place in our school.[6]

It was a sixty-second sear, and the speech went immediately viral.

"Phone calls came in like crazy," Xi told me. Major media programs highlighted her speech, and she appeared on several TV segments and interviews. Xi had one speculation as to why her speech had such an impact. "No one in the Chinese community either said much or said it in an environment where there was major media to pick it up." Yet her speech was one of the most brilliant short encapsulations of the Marxist Cultural Revolution's similarity to Critical Race Theory. In simple, obvious parallels, Xi Van Fleet summed up the stakes to an audience of millions. The number of Loudoun County parents protesting against CRT swelled from hundreds to thousands. Xi Van Fleet introduced a new framework, with game-changing, even world-altering implications, to the Critical Race Theory battle in the schools. It was the comparison to one of the world's greatest tragedies that lit the fuse that started the battle for the schools in Loudoun County.

Parents were not only seeing the indoctrination of their kids in the oppressed-oppressor dichotomy, they were also seeing how pro-CRT parents were treating them and their kids when they voiced their complaints.

Investigations. Facebook groups for the purposes of intimidating them. Holding their children hostage. These issues made the typically suburban and image-conscious parents livid with rage and galvanized people who otherwise wouldn't have participated—immigrants, political independents, religious people—into action.

In fact, on June 22, 2021, throngs opposed to these new LCPS policies and tactics gathered at the Loudoun County school board office in Leesburg, Virginia. "It's chaos around here; it's just chaos," said Drew Wilder, a reporter for NBC4, regarding the protests against policy 8040—which concerned the "rights of transgender and gender-expansive students"— as he whirled around his hands to pantomime a tornado.[7] "They usually did rallies before, [and] there would be speakers from all over northern Virginia, but that one...was particularly rowdy," Joe Mobley, a parent who attended the rally, remembered with a chuckle in a conversation with me. The mood was tense, anticipatory. "That whole summer was the kind where school issues exploded wide open, but the epicenter, ground zero, was definitely Loudoun County, Virginia."

As Winsome Earle-Sears, then running as a Republican candidate for lieutenant governor of Virginia, told me in an interview, "Political party is one thing—but your child is your child. And you don't care about a political party. You want to know who's going to be the best for my child."

The parents swarming into the meeting on June 22 were making it clear by their presence that LCPS's Critical Race Theory and policy 8040 were not the kinds of things they wanted mandated to their children— and furthermore, that they were *here*, they had a *right* to speak, and they *wanted* to have a seat at the table in the face of invidious retaliation.

You will recall that policy 8040 would have required every teacher and school staff member to refer to transgender students by their preferred pronouns, allow them to use their preferred bathroom, and allow transgender students to "come out" to their teachers without alerting their parents. Concerned parents were there to discuss the harmful effects of these policies—and protest if necessary.

The Loudoun County school board president, Brenda Sheridan, called the meeting to order by restating some rules. No clapping. Jazz hands only. Sixty seconds for every remark. Then the board went through its agenda as if walking on a bed of nails. Members were careful to draw out their sentences, knowing—finally—that they were under close supervision. By the time the board had to yield to public comment, parents were anxiously awaiting their turns to speak.

All the tense, unnerved audience needed was the spark that lit the fuse. That spark came just eighteen minutes into the meeting, when the very first parent commenter, Kellie Herring, sauntered over to the lectern to make her remarks. And she delivered a salvo that utterly obliterated any lingering pleasantries that could have been exchanged between the pro- and anti-CRT camps.

"I'm back here today as the proud *screaming* parent of a young transgender son in our Loudoun County school," Herring said, sarcasm exuding from her face. "Today, instead of focusing on the hate that seems to be dripping off the followers of *Jesus* in the room and from their kids in our schools, *I want to take the time*—"

Herring's sentence was interrupted by a squeal. Parents' boos and cheers cascaded down on her one after the other, and Herring egged it all on, clearly enjoying herself. "I can wait!" she insisted over the fracas, gloating, as rainbow hand fans became weapons of moral war and protest signs and pitchforks bobbed up and down in the packed, hot auditorium. "The board is in recess for five minutes!" barked the school board clerk as protesters exploded from their seats, spraying complaint carnage and hurling grievance grenades. This was no longer Old Virginia, with its gentility and white horses. This was the Grangerfords and Shepherdsons from *The Adventures of Huckleberry Finn*.

Eventually, things simmered down to the point where the next speech could be made—another supporter of policy 8040. Then, after a series of such speeches, a few critics were allowed to speak. One was Tanner Cross, a physical education teacher employed by Loudoun County who was suspended from his duties for refusing to call a transgender student by the student's preferred pronouns. He was sponsored by the Alliance Defending Freedom, a conservative legal advocacy group that was backing his effort to sue the school for violating his First Amendment rights.

Nearly every national media outlet came to film the brouhaha, while busloads of people representing every advocacy group under the sun filled the room. Ian Prior, a parent leader on the anti-CRT side, later alleged that progressives launched an effort to populate the room with parents outside the county: "What we see now is a school board who is working with special interests to pack the room...The Loudoun County Democratic Party put out a tweet where they said they'd be busing people [in] from who knows where, [including] special interests like the AFL-CIO, Planned Parenthood, [and] Equality Loudoun," he said.[8]

Special interest groups were all over this, but the biggest speech of the day did not come from any of their members. It was delivered by an older, grizzled-looking man named Dick Black, a retired Republican state senator from Virginia with nothing much to lose or gain from speaking— except his own self-respect.

The school board clerk said his name, and the stooped, white-haired figure marched from his seat to the podium, clutching his notes in his fist. His eyes were livid. When he spoke, a haughty obstinacy still lingered on the creases over his resolute brow. He spoke simply and plainly:

I'm retired senator Dick Black of Ashburn, Virginia. You retaliated against Tanner Cross by yanking him from teaching for addressing a public hearing of this board. The judge ordered you to reinstate Mr. Cross because if his comments were not protected free speech, then free speech does not exist at all. It is absurd and immoral for teachers to call boys girls, and girls boys...and even kids know that it's wrong.[9]

A murmur of agreement ensued. The crowd was locked in, getting louder.

This board has a dark history of suppressing free speech. We caught you red-handed with an enemies' list to punish opponents of Critical Race Theory. You're teaching children to *hate* others for their skin color, and you are *forcing* them to lie about other kids' gender. I am disgusted by your bigotry—

At the word "bigotry," the school board cut off his mike. Yet the retired state senator continued speaking, without amplification, and like a rising wave, a chorus of parents joined in on the confluence of indignation. Signs urging STAND UP VIRGINIA! waved, the image of a man on a horse positioned right above the words. All at once, the parents agreeing with Dick Black's speech began to rise, one after the other, the full width and breadth of their strength on full display.

Dick Black was speaker number 51 out of a scheduled 250, but the board could not sit through the other 199. "Madame Chair, I move to end public comment," a school board member said hurriedly, and then the board yanked the mike, cut off the live stream, and retreated behind a black curtain draped over the boardroom backdrop. Outside, throngs of parents waving signs and fans shouted and jeered. They took over the auditorium, making speeches and rallying long into the day, while police watched with more than a hint of interest in what this would eventually be compared to.

———

After the school board meeting ended, its president, Brenda Sheridan, gave an interview to the *Washington Post*'s Hannah Natanson, expressing disgust at the protesters for what she perceived as disruptive, racist, and anti-LGBTQ behavior. "I'm deeply concerned about the rise in hateful messages and violent threats aimed at progressive members of the school board," she said. "Opponents of the school board who are pushing false stories about 'critical race theory' have severely hurt our ability to do the jobs we were elected to do."[10]

The board was adamant that Critical Race Theory, a doctrine in direct opposition to the idea that America has gotten over its past racial sins, was not in fact being taught in the district's schools and that protesters were going after the new LGBTQ policies for no reason other than hate.

Meanwhile, in the aftermath of the meeting, a few parents were charged with trespassing, and one man, a father named Scott Smith, was handcuffed and arrested for "disorderly conduct" toward a deputy police officer and few of the other attendees there. (Scott Smith was the man who was angry over his daughter's violation by a transgender student at a Loudoun County school.) The meeting certainly provided fuel to Sheridan's argument that the parents were agents of chaos, of disruption. But these are harsh words overall to aim at your constituents. *False. Hateful. Violent.* Those are words aimed to wound. If Sheridan is to be believed, these parents protesting Critical Race Theory in the schools could be called "bigots," the last miked word in Dick Black's remarks at the June 22 meeting. Maybe even criminals.

A reasonable observer would look at the melee, the opposing speeches, the name-calling, the liberal use of the word "bigot," and think that this was a case of intellectual "he said, she said," a case of murky definitions taken to their logical ends by both the school board and the parents opposing them, broadly representing liberal and conservative factions. An observer might even say that both sides had reasonable grievances and that all the commotion was a bit extreme. Sure, the board isn't a friendly outfit, but these parents didn't have a right to march in and storm a meeting and level the kind of verbal attacks on board members they did.

Maybe everyone just needs to get along. A person making that point could be forgiven for having that perspective. He or she would be right if it weren't for one thing: everything Dick Black said in that speech about Loudoun County Public Schools' policies was true.

The Empire Strikes Back

The Loudoun County protests were attracting some serious attention—and not all of it from friends. While President Joe Biden was in the midst of limiting teachers' and parents' rights to speak out against transgenderism and Queer Theory, his compromised attorney general, Merrick Garland—who, as you'll recall, has a son-in-law who profits off the woke economy—was helping the Biden administration establish a surveillance state, the likes of which has never before been seen in American history, targeting what they both deemed to be bigoted, antigay parents.[11]

Garland's office sought to mobilize the FBI's Counterterrorism Division and its Criminal Investigative Division to "[address] a spike in harassment, intimidation, and threats of violence against school administrators" from parents opposed to CRT.[12] He broadened the statutory authority of the FBI to include investigation of Americans accused of harassing school board members. He asked the FBI to create a threat tag called EDUOFFICIALS, which the FBI could use to take action against people who display what the federal government (i.e., Attorney General Garland) defines as "criminal activity" toward school board officials.[13]

"Threats against public servants are not only illegal, they run counter to our nation's core values," Garland intoned hollowly in a letter dated October 4, 2021. "While spirited debate about policy matters is protected under our Constitution, that protection does not extend to threats of violence or efforts to intimidate individuals based on their views."[14]

In fact, Garland did not issue this letter recommending an FBI investigation of the anti-CRT parents because of reason or logic but because of an open letter that he received from Viola Garcia, the president of the National School Boards Association (NSBA), a relatively unknown group that up until then had a solid reputation for bipartisanship. But that changed dramatically with one letter.

The NSBA letter to Garland began by saying, "America's public schools and its education leaders are under an immediate threat."[15] Then it said that anti-CRT parents were waging violence against schools "equivalent to a form of domestic terrorism," begging the attorney general for government action against parent protesters. Right there on the letter, emblazoned as its chief example, was Scott Smith's scuffle with officers over his daughter's sexual assault by a transgender student at the June 22, 2021, meeting.

The real funny thing is that no one would care about Viola Garcia's letter had not Attorney General Merrick Garland picked it up, read it, and actually *did what she asked him to do,* even admitting that the letter compelled him to action. "I read the [NSBA] letter," Garland said rather plainly at a Senate hearing on the matter, confirming that it figured into in his decision making but refusing to go into detail about how involved an outside organization was in influencing him.[16]

In fact, new evidence shows that Garland and Viola Garcia had been orchestrating the release of both her letter and Garland's letter in response, sent just five days later. In a series of emails obtained by the advocacy group Parents Defending Education, one can see that Garcia tried to get Garland to supplement her letter with federal action. Emails popped up showing Garcia's efforts to persuade Garland's office to release both letters together. In one, Garcia wrote about her dalliance with the Biden administration: "In talks over the last several weeks with White House staff, [Biden's executive team] requested additional information on some of the specific threats, so the letter also details many of the incidents that have been occurring."[17] In an internal memo, the NSBA acknowledges that it had a meeting with the White House on September 14, 2021.[18] The release of the letter and Garland's response was, effectively, coordinated. The NSBA would label the parents "domestic terrorists" and provide the cover; Garland would come in, high-minded, with the objective of "preventing violence."

But putting the FBI in charge of investigating these parents?

For the FBI to get involved in an issue, there has to be a "federal nexus" for it, according to FBI-speak. A "federal nexus" is any kind of determination that an issue requires the federal government's attention and resources.[19] For example, the War on Drugs, whatever you think of it, was changed from a state-by-state issue to a federal issue during the Reagan administration, giving the Drug Enforcement Administration and the FBI broad authority to investigate drug kingpins and smugglers (and, sometimes, innocent people along with them). Now Merrick Garland was changing the issue of "harassment, intimidation, and threats of violence against school [officials]" from a state-by-state issue to a federal one so that he could issue FBI warrants, giving the Bureau powers of counterinsurgency against parent protesters.

Merrick Garland, who had once been a Supreme Court nominee, knew (or should have known) the consequences of labeling parents as intimidators. He just didn't care, and he laid on his callousness thickly. "I am directing the Federal Bureau of Investigation, in conjunction with each United States Attorney," he wrote, "[to] facilitate discussion of strategies for addressing threats against school administrators, board members, teachers, and staff."

Asra Nomani, a Muslim parent fighting Critical Race Theory in the schools, took personal umbrage at the declaration that Garland and the FBI considered her a prosecutable threat. "I am what a domestic terrorist looks like?" she asked plainly on national television.[20]

Under intense questioning from Republican senators, Garland attempted to assure parents such as Asra that he wouldn't weaponize the FBI against them, saying he could not "imagine any circumstance in which the Patriot Act would be used in the circumstances of parents complaining about their children, nor can I imagine a circumstance where they would be labeled as domestic terrorists."[21]

But he turned around and did the exact things he promised not to do. In fact, correspondence obtained by Republican representative Jim Jordan's office reveals that the FBI has been using the EDUOFFICIALS tag to monitor and even approach parents' houses after the parents have spoken out about political issues. Through Jordan, one mom alleged that an FBI official had knocked on her door and interviewed her after she said to one school board member, "We are coming for you." Jordan then told Fox News that he had learned of "more than two dozen" other cases of the FBI harassing and bothering parents, although none has been openly confirmed.[22]

An anonymous FBI whistleblower confessed to the *Washington Times* that his team had been asked to find "white supremacy" in places where there is none, saying there are quotas and "internal metrics" that FBI agents were asked to meet:

"The demand for White supremacy" coming from FBI headquarters "vastly outstrips the supply of White supremacy," said one agent, who spoke on the condition of anonymity. "We have more people assigned to investigate White supremacists than we can actually find."[23]

Merrick Garland, a man whom *Washington Post* columnist Ruth Marcus once described as "deliberative, hyper-methodical" based on her personal correspondence with him, responded to Viola Garcia's letter by directing the FBI, for the sake of "disrupting white supremacy" and *in the name of CRT*, to investigate parents who opposed their school boards' handling of their children.[24]

This is how power-drunk people take advantage of the racism narrative. They fool themselves into thinking that all their power is justified because of "white supremacy." When they attain such power, they take it upon themselves to rid the world of racism. And when they can't find racism, they make it up in order to give themselves the power to "solve it."

And in their own eyes, they are morally justified. More than that—they are morally *obligated* to create the society promised by twentieth-century progressives. Let liberty and freedom from government interference be cast aside.

Back to Santa Barbara

Santa Barbara PE teacher Christy Lozano remembered the fancy galas and government events at which liberal do-gooding was protected and abetted. She, too, could be part of high society's virtue signaling if she just kept her mouth shut about all the horrible antichild things she was seeing in her school. She had a nice salary—about 1.5 times the salary of a similar position at a Christian school down the street—and apparently had tenure. She had been a devoted PE teacher for eighteen years—why not let the sun set on her career in idyllic Santa Barbara? She could wine and dine with her fellow Californians, walk the sun-kissed beach, and live in paradisial retirement. It wouldn't be a bad way to go out.

But the unrest among the teachers in her district was brimming. Nine out of school superintendent Hilda Maldonado's ten cabinet members had already left. She felt the walls of Hilda's woke equity agenda start to close in.

But what convinced Christy that she needed to stay and speak out was something tugging at her conscience. It was the voice of a child. A girl named Paola Padilla. When I called Paola, she was taking a break from her shift as a gas station worker. Christy was Paola's adoring PE teacher, and the adoration was mutual. "Christy always encouraged me when I needed it," she said. "She had such positive energy."

A Mexican girl and the child of immigrants, Paola, who graduated from high school in 2019, was precisely the type of student that Santa Barbara Unified was targeting with its equity programs. In her short time out of high school, Christy had become her mentor and confidant.

"There's been a lot going on, and I just didn't like it," she told me bluntly. "It's definitely, it's always about racism. I'm sorry—I think it's always about racism and the gender pronouns because you don't want to offend people and stuff. So definitely school, I feel like, was surrounded by that instead of education."

I asked Paola when she started realizing this. "I'd say junior year," she replied. "Eleventh grade. That's when everything started hitting me. I was like, 'Wait—how am I in junior year and I don't know how to write an essay?' Like, I couldn't write an essay. You can ask my teachers. I would have to ask them, 'Hey, I can only tell you verbally, but can you write it down for me?' That's when I was like, something is not right. And my other friends across the country, they could do it. And I couldn't."

Paola told Christy how much she struggled in school, how much she was told the world was against her, how few real skills she was really taught, and Christy's heart broke for her.

The former aeromedical evacuation officer in Iraq and Afghanistan was trained to rise to the occasion, not shrink back. "Sometimes I feel like the job the Lord has given me to do is not necessarily to sit back but to be the one to expose what is actually going on," Christy says. And after another round of failed reeducation therapy and brain-burning training, the PE teacher decided she couldn't remain silent. She decided to go public with what she knew about the school she worked for.

Christy posted a public YouTube video, which quickly went viral in her community.[25] It started off with some photos of her playing and hanging around with Dos Pueblos High School's Latino kids, playing basketball, soccer, and running with them. But the heartwarming intro gave way (with Adobe fade-in and out transitions) to a serious Christy, blond hair down and hoop earrings framing a sober face.

Christy did not hold back in the video, which got more than 14,500 views. "For a teacher who is committed to being a positive force in the Santa Barbara Unified District, and invested in team building and confidence lifting, this curriculum does the opposite. This curriculum brings negativity. It's not going to build confidence, security, love, trust, teamwork, unity, and all the elements that are needed to educate our kids."

Then we see Christy log in to a password-protected school district website, meant only for the eyes of school staff. But not anymore, Christy said. She was going to make it available for *everyone* to see. It was like going through a rogues' gallery. There was a section devoted to a "National Black Lives Matter Week of Action," during which kids learned how to be activists for Black Pride. There was also a section called "Specifically for White Folx" with links to some of the resources Christy encountered in her teacher training—a *Vox* article on how to be a "good white ally, according to activists," Black Lives Matter curricula, and even a bizarre digital cartoon of a Black Wonder Woman waving a Confederate battle flag (on Etsy, it's advertised to be a superwoman taking down the Confederate battle flag from the South Carolina state house in 2015).[26] On the gender side, Christy showed a link to a section called "Pronouns Matter" and a video guide for *Sparkle Boy*, a book about a young boy who enjoys cross-dressing. The guide claimed, "Teachers can challenge traditional gender bias" via the story and called on teachers to help kids "explore gender identity."

Within days, Christy's video was picked up by Fox News, leading to an appearance on Laura Ingraham's popular prime-time show, where she made her point: "It's psychological warfare...I will go down fighting if I need to."[27]

Not two days after the show was aired, the fight was taken to her. Columns written by the woke mind police began to flood into Santa Barbara's newspaper and media apparatus, one of them written by a pink-haired woman named Starshine Roshell who called out Christy for being a "ranting white gal" (a descriptor that would fit Starshine Roshell).[28] Another article said Christy's video came in line with "conservative and right-wing attempts to win control of public-school systems around the country."[29] Okay, that part is true. But so is *Christy's video*. If it is now "conservative and right-wing" to *state the truth* about the subjects taught to students, then let the right-wing river floweth.

Christy made a very important point in her video. "I would imagine that if you mention 'ally,' that must mean there are enemies at the moment."

Who are these enemies to progressive wokeness? Well, clearly, parents and teachers like Christy. Parents who want CRT and Queer Theory out of the classroom because they believe—with strong evidence—that these theories are damaging children.

And it saddens Christy that she is treated as an "enemy" simply for speaking out against these courses. "I've always just wanted to help people," she said. Why is she the enemy, not the lack of education pervading our country? Why is she the enemy, not the perverted teachers and activists' curricula foisted upon students? It is because the School of Woke treats the education system as a Marxist activist zone, where there have to enemies because there *has* to be conflict. Lower the standard of nefariousness until people who have even one dissenting opinion about race or gender can be seen as an enemy.

There was a sadness in Christy, who has now been publicly ostracized in her highly progressive Santa Barbara community. But in the month after her exposé went viral, conviction began to replace negativity. "I won't stay in the discouragement; I'll keep my head up," she said to me as support rallied around her from ordinary parents and even children—children she had taught and mentored for years of their lives.

Then I asked Paola about the woke concerns Christy brought up in her video. Are Christy's concerns well founded? There, too, Paola was unequivocal: "What I noticed was they would always kind of segregate us brown people and always talk about white privilege and stuff like that. Like, they would mention it and I was like, 'Okay.'" It was a seductive theory because it allowed people like Paola to cast the blame for her problems on other people instead of taking personal responsibility for her life. "At first you're kind of like, 'Oh, it's true—maybe there is privilege with white people and stuff.'"

But Paola had enough self-confidence to shield herself against that indoctrination. "I don't think we have privilege. We're in America. You have clean running water, you have a house, food, [a roof] over your head. And if that's privilege, we work hard. That's what it is."

Eventually, Paola found a confidante in Christy, bonding over their mutual opposition to these woke tactics. "I was telling Ms. Lozano, I'm all about inclusivity, loving people and not discriminating. I'm all for that. But when it starts trying to indoctrinate and force kids, it's kind of information, I guess, at a very young age, without their parents' consent. It's just some other type of evil."

Christy saw kids like Paola go through this garbage training day after day, and although Paola could resist its lure, others couldn't. And the people training them were starting younger and getting more hateful and spiteful by the year. Christy knew she had to take a stand.

She knew she had to run for office.

The position of superintendent of Santa Barbara County is an elected one that hadn't been contested since the time of Reagan. The superintendent earns a plush $200,000-a-year salary and manages a team of more than five hundred employees. The responsibility is huge. "It oversees the credentials of teachers and...making sure teachers are put into the correct positions. It oversees budgets, signs off on budgets, and facilities and things like that,"[30] Christy said in the online magazine *edhat*. (The position is not to be confused with that of the school district superintendent, Hilda Maldonado, who is appointed by the school board.)

One of the draws of the elected position was that if Christy won, she could oversee Hilda Maldonado and frustrate her woke agenda. That was worth it all, in her eyes. It was worth going public, putting in the work to run for this position, if she could be Hilda Maldonado's *boss!*

At the time of this writing, the superintendent of the education office is a woman named Susan Salcido, who was appointed by the previous superintendent and had subsequently run unopposed for years. Christy Lozano, despite never attaining a rank higher than teacher, decided she would be Salcido's first challenger.

Susan Salcido is a woman used to staying out of the spotlight, but her résumé reveals that she is a creature of the progressive establishment. The Korean American woman (she married into her last name) touts her heavily credentialed résumé on her personal website and LinkedIn. It includes several degrees in education, a PhD focused on "student equity," and a corporate climb from high school English teacher to junior high school principal, deputy superintendent, and finally superintendent of the Santa Barbara County Education Office.[31] Those credentials also brought her into significant alignment with the state's Democratic political machine, which works to keep its preferred candidates in power and voters unaware.

Christy could only see this machine in action the hard way.

She found out while eating breakfast one morning about a lawsuit filed in the county of Santa Barbara aimed at preventing her candidacy for superintendent. The lawsuit alleged that Christy didn't have a certain "administrative credential" that was needed to run for the position, even though she had just obtained it (but had not activated it at the time).

The woman suing Christy was named Mollie Culver, a pot-industry lobbyist working within the district. But make no mistake: Culver was a chump hire protected by a larger progressive umbrella. She had previously done dirty work for Lois Capps, a former Democratic United States congresswoman and the mother of *current* school board member Laura Capps.[32] Remember? Laura Capps was the one who blocked AHA! from being excised from the district because the nonprofit organization would lose private funding. *That* Laura Capps.

It was a frivolous lawsuit that sent a clear message from the educational establishment clique: *You are not welcome.* The tolerant-and-inclusive party had, of course, become intolerant when it came to people threatening its power.

Of course, Christy lawyered up and won the right to run. For the first time in many election cycles, voters in Santa Barbara were going to be given a chance to make a real, consequential decision on the future of their schools. Sleepy-eyed voters who had gone party line in the past could not anymore—because Christy was not running as a member of a party but under a framework of ideas that directly addressed the faults present in the school system as she saw them. Her message was simple and hard-boiled: "Over half of the 67,470 Santa Barbara County students are performing below California state achievement levels," she stated on her campaign website. To solve this crisis, Christy proposed a "four-part plan":

- creating a literacy task force to address students struggling to read at their grade levels;
- using best practices in the classroom, which means getting politics out of it;
- meeting with every member of the cabinet and relevant stakeholders, including parents; and
- leading by example.

Christy wasn't playing around anymore. After years of tolerating the establishment, she was going after its corruption and excesses.

The candidate got at least one supporter: Paola Padilla. "She did tell me [that] she's running, and I was so excited. I was like, 'Go, go, go, girl—go do it.'"

There is a time to stay silent. But this is not the time. If we don't stand our ground against the woke infiltrators, we'll see Santa Barbara County's and Loudoun County's race and sex dystopias establish themselves in schools across America. Get your crossbows and your coffee. It's time to defend our gates from the breach.

CHAPTER 11

Fight Back Against Tyrants

In some ways, the battle for the schools was inevitable. But in other ways, it's a wonder it even got started. Progressives have been in control of our school systems, our graduate schools of education, and our educational bureaucracy for decades. They built a system designed to protect *themselves* and *their* woke interests from harm, while the children they purportedly shepherd bear the long-term costs. That's why the system could continue to spend more and more money and get fewer and fewer results for Black and Latino kids. Progressives created a created a system *designed* to avoid accountability by tearing down No Child Left Behind, embedding CRT into their self-justifications for failure, and controlling the narrative on children—even controlling children *themselves*—through Queer Theory and LGBTQ inclusion initiatives.

So it's a wonder that this battle wasn't over before it began. But every system, no matter how menacing, has a flaw.

The flaw in the woke system lies in its purveyors themselves.

The Inevitable Terry McAuliffe

In January of 2021, it sure looked like Terry McAuliffe was going to become the governor of Virginia. The Democrat grinned eagerly from his prime seat at the US Capitol as Joe Biden came out on a soggy morning in the middle of a coronavirus-abridged inauguration to take the oath of office.[1] Nowhere to be found was Donald Trump, humbled and sent to exile in Mar-a-Lago, in Florida, his supporters scattered and the Republican Party damaged. Virginia had swung heavily for Biden in the 2020 election. To the invitation-only crowd of fewer than one thousand Democratic elites present at Biden's inauguration, the outcome of Virginia's elections in 2021 was bound to be a repeat of the gubernatorial election of 2020—that is, blue as a bruise. And McAuliffe, a former governor and longtime party operative close to both the Clintons and the Bidens, was a blue blood of a blue party in a blue state.

McAuliffe could feel it in his veins. Everything was lining up perfectly for the ambitious Virginian to replace the disgraced Ralph Northam as governor come Virginia's off-year election day in November of 2021. He had set the record for Democratic Party fundraising in his tenure as party chairman, stumped for Hillary Clinton and Biden, and gained the respect of the Democratic establishment as its up-and-coming leader. He had even openly flirted with the idea of running for president in 2020 and bragged to a group of union leaders, "If I can wrestle with alligators, I can certainly wrestle with Donald Trump."[2] He ultimately chose not to run for president, focusing on supporting Biden and the Democrats instead. In exchange, he must have felt sure that the governorship of Virginia would practically be handed to him on a silver platter. McAuliffe relaxed in his seat. For now, he would let the Democratic machine in Virginia work in his favor. Politics was for another time; celebration was for now.

Biden stood up to give the presidential inauguration speech: "Let us listen to one another. Hear one another. See one another. Show respect to one another," he said from the presidential pedestal, a typical display of good sportsmanship from the winner's circle. McAuliffe listened blithely, head nodding—the well-practiced bob of a man who spent his days regaling high-profile donors and activists.

At one point, during the presentation of the colors, Biden appeared to briefly glance at the former governor and even, according to McAuliffe himself, gave him a thumbs-up.[3] In that moment of eye contact, a shared understanding could have been symbolically communicated. Biden would quickly become the past, the grandfather of all that would come to be. And McAuliffe was going to be the future. He was going to be the future of a long line of Democratic governance, a coalition that would stretch for generations, built off the new Democratic platform of friendliness to big bureaucracies and moral high-mindedness on social issues.

Neither Biden nor the man he briefly looked at could have predicted the storm coming. It was a storm fifty years in the making by the Democratic Party. It was a consequence of the party's utter failure—a failure its members are still unwilling to acknowledge today—to confront the real problems that its governance over our schools has caused.

Glenn Youngkin and Winsome Earle-Sears

"I don't think there's any voters out there who believe Terry McAuliffe is for sex assault in schools."[4]

—Ben Tribbett, Democratic consultant, in *Politico*

Winsome Earle-Sears's eyes beckoned the listener to lean in. If you were to get close to the newly minted lieutenant governor of Virginia, you would see there was a glint of fire in them.

"You can either light a candle or curse the darkness," she told me in an impromptu interview in the back of a ballroom at the Gaylord Opryland Resort and Convention Center, in Nashville, Tennessee—an accurate summation of both the reasons behind her decision to run for office and the choices facing instructors who teach children about race in America. "Critical Race Theory is teaching that one race is above another. This thing called equity is that all things must be equal. Nowhere on God's green earth does that work."

Her formula for winning was as simple as "light a candle." When the lights come on, the cockroaches flee.

Winsome Earle-Sears was motivated to run for Virginia's lieutenant governorship on the same ticket as Glenn Youngkin (the positions are contested independently of each other) because of one word: "education," she said.

"I'm the former vice president of the state board of education, and I saw the scores, and they're horrific." To the Jamaican-born immigrant, the first in her family to enroll in college, nothing could replace a firm foundation in literacy and basic math skills. She justified her philosophy to me in the language of economics: "Businesses will not relocate to an area where the population is undereducated or uneducated. You gotta have the workforce talent." Perhaps she was looking over her shoulder at the business-minded Glenn Youngkin, who had come into politics from private equity and was approaching education in a scientific, skills-building manner. But you could tell that Winsome's motivation was fundamentally spiritual.

Invoking Jesus' famous dictum "Render unto Caesar the things that are Caesar's," Winsome shouted to a rowdy Nashville crowd the night I met her, "Our children don't belong to Caesar—they belong to us!"

Glenn Youngkin was a longtime northern Virginia resident and financier, for many years part of that comfortable multimillionaire elite in the DC ecosystem. Although he hadn't run in any election before, don't mistake him for a political novice. Even in DC high-finance circles, business and politics mix like orange juice and vodka. He made dutiful donations to Republicans and presided over a Republican system in much the same way that Terry McAuliffe presided over the Virginia Democratic system. The difference, of course, was that Terry McAuliffe's Democrats were slaughtering Youngkin's Republicans in election after election and taking over every meaningful cultural institution in Virginia. And for a while, he tolerated the whipping, because that's the kind of Republican the cognoscenti assumed he was: a comfortable country-club protector of a declining old guard.

But it turns out that Youngkin, a six-foot-six former basketball player, was tired of getting dunked on. He made a career switch from co-CEO of his private equity firm to political candidate. He poured his own millions into a self-funded campaign for governor of Virginia, outblocking, outmaneuvering, and layupping six other candidates for the Republican primary win.

But that was the easy part. It was going to be difficult to take down Terry McAuliffe, whom inner-circle political strategist Jeff Roe described in *Politico* as "a political boss. If you constructed what a political boss looks like, it would be him."[5] Terry McAuliffe was a legitimate, A-list, blue-blood Democratic party candidate on paper. Polished, ruthless, overflowing with money and connections—he was like a video game's final boss.

But for all his money and connections, the Democrat had one weakness—he was truly out of touch; politicians often try to paint others with this brush, but in McAuliffe's case, it was true. As McAuliffe had gotten rich pulling the levers of a rich party, he had also gotten sclerotic, unable to respond to the concerns of the voters he claimed to serve. He preferred the company of the Hillarys and Bidens of the world to that of ordinary Virginians. Terry McAuliffe simply could not put on a campaign of significant ideas, even when given the opportunity. Rather, he spoke endlessly about Trump, who was already out of office: Trump, Youngkin, and Trump again. CNN correspondent Dan Merica even said the former governor invoked the forty-fifth president's name "perhaps more than any other political figure."[6]

"Terry focused so much on Trump and made his campaign so much about Trump, then abortion, and then I think climate change was in there for a minute," Kristin Davison, a Youngkin adviser, said candidly in *Politico* after the election.[7] The attacks against Youngkin for being a suburban "Trump in a Patagonia vest" got tired eventually, especially since the uber-Christian Republican (Youngkin himself financed the construction of Holy Trinity Church in McLean, Virginia) looked, talked, and presented himself in a way that was completely different from the style of the orange man.

However, Youngkin didn't exactly want voters to think he was Virginia's Mitt Romney, either. He needed to find a way to rally *with* the people instead of just preside over them. His campaign allies were exceedingly aware that the candidate was searching for a populist opportunity, lest Terry McAuliffe start to rip into the Republican for "avoiding $75,000" in property taxes by characterizing his northern Virginia horse farm as "agriculture." (McAuliffe dipped into this issue during the second gubernatorial debate.)

And then the revelations of CRT in schools came down like a comet, entirely grassroots, and completely within the campaigns' frame of mind.

"I didn't hear about CRT until I started running," Winsome Earle-Sears confessed during my interview with her, and Youngkin likely hadn't, either. But the candidates both understood, implicitly, that something in the education system was amiss and that the parents revolting against it had a point. Namely, the school staff was feeding itself and its associated special interests bigger and bigger pieces of the pie, and students weren't learning as they should have been.

With protests against schools boards raging out the front doors of administrative buildings across Virginia, Youngkin's campaign team was finally able to get a grip and seize the education issue in a way that Republicans had never been able to, at least in the previous fifty years.

Campaign strategists Jeff Roe and Kristin Davison were on target with their diagnosis: "The days of the [school] superintendent of your local county being the most powerful politician of your county are over, and it's about damn time," they said in a speech in Palm Beach that I attended.

Still, CRT was the lightning-rod issue that tied it all together—legitimately, as I have tried to show. At every campaign stop, Youngkin pledged passionately to ban Critical Race Theory by executive order.[8] Once he decided to embrace the controversy, he threw himself all in. He became the voice of all the moms and dads who were seeing their kids' brains rot in pits of depression and stagnation in the name of a race- and gender-driven agenda.

In the run-up to the election, every community had different concerns, but each concern reflected a particular facet of Critical Race Theory. Many Asian voters were concerned about the end of merit-based education at the top public school in the region, Thomas Jefferson High School, in Arlington County. Many socially conservative parents (of all races) were absolutely shocked by the revelations of sexual-assault allegations and the resulting cover-up by Loudoun County, primarily because they involved a gender-fluid student. And many Black and Latino parents seethed with anger about the fact that Democratic administrations had been rolling back school choice in Virginia, leaving them with fewer alternatives for their children.

It was all leading up to the climactic event of the election cycle: the gubernatorial debates, aired on national television, the second of which crystallized the contentious nature of the campaigns in ways that had only been implied before.

Terry McAuliffe came into the debate two minutes late, almost too smug and confident. He had his talking points, including those on education, locked and loaded. "I invested $1 billion in education during my governorship, [and] I'm gonna invest $2 billion in education when I'm governor next," he cracked during his opening statement. It was a nice, if vague, attempt to own the issue. But it was full of the same generalities Democrats had used for many years. They continued to make education a fundamentally monetary issue, even though voters were waking up—the money wasn't being used *for* their kids but against them.

During the debate, someone asked whether the candidates would mandate transgender policies like Loudoun County's policy 8040 (the bathroom and forced-pronoun-usage policy) or whether they would leave these matters up to local districts. Terry McAuliffe made a perfunctory nod toward local control before addressing what he really wanted to focus the transgender debate around: protecting kids from homophobic parents.

"These children are going through very stressful situations. Why people continually want to demonize children, I just don't understand," he said. McAuliffe then went on about ensuring that these LGBTQ kids feel affirmed and safe. It was a pretty good answer that showed at least a veneer of heart and played to 2010-era gay-rights politicking. It would require a good response.

And Youngkin delivered in the most brilliant way—by sidestepping McAuliffe's LGBTQ baiting and turning attention to the issue he had been campaigning on for several months: parental rights.

> We are called to love everyone. To love everyone. And I agree with your conclusion, Terry, that we must let local districts make these decisions. But we must ask them to include concepts of safety, privacy, and respect in the discussion. And we must demand that they

include parents in this dialogue…What we've seen in the past few months is that we have watched parents that are so upset because there was such sexually explicit material in the library that they've never seen, it was shocking. And in fact, you vetoed the bill that would have informed parents that they were there. You believe school systems should tell children what to do…I believe parents should be in charge of their kids' education.[9]

Terry McAuliffe responded:

I'm not gonna let parents veto schools and take books out…I don't think parents should be telling schools what to teach. I get really tired of everybody running down teachers. I love our teachers and what they did through COVID. These are real heroes that deserve our respect.

Alberto Pimienta, a panelist in the debate, hurriedly moved to ask another question. And Youngkin even clapped sympathetically when McAuliffe dispensed his applause line about teachers being heroes. It was a classic case of situational irony—when an audience knows more about the consequences of what has just been said than the debate participants themselves do. Because Terry McAuliffe had just made the biggest mistake of his entire career. He said the line that revealed what he really thought.

"I don't think parents should be telling schools what to teach."

McAuliffe's inadvertent confession changed the course of the campaign. "In our poll, we were showing that we were hitting, like, a 45 [percent]" polling average before McAuliffe's debate comments, Winsome Earle-Sears admitted. But McAuliffe's comments (and the campaign materials printed about them) opened the spigot, and the votes for Youngkin came pouring out. Virginia had turned against McAuliffe. "That's when all things broke loose, as people say, and we got Democratic votes, we got Reform Party votes," Earle-Sears recalled.

The reason why McAuliffe's comments broke open a blue state was because they showed the true nature of the Democratic Party's thinking about children. *They are ours; we control them.* You could feel McAuliffe hissing like a viper protecting its young. And the truth is, the Democratic Party in general has made it a priority to control and possess children. The rhetoric started with Hillary Clinton's devilish-grandmotherly comment, "It takes a village to raise a child," which provided the party's justification for building an arsenal of bureaucrats around each and every child.

A single kid in a public school could have a teacher; a counselor; a Diversity, Equity, and Inclusion officer; a lawyer; an HR consultant; and a tech services coordinator—an overprotective cocoon that subordinates learning to protection and affirmation and that smothers the mind of a child with various concerns that fight for control of him and his thoughts. The Democratic Party is the preferred choice, too, of tech billionaires who want to seduce children with technology and of social-emotional learning predators who want to seduce children *period*. At least in the field of education, the Democratic Party has evolved into a reactionary party that wants to keep and expand this tyrannical system—even if it means keeping parents out.

But it would have taken an extraordinarily farsighted person to see that and say that in the September 2021 debate. So I forgive Glenn Youngkin for not pouncing on that issue right then and there.

With a more concerted and earlier effort to court the parents questioning school policies, Glenn Youngkin could have won far more than 50.6 percent of Virginia voters, the final tally on that November 2, 2021, election. But at least he did that. On election night, he and Winsome Earle-Sears pulled off the most dramatic recent upset election since, well, Trump in 2016. They ousted a former Virginia governor and Democratic Party boss. They won over enough concerned parents—independents—to pull them across the finish line. Ironically, just as it was in Obama's 2008 presidential campaign, education was the third-most-important issue on the voters' docket—except this time, the Republican won.[10]

An October 2021 *USA Today*/Suffolk University poll found that when it came down to the matter of whether parents or school boards should have more influence over their children's education, "79 percent of Republicans and 57 percent of independents said parents—but just 16 percent of Democrats did."[11] Youngkin was able to win the election with the help of those independents, a majority of whom supported his side.

Virginia is not the only state where an education platform could be effective for Republicans. A 2022 Impact Research poll found that 43 percent of likely voters nationwide trust Democrats on education compared to 47 percent for Republicans—a far cry from the Obama coalition's 50-percent-plus majority on education issues.[12] Republicans need to seize the opportunity to remind voters that it was Democrats—Democrat-controlled school boards, bureaucracies, and politicians—who got American education into this mess. Were Republicans complicit? Sure. But the American memory still sees the Democratic Party as owning the machinery of education.

Republicans also need to act on their message. On day one of his tenure, Glenn Youngkin did what he promised to do: he signed an executive order to ban Critical Race Theory from the public school system in Virginia. What that means in practice is still playing out at the time of this writing. But the mood was set. We can teach about racism without turning our children against each other. We can affirm our students' feelings while protecting their privacy.

The election of Glenn Youngkin and Winsome Earle-Sears in 2021 signaled to the country a new, broader social agenda that could truly win the minds and hearts of voters, including independents and Democrats. Here's what Youngkin said rather eloquently during his debate with McAuliffe to summarize his final message to the Virginia electorate:

I think we recognize in Virginia that America has chapters that are abhorrent. We also have great chapters. We need to teach our children real history. We need to teach our children to come together and have dreams that they can aspire and go get. We don't need to teach our children to view everything from the lens of race and then pit them against one another. On day one we're going to get education moving. We're going to reestablish standards of excellence.[13]

That's why at the Nashville Road to Majority conference I attended, Winsome Earle-Sears drew a parallel with the biblical directive to "render unto Caesar." But Caesar, in this case, was demanding more than taxes and money. He was demanding children's souls—and parents were finally realizing that the buck stopped here.

A Few Tips to Save Our Schools

The effort to rid an education system of woke ideas and rebuild one that's truly founded on the needs of children will be a long one—and there is simply no substitute for engaging with the public school system. Republicans risk looking out of touch if their only solution to the travesties of public education is to demand its dismantling. Worse, they risk looking like they don't care about the children currently in public schools.

Winsome Earle-Sears's three-pronged approach, which she outlined to me in that impromptu interview in Nashville, offers a much better path forward for Republicans. At first, she just pushed classic school-choice talking points, including the establishment of more charter schools and private schools. When I pushed back, saying that "90 percent of Black and Latino kids are still in public school; what are you going to do about them?" Winsome thought carefully. "Students first; set high expectations; hold people accountable for everything," she finally said, almost spontaneously, as if she had come up with the plan in the moment.

But I agree with her. These are good principles that will help save public schools. What do they look like in practice? The following action items are for elected officials, public school administrators, and teachers who want to make a *positive* difference in children's lives while respecting the rights that the children and their families have.

One: Reset the Teacher-Student Relationship to One of Authority Rather Than One Without Boundaries

Fifty years of Marxist and liberal indoctrination in teachers' colleges have taught the new generation of educators that their purpose is to build an "equal" and "friendly" relationship with students and to indulge them. This has led to confused students, purposeless teachers, and even inappropriate crossings of adult-child boundaries. A teacher's purpose is to teach a student how to think. A student does not know how to think before he is taught; otherwise, there would be no need for a teacher. A teacher, and policies addressing teachers, need to work from the premise that a teacher has a unique role in a child's life that no other person can really have. Teachers are responsible for a child's cognitive development. Not even parents can provide that, unless those parents homeschool their children.

By buying the critical pedagogists' rhetoric that a teacher's fundamental purpose is to build an emotional relationship with a student, not only are teachers putting themselves in competition with parents for that emotional relationship, they are also actually undermining their own special place in that child's development. All the teachers' colleges and Freirean indoctrination in the world cannot subvert this simple truth.

Schools are edifices that were built for the fundamental purpose of preserving the core teacher-student relationship for the sake of the student's cognitive development. They have since strayed from this purpose and become social welfare dispensers—at least in the social welfarists' imagination. Education writer Stephen Sawchuk points out that the transformation of US schools from centers of teaching and learning into places that serve social-welfare functions accelerated between 1900 and 1930.[14] He writes (with a liberal edge): "As politicians have scaled back supports for other social programs, the resulting challenges—drug epidemics, vaping, gun violence, severe weather events, a pandemic—have been foisted by default on schools."

Whether the other social programs have truly been significantly scaled back in recent history is an open question. But one thing is for sure: we have made school into a beast it was never meant to be. Instead of asking these institutions to do one thing really well—that is, teach—we have asked them to do many things inadequately, including close racial achievement gaps. That lies at the heart of this woke crisis and suggests that a reformation of ideals is at hand.

Two: Facilitate Parent Involvement Rather Than Limit Teachers and Administrators

Legendary mathematics teacher Jaime Escalante shepherded more than one hundred poor Mexican kids in East Los Angeles through the educational rigors necessary to pass the AP calculus exam. But he was only able to do this because he actively courted the parents of the students—some of whom were quite skeptical that their children would ever be able to achieve success in math in the first place, despite the children's protestations to the contrary.

There is simply no substitute for an involved parent in a child's life—and in many low-income minority communities, parents who are juggling more than one job and going through mental and physical heath challenges need to be persuaded to maintain a presence in their children's education.

Florida's Parental Rights in Education law, signed in 2022, does some of this, but it doesn't go far enough. I spoke with with Aaron DiPietro, a legislative director at the Florida Family Policy Council, who said that the law "requires schools to send parents any change they make to their child's school services," meaning that if a school wanted to, for example, assign a child a new gender pronoun, it would be required to let the parents know of this change. That is fine in terms of preventing controversial programs from being imposed on children without parental notification, but it doesn't get at the root of the problem: lack of parental involvement in a child's educational life.

An improved policy, building upon the gains won by the law, would help parents understand teachers' visions for the classroom and give them some level of choice in the teachers to whom their kids are assigned. Teachers could make presentations to parents early in the year, so parents can get a sense of who they are and how they teach, then parents could match their kids to teachers through a specific process—a first, second, and third choice. Although it's not a perfect system, the key to ending the hostility between parents and teachers is to give parents a chance to appreciate a teacher's vision. Some level of parental choice *within* the public school system should be allowed so that parents don't feel trapped.

In the early 2000s, when I was a child, I had the privilege of growing up in one of the nation's best parental-choice systems at work—in Henrico County, Virginia—during its "golden age" of development. The county's reform-minded superintendent initiated a program of parental choice that included five specialty-center high schools—for the arts, for math and science, for the humanities, for engineering, and for communications (now, there are many more).[15] The specialty centers—located in each of the county's school districts—mixed and mingled with the neighborhood population, meaning that students experienced both an accelerated program in whatever subject they chose and, for some, the experience of being in a different community from the one they resided in. Unlike forced integration, this was integration by choice, meaning that parents were under no obligation to send their students to the specialty centers if they didn't want to. But it also meant that the teachers serving the students in each of these alternative programs knew they were getting students whose families were on board with them. This gave teachers the confidence to teach the way they wanted to while facilitating parental involvement in their children's education.

Either of these policies—parent-teacher matching or the establishment of specialty centers—allows for more parent-teacher cooperation in the educational process, helping students get a holistic learning experience that is well integrated and can be supported both at school and at home. Parental involvement and cooperation, as I've emphasized, is essential to student success, and when parents and teachers collaborate on a shared vision, so much more is possible together than apart.

What about the crazy parents?

It is a question I can hear jaded teachers asking. And it is true—there are "crazy" parents who will march into classrooms and disrupt the learning experience in pursuit of their own agendas. But parental choice gives teachers the authority to say to such a parent: "You *chose* me; you *chose* this program; now let me teach it." If a parent comes in to complain, a teacher can appeal to the facts: other parents have chosen this program, and they like it. If you don't, you're free to choose something different for your child next year. But it's a parent's choice, and a parent has to accept responsibility for his or her choices. That's the message we should strike at the heart of all this. Schools should be facilitators for parents' decision making, because it is the parents who pay the taxes that pay for the schools. That means that parents should learn how to live with the consequences of their choices—if they get them. That's the vision of what a truly republican educational system could be and should be.

Three: Bring to Light the People the Public School System Is Working With

After the Soviet Union's launch of the first Sputnik satellite, in 1957, the United States made a historic investment in math and science education. One estimate pointed to roughly $1 billion ($9.9 billion in 2022 dollars) in federal funding that went to state governments for that purpose.[16] Undoubtedly, some of this funding supported good, positive initiatives that boosted student math and science skills. However, a side effect of this massive federal expenditure—which, perhaps because of its apparent success, doubled the number of American students going to college, from 3.6 million in 1960 to 7.5 million in 1970[17]—was that the federal government approached future expenditures in education rather more cavalierly.

Consider the COVID-19 pandemic in 2020. In response to the shutdown of schools, the Trump administration passed a $13.2 billion federal appropriations budget designed to address "the impact that COVID-19 has had, and continues to have, on elementary and secondary schools across the Nation." In 2021, the Biden administration passed a $122 billion follow-up—more than ten times the 2020 iteration. Grouped together, the expenditure was dubbed the Elementary and Secondary School Emergency Relief Fund (ESSER), and it was distributed to state and local districts to, in the administration's words, "help safely reopen and sustain the same operation of schools and address the impact of the coronavirus pandemic on the Nation's students."[18]

The ESSER charter specifically said, "Allocating resources in ways that advance equity and ensuring they are adequate for providing the opportunities and supports students need to succeed are particularly important as we recover from the disproportionate impact of the COVID-19 pandemic on communities of color and communities experiencing poverty."[19]

But Marguerite Roza, the head of Georgetown University's Edunomics Lab, which studies education finance, told me in an interview that the ESSER funds basically have no guardrails attached to them at all. "There wasn't much of a restriction on any of the ESSER funds," she said. "Districts decide on using the money to help whatever they're in need of."

As it turns out, in many of these progressive districts, what is needed is installing the racism narrative. Consider that North Carolina's Cumberland County spent $500,000 of its ESSER funds specifically on an "equity plan" designed to install equity reasoning and thinking at every level of the school district. The budget plan reads: "As equity becomes our universal approach, specific measures are needed to ensure that this is done effectively." This is, of course, chilling. What's worse is reading what the specific measures are. The county will devote $70,000 of this $500,000 to unnamed "professional development" training. It took some sleuthing to eventually determine that Cumberland County hired the Equity Collaborative in 2019 to conduct Critical Race Theory trainings for its teachers, and there are more collaborations with these appalling organizations in the budget for the future.[20] And, in its Diversity, Equity, and Inclusion plan for 2022, the county stated its intention to conduct an expensive headhunting effort to find a chief diversity officer who will surely work to inject more CRT into the veins of this school system.[21]

The progressive machine had clearly been waiting for years for an opportunity like COVID-19. It may surprise you to see how closely the timing of the pandemic corresponded with the instigation of social unrest—but it shouldn't. The rats were simply waiting to get fed.

I don't want to take away local authority to handle finance, but I want to make it more transparent. School districts should alert the public as to which specific organizations they are planning on funding and working with before submitting budget requests. If they do not, our elected officials and community members need to force that data to come to light. They must demand the names of the organizations that districts are contracting with. They will find that the school system is rife with stinking rats.

"You shine a light, the cockroaches flee," says James Lindsay, the coauthor with Helen Pluckrose of *Cynical Theories: How Activist Scholarship Made Everything About Race, Gender, and Identity—and Why This Harms Everybody*, an influential book about the ways in which race and gender scholarship have corrupted the academy. Lindsay runs an organization called New Discourses, dedicated to helping legislators and advocates learn the tactics of the woke and fight back against them. His first step is exposure—which may get rid of 20–30 percent of the most evil actors in the wake of sheer popular anger. However, 70–80 percent of the woke will remain, because they're funded to be woke, often privately and in secret. They have backgrounds like Hilda Maldonado's: head of Diversity, Equity, and Inclusion here, director of inclusion and learning there. That's why Lindsay suggests having mission-driven legislators and budget trimmers going after woke funding streams: "If you actually want to deal with the woke, you have to cut off their funding, cut off their popular support, starve them of the thing that keeps them going," he says. "If no one pays for what they're doing, it makes it a lot more difficult for them to dedicate all their time to doing it."

Passing funding transparency requirements or provisions that rescind funds from schools that divert them to contractors who peddle CRT or Queer Theory would do a lot to chill school spending on these apparatuses.

Of course, liberals will argue that these funds are necessary to "stop racism" and "protect gay kids." Disputing that, of course, is why I wrote this book.

Four: Make the New Measure of School Success TSL—Time Spent Learning

The true statistic of educational value is not test scores. Nor is it money spent per child. But we desperately need an accountability metric for schools. No Child Left Behind became unpopular. But at least it did *something* to force horribly performing schools to get in line. When NCLB was replaced by Obama's Every Student Succeeds Act, Critical Race Theory and the diversity bureaucracy flourished. Now we need to refocus our schools on their primary objective—educating students.

So rather than test scores as an accountability metric, consider TSL—time spent learning.

The measurement is relatively simple to take. Once a month or once every two months, you bring an independent auditor into a classroom (or into a place where he can watch a video of a class in session) simply to monitor how much time the teacher spends on the material relevant to his subject and the time the students spend working independently on their assignments. The auditor stops his stopwatch when the teacher tries to control the classroom—for example, to prevent noise and distractions—or when a nonprofit activist tries to steer the class away from the material. He also stops the stopwatch when the students take tests or when class is interrupted for any reason. A school can bring in several auditors just in case one auditor's standards are different from another's. Then you compile all the auditors' time measurements and average them. That will generate one number—TSL, the time spent learning per day—that can be compared to those of schools across the county and the nation. It's a relatively inexpensive measurement that can add or replace standardized tests to encourage strong discipline and class engagement without running into the pitfalls typical of standardized tests.

Yes, truly great once-in-a-blue-moon teachers like Jaime Escalante can accelerate a child's development in an unprecedented way. But by definition, the vast majority of teachers are not great. Therefore, the best way to better learning is to *spend more time learning and practicing*. This means that teachers and administrators should work together to make the primary focus of the classroom experience (1) learning, (2) internalizing material, and (3) teaching self-control—all while eliminating unnecessary distractions that undermine this goal. Teaching CRT and Queer Theory in class, obviously, does not count as contributing to a student's TSL.

Another good thing about this metric is that its measurement, unlike standardized testing, does not impinge upon the time spent on learning itself. In Montgomery County, Maryland, the time spent on standardized testing came to around seven hundred minutes a year, or nearly two whole school days.[22] Rather than put students through frequent compulsory testing, an auditor can simply sit in the back of the class, unobtrusive, while students proceed with the day. I recognize parents' frustrations with the litany of standardized tests their kids must sit through, so I propose this noninvasive measure that still helps answer the question about how effective a school system really is at driving learning forward.

Our Obligation and Our Reward

Not everyone who fights wins. Christy Lozano lost her bid for superintendent of the Santa Barbara County Education Office. She got 32,000 votes, while incumbent Susan Salcido, who had previously never faced an opponent for her seat, got 52,000. It was a low-turnout election, but Christy put her heart into it. When I called her, inquiring about the vote, she seemed solemn and disappointed but not bitter.

"Count the costs," she said, ruminating on her experience and offering advice to others who might want to follow in her footsteps. After Christy lost the election, she was immediately forced to resign by her school. "They made my life hell," she said. An eighteen-year tenured teacher, the teachers unions like to say, is safe. Certainly, *safe* was how the convicted sexual predator Matef Harmachis felt in his role. But after Christy decided to run for office, and spoke out on video in a way that threatened the educational order, the teachers union showed how little that feeling of safety really means if it doesn't like you.

Exhausted by the campaign, the forty-eight-year-old single mother resigned under pressure, which included harassment and social ostracizing, and took a job, at two-thirds of her previous salary, at Coastline Christian Academy, the small Christian school down the street. "Nobody can live on $50,000 a year in Santa Barbara," she says about her pay. But she still views her situation at the school as superior to the environment she faced at Dos Pueblos.

Her antagonists could chase her out of the school, but they weren't able to break her spirit. Even with a lower salary and fewer resources, Christy discovered just how much learning could be done and just how much potential kids have if the right environment is in place.

"What takes weeks to teach these kids in public schools these kids can learn in a day," she said, astounded. "I always start my classes with fitness training. How many push-ups can they do? How many sit-ups can they do? How fast can they run a mile? And then we work on it through the school year. So it's a series of maybe five or six tests. In the public school I could do maybe one test per day. But in the Christian school I can get them to do all the tests in one day."

For Christy, the school culture is the reason why this is the case. "It's primarily the expectations...In Coastline, all the teachers have a behavioral expectation. In the public school, some do, some don't." It's the difference between the students knowing what the teachers expect of them at all times and students being able to take advantage of a lack of expectations, Christy said. The teachers in the public school are paid much more, she reminded me. But the teachers in the small Christian school are much more effective in part because the students are well behaved. So inspiring is this environment that Christy "would rather keep this job and find a second job than take higher pay elsewhere."

That was not the only opportunity Christy received after her election loss. She was on the verge of accepting an offer to start a "learning pod" at the United Boys & Girls Club of Santa Barbara. This alternative to public schooling would require parents to pay $100 a day (around $15,000 a year, a midlevel price for schooling considered private) to teachers and volunteers who would teach from 8:30 a.m. to 2:00 p.m., after which the children would receive care from the Boys & Girls Club until 6:00 p.m. "It's for working moms," Christy, a working mom herself, explained. "I met with [Michael Baker,] the ED of the Boys & Girls Club, and the director of the Westside club, and he said you can use any of our clubs, whatever location you want—we're not going to charge you anything." And she was excited about the prospect of "bootstrapping" a school, relying on donations and fundraising for the first two years while applying for grants and other funding that would eventually make her little learning pod (thirty-five parents had already signed their kids up) a self-sustaining school.

But the opportunity was dead on arrival as soon as Santa Barbara's progressive establishment heard of it. "We were publicizing it—two to three articles. People read them and started complaining to Michael Baker," she said. "So then he twenty-questioned us. 'Is this a religious organization?' 'Does it discriminate against people?' And we were like, 'No!' "

But it was guilt by association, and the Boys & Girls Club suspended its arrangement with Christy and the learning pod. Another loss precipitated by the woke establishment, bent on punishing its enemies. Still, Christy maintains a fighting spirit. "I'm running for school board this year," she said with a mischievous smile, not giving up despite her initial loss. "And in fact, it's easier than it was when I was running for superintendent, because everyone already knows me." She grinned. "Sorta like cashing in on your hard work."

She lost that school board election as well. But she started a wildfire in her county. "She was everywhere...you either loved or hated her," Joshua Molina, a reporter for *Santa Barbara Talks*, said, complimentarily, about her influence.[23] The laser focus on Christy also sparked a minor teacher revolution in the otherwise highly progressive county. The murmurs about SB Unified superintendent Hilda Maldonado became all-out protests. On May 24, 2022, Santa Barbara's teachers gathered around the district's administrative office and staged a mini Loudoun County melee, waving signs reading WHERE DID 12 MILLION TAXPAYER DOLLARS GO? and OUR BOARD IS FAILING TEACHERS AND STUDENTS.[24] Santa Barbara High School and Goleta Valley Junior High are the latest schools to send formal letters demanding that Hilda respond to their concerns or resign. It's actually incredible. Working teachers are openly revolting against their superintendent. It looks like despite Christy's initial loss, she raised enough awareness to inspire other people to speak out.

Christy expected to raise $10,000 for her campaign for superintendent. She ended up raising nearly $100,000—a very large sum for a countywide position. "Only five or six people gave $4,900," she said, referring to the maximum possible donation. The rest gave "mostly between $100 and $1,000." Her army of support was much bigger than she could have imagined. And although Christy risked her job and her reputation for the kids she taught, she found a landing place better than she had hoped. She found a web of support that would help her and nurture her when she was down so she could come back fighting even harder. "I'm like a celebrity in that Christian school," she confessed happily.

Perhaps not all of us are as courageous as Christy, who stepped up and made that leap of faith. But her story of running for office in the most progressive county in America, facing unimaginable odds, and losing both an election and her job in the process, shows us that courage *is rewarded* in America. Perhaps not enough, and perhaps not until we make wokeness in our public education system a national issue, but win or lose, people remember the person who will fight for their kids.

Derrick Bell, the Harvard Law School CRT progenitor, wrote that "the interest of blacks in achieving racial equality will be accommodated only when it converges with the interests of whites."[25] In other words, white people will only help Black people when it helps themselves.

The battle against CRT shows that Bell is wrong. Americans of all stripes are banding together to fight back against tyrants who care more about themselves than they care about our kids. There is absolutely no question anymore: CRT and liberal governance of schools has contributed markedly toward the stagnation and even decline of student achievement and physical health in our country. And we have a moral obligation to save our schools from these distractions, from these ideologues, from the business interests trying to turn children into data mines, and from the federal government trying to use the CRT narrative to amass unprecedented prosecutorial power.

As an American reading this book, you may feel the temptation to flee the public school system entirely and to live in ignorance of what's going on there. But whether your children go to public school or private school, or even if you choose to homeschool, you cannot give up now, when so many children are counting on us. We must stay and fight.

This is how the battle must be framed. Education should be an empowering endeavor. It should enrich children with learning, not depress them. And it should exist for the purpose of helping children succeed, not for personal profit. The vertical, authoritative, and trusting relationship a teacher has with a child is the entire foundation upon which the edifice of the educational system is built. Everything else is ancillary or, at worst, detrimental. Let's focus on making that relationship as strong and fruitful as it can be. When that relationship is rich and tightly woven, no amount of money or political influence can break or overcome it.

Afterword

Minority Experience

I made a best friend at the age of nine whose name was Dave. His parents were South Carolinian white people and quite honestly the nicest people I had ever known. Dave and I would play together on the front lawn of his house. I would dream up the most ridiculous games to play, and he would play them. It was a carefree childhood, and it was that way in large part because of Dave.

Meeting Dave and his parents inspired me to get to know people of different cultural backgrounds from mine. For white people, "different cultures" could mean Chinese, Indian, African American, Mexican, and so on. But for me, it meant *southern white people*. At any point, I could go back to my Chinese church, my Chinese friends, my Chinese parents. When I wanted to extend myself, however, and learn something different, I would go to the Southern Baptist church down the road, called Mount Vernon Baptist Church. I would listen to the preacher talk about Jesus. I would even experiment with talking to some of the southern girls at the church. (They were always polite. But none of them took my bait.)

When I was in ninth grade, my first real girlfriend was a farm girl from Powhatan County, Virginia. Her parents were the only Democrats in a Republican stronghold (I am barely exaggerating). She was also a rock chick who loved the band Scorpions. Yet even she was opposed to things like smoking marijuana and cursing. If I hadn't learned before, I certainly learned then: people are nuanced. There's no one thing that defines a person—whether white or Black, liberal or conservative, boy or girl.

My girlfriend and I broke up because I moved to New Jersey. And it was there, in Princeton—my parents moved there so they could send me to a good public school while my dad worked near Philadelphia—where I first got a whiff of what I would later come to know as Critical Race Theory. It wasn't overly aggressive, but I remember, for example, that my friends in the debate club would bring up Critical Race Theory to show that my team's position reinforced racism. When I asked the captain how I should respond, he just shook his head and said, "You don't."

But it wasn't until I went to college, at Davidson College, in North Carolina, that I really felt pressure to act a certain way and believe certain things because of my race. My first year, I tried joining the AAPI (Asian American Pacific Islander) club on campus. But it turned out to just be a group about Asian self-victimization and brooding. We read a poem about a white man lynching a Chinese man named Vincent Chin in Detroit. I understood the horrific nature of the incident, but I did not come to an AAPI club to learn about ways in which I was "like" Vincent Chin, oppressed by the white man. I wasn't, and America wasn't, either.

But even after I left the AAPI club, I couldn't escape the victimization narrative. During my freshman year, Davidson brought in an Asian American studies professor to teach a mandatory class called Diversity. The professor pulled out a diagram that depicted a pyramid of privilege and oppression. She put white people at the top of the privilege hierarchy. She put Black people at the bottom. And squeezed in the middle she put Asian people—like me. I was appalled. This wasn't about celebrating our diversity. This was about shaming white people and anyone who admired them or grew up with them.

Later, I learned about the Critical Race Theory term "white-adjacent": the minority kid who conforms to "white" values and therefore abets white supremacy. They were referring to me, I realized with horror. I went to a "white" church. I dated "white" girls. I chose to go to a "white" college. I realized how much Critical Race Theorists hated the thought of me: someone who assimilated well into my hometown, someone who even admired the values of my hometown and the people who brought me up and nurtured me there.

Was I "whitewashed," as my Asian friends would say, teasing me? These thoughts and doubts resurfaced in 2019, when I was getting started with my career, working as a fundraiser. My job required me to be strong and extremely confident in my identity—but all the while I was looking in the mirror and questioning its value. Did I not want to be just like another white person, raising money from white people? What would people say about me if I did?

Critical Race Theory, obviously, would say that I'm a race traitor. The self-doubts threatened to split me apart: at the time, I was writing a book about the Asian Americans who were suing Harvard, a book that later became *An Inconvenient Minority*. Was I even qualified to write such a book, given that it appeared in the world's eyes that I was trading in my "Asian card"? There were a few nights where I thought about abandoning the project altogether, given my fear that my Asian friends wouldn't respect me for writing it even if I completed it.

I prayed and I prayed. "God," I said under my breath on sleepless nights when my self-doubt, dressed as moral compunction, threatened to overwhelm my creative momentum, "I don't know if I'm doing the right thing. I don't know if I'm being the right person."

I knew theoretically that I am not obligated to any race under the Bible's covenant with humanity. "There is neither Jew nor Gentile, neither slave nor free, nor is there male and female, for you all are one in Christ Jesus" (Gal. 3:28 NIV). But did I really believe it? That verse seemed so far away from what America was turning into in the 2020s. When nothing else remained, when I had nothing else left, no energy to spend on litigating race and racism and progressive racism in America, I clung to this verse like a baby clings to his mother's breast—by faith alone. We are all one. We are all one race. We are all united under God's grace, I repeated to myself, barely believing it, barely holding on, as George Floyd and the summer riots and talk about "systemic racism" and our need to be allies against "white supremacy" exploded everywhere. I knew that wasn't my experience, but I was losing confidence in what I remembered from my childhood.

On September 15, 2020, on a vacation trip to the Outer Banks, in North Carolina, I had a breakdown. Tears filled my eyes over my self-doubt, my indecisiveness, the burden I felt to either be for or against my race. I sunk to my knees, sweating, crying, not knowing if I was any good in this world. And God spoke, gently, calmly, like the waves lapping the shoreline: "I made you who you are because who you are is good."

God made me in my skin. God raised me in Richmond, Virginia. God gave me a friend named Dave with beautiful parents who treated me with the utmost love. God brought me to write this book.

He gave me every experience in my life because He knew it was good. Not because I was "white" or "white-adjacent." But because I was individually unique, designed to be exactly who I am. And because I experienced the generosity of this nation in exactly the way God intended.

And it wasn't just I who experienced such kindness from people who looked different from me. It was my parents, too. When they immigrated to America from China, in 1990, they had no friends, no social connections of any sort. But a loving white couple named Barbara and Jack Tapping took them in and became their friends. They introduced Mom and Dad to their local church and their local international student ministry. Having no children themselves, they shepherded Mom and Dad through life like surrogate parents, guiding and loving them and always keeping in touch. And when I was born, a wee bean with a big forehead, they held me in their arms.

Barbara and Jack visited me many times when I was little—so many times that when I was in fifth grade and asked to profile a member of my family, I decided to make a presentation about Barbara and Jack. Because they are family. They loved Mom and Dad and me. I love them. I dedicated this book to them, and now you know why.

They're so much more to me than the color of their skin. What Critical Race Theory wants to reduce, I want to reconstruct. I want to reconstruct the color-blind foundations of our country: my hope is that we can truly be a loving country filled with people who look past physical differences and treat one another by the content of our characters, not the color of our skin.

I know some people think that's a cliché. But I still believe in that color-blind dream, and I am willing to repeat that over and over, even when no one else does and it risks being forgotten. I believe in it because I've lived it. I've seen and done and been around things that would be impossible in a racist country. But in order for me to accomplish any of it, I had to overcome my self-doubt, my paralysis, my fear that I was "going against my heritage" for doing something different. I wasn't. I was doing my heritage proud by advancing my values in a country that welcomes them, the values I was raised with. These are not "white" values. These are the *values of my hometown*.

That's the message we should be teaching our children. Rather than torture ourselves with self-doubt and guilt over our lack of conformity to a racial script, we should live hungry for opportunity and be appreciative of the love, the experiences, and the qualities we've each been given. That is my minority experience.

Acknowledgments

My understanding of the issues surrounding Critical Race Theory and education have been shaped by countless allies and friends who helped bring this book to publication. Thank you to my publisher, Hachette Book Group's imprint Center Street, for shepherding me through this whole process. Thank you to my editor, Kathryn Riggs, for her great treatment. Thank you to Andrew Stuart, my agent, for representing yet another groundbreaking book. Thank you to my "inside sources," only a few of whom I can publicly name, including Sheridan Rosenberg, Christy Lozano, Mark Robinson, Winsome Earle-Sears, Allison Coates, Jian Chen, Karen Lithgow, Ian Prior, Luke Rosiak, and many others. Thank you to Frayda Levy for supporting and encouraging me in my mission. Thank you to my family—Grace, Kenneth, Connie, Kathleen, Barbara, and Jack—for supporting me in every way as I turned this book out in a tight window. All praises go to the Lord, whose love endures forever. Psalm 136.

Notes

What Is Critical Race Theory?

1. *Encyclopaedia Britannica Online*, "Critical Race Theory," accessed November 27, 2022, https://www.britannica.com/topic/critical-race-theory.
2. Richard Delgado and Jean Stefancic, *Critical Race Theory: An Introduction*, 3rd ed., Critical America 20 (New York: New York University Press, 2017).
3. Panorama Education, "Panorama for Social-Emotional Learning," accessed November 24, 2022, https://www.panoramaed.com/social-emotional-learning-sel.
4. Gloria Ladson-Billings, "Just What Is Critical Race Theory and What's It Doing in a Nice Field like Education?," *International Journal of Qualitative Studies in Education* 11, no. 1 (1998): 7–24, https://doi.org/10.1080/095183998236863.

Introduction

1. "Rebecca Garland, Xan Tanner," *New York Times,* June 17, 2018, https://www.nytimes.com/2018/06/17/fashion/weddings/rebecca-garland-xan-tanner.html.
2. Panorama Education, "Panorama for Social-Emotional Learning."
3. Kyle Alspach, "How Panorama Education Got Mark Zuckerberg as a Backer and Picked Boston for Its HQ," *Boston Business Journal*, January 27, 2014, https://www.bizjournals.com/boston/blog/startups/2014/01/panorama-education-mark-zuckerberg-tech.html.
4. Adam Andrzejewski, "Panorama Education, Co-Founded by U.S. AG Merrick Garland's Son-in-Law, Contracted with 23,000 Public Schools & Raised $76M from Investors," *Forbes*, October 12, 2021, https://www.forbes.com/sites/adamandrzejewski/2021/10/12/panorama-education-owned-by-us-ag-merrick-garlands-son-in-law-contracted-with-23000-public-schools-for-social--emotional-climate-surveys/?sh=6aaa01b44e60.
5. Dale Russakoff, *The Prize: Who's in Charge of America's Schools?* (New York: Houghton Mifflin Harcourt, 2015), 213.
6. Alspach, "How Panorama Education Got Mark Zuckerberg as a Backer and Picked Boston for Its HQ."
7. Jonathan A. Knee, "The Melting of Mark Zuckerberg's Donation to Newark Schools," *New York Times*, August 26, 2015, https://www.nytimes.com/2015/08/27/business/dealbook/the-melting-of-mark-zuckerbergs-donation-to-newark-schools.html.

8. "Panorama Education School District Payment Survey 2017–2020," accessed November 27, 2022, https://www.openthebooks.com/assets/1/6/Panorama_Education_School _District_Payment_Survey_2017-2020.pdf.

9. "Fairfax County Increases Five-Year Contract to $2.4 Million to Panorama Education, a Government Contractor Cofounded by Son-in-Law of U.S. Attorney General," Parents Defending Education, October 7, 2021, https://defendinged.org/incidents /panorama-education-datamining/.

10. "District of Columbia Universal Health Certificate Instructions," District of Columbia Public Schools, accessed November 28, 2022, https://dcps.dc.gov/sites/default/files /dc/sites/dcps/publication/attachments/English%20-%20DC%20UHC%20Instructions %20SY17-18.pdf.

11. Andrzejewski, "Panorama Education, Co-founded by U.S. AG Merrick Garland's Son-in-Law, Contracted with 23,000 Public Schools & Raised $76M from Investors."

12. 2022 Virginia School Survey of Climate and Working Conditions, Loudoun County Public Schools. http://inconvenientminority.com/wp-content/uploads/2023/01/Broad -Run-Student.pdf

13. "District of Columbia Universal Health Certificate Instructions."

Chapter 1

1. Hannah Natanson, "Loudoun School Board Cuts Short Public Comment During Unruly Meeting; One Arrested," *Washington Post*, June 23, 2021, accessed December 6, 2022, https://www.washingtonpost.com/local/education/loudoun-school-board -closes-meeting/2021/06/22/30493128-d3ad-11eb-9f29-e9e6c9e843c6_story.html.

2. "Ziegler Proposes $1.56B Loudoun Schools Budget," *Loudoun Now*, January 5, 2022, https://www.loudounnow.com/news/education/ziegler-proposes-1-56b-loudoun -schools-budget/article_f951ebe8-6a2e-5f54-904c-d2aa61d231d0.html.

3. Extrapolated from LCPS budget, 2009–2010, and LCPS budget, 2021–22. See "FY10 Appropriated Budgets," Loudoun County Public Schools, https://www.lcps.org /cms/lib/VA01000195/Centricity/Domain/64/FY10_Appropriated_Budgets.pdf.

4. Virginia Department of Education test results tables, accessed November 24, 2022, https://p1pe.doe.virginia.gov/apex/f?p=152:1:110397162599842:SHOW_REPORT.

5. Andrew Parker, "Report: Work to Be Done on Race, Equity in Loudoun Schools," *Loudoun Now*, June 7, 2019, accessed December 6, 2022, https://www.loudounnow .com/news/education/report-work-to-be-done-on-race-equity-in-loudoun-schools /article_38ee126b-deee-53a3-a85b-13e91b928e1b.html.

6. Luke Rosiak, "Loudoun's NAACP Head Claims Embarrassing Comments Were Made by an Imposter," *Vancouver Times*, May 20, 2022, https://vancouvertimes.org /loudouns-naacp-head-claims-embarrassing-comments-were-made-by-an-imposter/.

7. Luke Rosiak, *Race to the Bottom: Uncovering the Secret Forces Destroying American Public Education* (New York: Broadside Books, 2022).

8. Sandy Frasch, "Simulated Underground Railroad Experience," Indiana University– Purdue University Indianapolis, July 24, 2001, https://scholarworks.iupui.edu/bitstream /handle/1805/3051/Simulated%20Underground%20Railroad%20Experience %20Part%20A.pdf;sequence=1.

9. Veronike Collazo, "For Black History Month, This Loudoun County Elementary School Played a Runaway Slave 'Game' in Gym Class," *Loudoun Times-Mirror*, updated February 24, 2019, https://www.loudountimes.com/news/for-black-history-month-this-loudoun-county-elementary-school-played-a-runaway-slave-game-in/article_9cecd568-35ef-11e9-8540-6372d03d3025.html.

10. *2nd Tuesday School Board Meeting 4:00 p.m. & 6:30 p.m.*, LCPS, 2019, https://go.boarddocs.com/vsba/loudoun/Board.nsf/Public.

11. Collazo, "For Black History Month, This Loudoun County Elementary School Played a Runaway Slave 'Game' in Gym Class."

12. "Loudoun County Public Schools Service Agreement," April 2019, https://defendingedstg.wpengine.com/wp-content/uploads/2021/10/Equity-Collaborative_Loudoun-County-VA_2019.pdf. Also see "Consultant Report Card: Equity Collaborative (the)," Parents Defending Education, https://defendinged.org/report/the-equity-collaborative/.

13. Chrissy Clark, "Loudoun County Schools Spend Hundreds of Thousands on Critical Race Theory," *Washington Free Beacon*, September 28, 2020, accessed December 7, 2022, https://freebeacon.com/campus/loudoun-county-schools-spend-hundreds-of-thousands-on-critical-race-theory/.

14. Equity Collaborative, "Initial Report: Systemic Equity Assessment: A Picture of Racial Equity Challenges and Opportunities in Loudoun County Public School District," June 6, 2019, https://docplayer.net/190535032-Initial-report-systemic-equity-assessment-a-picture-of-racial-equity-challenges-and-opportunities-in-loudoun-county-public-school-district.html.

15. Aaron Parsley, "Gov. Ralph Northam Says He Is '99% Sure' Who's in Blackface in Racist Photo That Rocked Va. Politics," *People*, January 13, 2022, https://people.com/politics/ralph-northam-99-percent-sure-who-is-in-blackface-racist-photo-virginia/.

16. Mark R. Herring, "Final Determination of the Office of Attorney General Division of Human Rights," November 18, 2020, LCPS, https://www.lcps.org/cms/lib/VA01000195/Centricity/domain/60/voag/FINAL_DETERMINATION_2020-11-18_NAACP_Loudoun_Branch_v_Loudoun_County_Public_Schools.pdf.

17. Gurinder Badwal, "4 Criticisms," https://www.lcps.org/cms/lib/VA01000195/Centricity/Domain/19189/4%20Criticisms.pptx.

18. James F. Lane, "Resources to Support Student and Community Dialogues on Racism," Commonwealth of Virginia Dept. of Education, Published February 22, 2019, accessible at http://inconvenientminority.com/loudoun-county-evidence.

19. Robin DiAngelo, *White Fragility: Why It's So Hard for White People to Talk About Racism* (Boston: Beacon Press, 2020), 152.

20. Lauren Fruen, "Cops Investigate Virginia Teachers' Facebook Group for Naming Parents Who Were 'Against Critical Race Theory' and Urging Members to 'Gather Information' on Them," *Daily Mail*, updated March 30, 2021, https://www.dailymail.co.uk/news/article-9415407/Cops-investigate-Facebook-group-named-parents-against-critical-race-theory.html.

21. Jordan Boyd, "Loudoun County Schools Institutionalized Critical Race Theory Despite Public Opposition," *The Federalist*, October 22, 2021, https://thefederalist

.com/2021/10/22/loudoun-county-schools-institutionalized-critical-race-theory -despite-public-opposition/.

22. Rae Yang, *Spider Eaters: A Memoir* (Berkeley: University of California Press, 2013), 94.

Chapter 2

1. Ian Prior, "You Won't Believe How Activists Pushed Loudoun County Schools into Critical Race Theory," *The Federalist*, May 28, 2021, https://thefederalist .com/2021/05/28/you-wont-believe-how-activists-pushed-loudoun-county -schools-into-critical-race-theory/.

2. Caroline Downey, "Consultant Hired by Loudoun County Says Public Education Should Not Focus on 'Learning,'" *National Review*, November 8, 2021, https://www .nationalreview.com/news/consultant-hired-by-loudoun-county-says-public-education -should-not-focus-on-learning/.

3. Chrissy Clark, "Loudoun County Schools Spend Hundreds of Thousands on Critical Race Theory," *Washington Free Beacon*, September 28, 2020, accessed December 7, 2022, https://freebeacon.com/campus/loudoun-county-schools-spend-hundreds-of -thousands-on-critical-race-theory/.

4. Mark J. Perry, "Chart of the Day: Administrative Bloat in US Public Schools," American Enterprise Institute, March 9, 2013, accessed December 7, 2022, https://www.aei .org/carpe-diem/chart-of-the-day-administrative-bloat-in-us-public-schools/.

5. Steven Bruhm and Natasha Hurley, eds., *Curiouser: On the Queerness of Children* (Minneapolis: University of Minnesota Press, 2004).

6. Bruhm and Hurley, 10.

7. Bruhm and Hurley, xii.

8. "Indoctrination in North Carolina Public Education," Office of the Lieutenant Governor, August 24, 2021, https://drive.google.com/file/d/1NfHOpZGD4EeHcGD6y1 AeVBuGUZkpNUia/view.

9. Terri Wu, "'My Duty as a Parent': Inside the Fight to Remove Sexualized Content from School Libraries," *Epoch Times*, January 13, 2022, https://www.theepochtimes.com /mkt_morningbrief/my-duty-as-a-parent-inside-the-fight-to-remove-sexualized -content-from-school-libraries_4204333.html.

10. Monica Helms, "My Princess Boy, by Cheryl Kilodavis," YouTube video, November 23, 2015, accessed December 9, 2022, https://www.youtube.com/watch?v =n0vMomKhY2Q.

11. Loudoun County Public Schools policy 8040, "Rights of Transgender and Gender-Expansive Students," August 11, 2021, https://go.boarddocs.com/vsba/loudoun/Board .nsf/files/C35H9N449351/$file/Draft%20%20POLICY_%208040%20Rights%20 of%20Transgender%20Students%205-6-21.pdf.

12. Sherry Everett Jones et al., "Mental Health, Suicidality, and Connectedness Among High School Students During the COVID-19 Pandemic—Adolescent Behaviors and Experiences Survey, United States, January–June 2021," Centers for Disease Control and Prevention, *Morbidity and Mortality Weekly Report* 71, no. 3 (April 1, 2022): 16–21, https://www.cdc.gov/mmwr/volumes/71/su/pdfs/su7103a3-H.pdf.

13. "Gender Support Plan," Charlotte-Mecklenburg Schools, http://inconvenientminority .com/loudoun-county-evidence.

14. Mayo Clinic Staff, "Pubertal Blockers for Transgender and Gender-Diverse Youth," June 18, 2022, https://www.mayoclinic.org/diseases-conditions/gender-dysphoria/in-depth/pubertal-blockers/art-20459075.

15. David Finkelhor, Richard Ormrod, and Mark Chaffin, "Juveniles Who Commit Sex Offenses Against Minors," *Juvenile Justice Bulletin*, December 2009, https://www.ojp.gov/pdffiles1/ojjdp/227763.pdf.

16. Justin Jouvenal, "In Case at Center of Political Firestorm, Judge Finds Teen Committed Sexual Assault in Virginia School Bathroom," *Washington Post*, October 25, 2021, https://www.washingtonpost.com/local/public-safety/in-case-at-center-of-political-firestorm-judge-finds-teen-committed-sexual-assault-in-virginia-school-bathroom/2021/10/25/42c037da-35cc-11ec-8be3-e14aaacfa8ac_story.html.

17. "Report of the Special Grand Jury on the Investigation of Loudoun County Public Schools," December 2, 2022, https://www.loudoun.gov/specialgrandjury.

18. "Report of the Special Grand Jury."

19. "Report of the Special Grand Jury."

20. Jouvenal, "In Case at Center of Political Firestorm, Judge Finds Teen Committed Sexual Assault in Virginia School Bathroom."

21. Jennifer Smith, "Loudoun County Judge Finds Boy 'in a Skirt' GUILTY of Sexually Assaulting Female Student in Girls' Bathroom," *Daily Mail*, updated October 26, 2021, https://www.dailymail.co.uk/news/article-10132015/Loudoun-County-judge-finds-boy-skirt-GUILTY-sexually-assaulting-female-student.html.

22. Smith, "Loudoun County Judge Finds Boy 'in a Skirt' GUILTY of Sexually Assaulting Female Student in Girls' Bathroom." Perhaps Ziegler thought no one would investigate his sourcing. Because boy, is it bad. There indeed is a 2016 *Time* magazine article about transgender people and bathrooms, but its title is "Why LGBT Advocates Say Bathroom 'Predators' Argument Is a Red Herring" (https://time.com/4314896/transgender-bathroom-bill-male-predators-argument/). The title gives away the entire article: in other words, it's a piece that cites activists, not scientists. The article cites zero scientific studies about the long-term rate of transgender sexual assaults compared to cisgender sexual assaults. The best the article can do is quote a couple of assertions from a few groups and activists saying that there is "no record" of transgender sexual assaults increasing (given the novelty of the issue, the lack of a record should not be surprising). But it's hardly a definitive voice on the debate. And it certainly does not excuse what Ziegler was about to say.

23. Nathaniel Cline, "Updated: Judge Finds Facts Sufficient for a Finding of Guilt in Teen Sexual Assault Case," *Loudoun Times-Mirror*, October 25, 2021, https://www.loudountimes.com/news/updated-judge-finds-facts-sufficient-for-a-finding-of-guilt-in-teen-sexual-assault-case/article_20fbf3fa-35ef-11ec-9e48-1393251238db.html.

24. Nathaniel Cline, "Family of Sexual Assault Victim to File Lawsuit Against LCPS," *Loudoun Times-Mirror*, updated November 26, 2022, https://www.loudountimes.com/news/family-of-sexual-assault-victim-to-file-lawsuit-against-lcps/article_383c4154-3203-11ec-8fbf-f3535a69b103.html.

25. Cline, "Updated: Judge Finds Facts Sufficient for a Finding of Guilt in Teen Sexual Assault Case."

26. Asra Nomani (@AsraNomani), "Breaking NEWS: The Stanley Law Group, PLLC From the Desk Of: William M. Stanley Jr., Esq. Family of Loudoun County girl

sexually assaulted at Stone Bridge High School to pursue civil action against Loudoun County Public Schools," Twitter, October 14, 2021, 12:24 p.m., https://twitter.com /asranomani/status/1448686187535818764.

27. Neal Augenstein, "Email from Loudon Co. Superintendent Alerted School Board on Day of Bathroom Assault," WTOP News, October 21, 2021, https://wtop.com /loudoun-county/2021/10/email-from-loudoun-co-superintendent-alerted-school -board-on-day-of-bathroom-assault/.

Chapter 3

1. Maria Miles, "Paulo Freire's Method of Education: Conscientisation in Latin America," *Economic and Political Weekly* 8, no. 39 (September 29, 1973): 1764–67, https://www .jstor.org/stable/4363063.

2. Paulo Freire, *Pedagogy of the Oppressed*, 30th anniv. ed. (New York: Bloomsbury Academic, 2000).

3. Roberta Clare, "Paulo Freire," Biola University, accessed November 24, 2022, https://www.biola.edu/talbot/ce20/database/paulo-freire.

4. Paulo Freire, "Paulo Freire on Marx and Christianity," YouTube video, uploaded by hiperf289, March 18, 2011, https://www.youtube.com/watch?v=LLXHWM6TCDc.

5. Bess Keller, "Education School Courses Faulted as Intellectually Thin," *Education Week*, November 12, 2003, https://www.edweek.org/teaching-learning/education-school -courses-faulted-as-intellectually-thin/2003/11; Sol Stern, "Pedagogy of the Oppressor," *City Journal*, Spring 2009, https://www.city-journal.org/html/pedagogy-oppressor -13168.html.

6. Blanca Facundo, "Who Are We?," in *Freire-Inspired Programs in the United States and Puerto Rico: A Critical Evaluation* (Washington, DC: Latino Institute, 1984), accessed November 24, 2022, https://www.bmartin.cc/dissent/documents/Facundo/section3.html.

7. Facundo, "Who Are We?"

8. Thomas W. Heaney, "Adult Learning and Empowerment: Toward a Theory of Liberatory Education" (PhD diss., Union Graduate School, 1980), https://www.proquest .com/openview/df9e0326a90914c157e7ccc16fd66ae2/1.

9. Heaney, "Adult Learning and Empowerment: Toward a Theory of Liberatory Education."

10. Blanca Facundo, "Working in the System," in *Freire-Inspired Programs in the United States and Puerto Rico: A Critical Evaluation* (Washington, DC: Latino Institute, 1984), https://www.bmartin.cc/dissent/documents/Facundo/section5.html.

11. Kester Oshagae Ojokheta, "Paulo Freire's Literacy Teaching Methodology: Application and Implications of the Methodology in Basic Literacy Classes in Ibadan, Oyo State, Nigeria," DVV International, accessed November 24, 2022, https://www .dvv-international.de/en/adult-education-and-development/editions/aed-692007 /10th-anniversary-of-paulo-freirersquos-death/paulo-freirersquos-literacy-teaching -methodology.

12. "Adolf Hitler Issues Comment on the 'Jewish Question,'" United States Holocaust Memorial Museum *Holocaust Encyclopedia*, accessed November 24, 2022, https://www .ushmm.org/learn/timeline-of-events/before-1933/adolf-hitler-issues-comment -on-the-jewish-question.

13. Adolf Hitler, "September 16, 1919 Report of Corporal Adolf Hitler to Captain Karl Mayr," *Famous Trials*, University of Missouri–Kansas City School of Law, https://famous-trials.com/hitler/2530-hitler-s-first-writing-on-the-jewish-question-1919.

14. Max Horkheimer, *Critical Theory: Selected Essays*, trans. Matthew J. O'Connell et al. (New York: Continuum, 1982), https://criticaltheoryworkshop.com/wp-content/uploads/2018/03/horkheimer_traditional-and-critical-theory.pdf.

15. Claudio Corradetti, "The Frankfurt School and Critical Theory," *Internet Encyclopedia of Philosophy*, https://iep.utm.edu/critical-theory-frankfurt-school/.

16. Malcolm X, "Malcolm X Speech," *Digital History*, accessed November 24, 2022, https://www.digitalhistory.uh.edu/disp_textbook.cfm?smtid=3&psid=3619.

17. Lisa Trei, "Black Children Might Have Been Better Off Without *Brown v. Board*, Bell Says," *Stanford Report*, April 21, 2004.

18. Trei, "Black Children Might Have Been Better Off Without *Brown v. Board*, Bell Says."

19. "Obama Speaks at Harvard Law in '90," *Frontline*, PBS, https://www.pbs.org/video/frontline-obama-speaks-at-harvard-law-in-90/.

20. Gloria Ladson-Billings, "Just What Is Critical Race Theory and What's It Doing in a Nice Field like Education?," *International Journal of Qualitative Studies in Education* 11, no. 1 (1998): 22, https://doi.org/10.1080/095183998236863.

21. Interview with Daniel Buck conducted by phone on June 28, 2022.

22. Such studies on racial outcomes in the United States were eventually further corroborated by international studies of countries such as South Africa directly after apartheid, where University of Chicago economists Germano Mwabu and T. Paul Schultz found that after controlling for location (that is, rural versus urban) and education, Black and white South Africans could close up to 61 to 68 percent of the racial wage gap for men and women respectively. This study is here: https://www.journals.uchicago.edu/doi/abs/10.1086/452460.

23. Bob Herbert, "Throwing a Curve," *New York Times*, October 26, 1996, https://www.nytimes.com/1994/10/26/opinion/in-america-throwing-a-curve.html.

24. Derrick A. Bell, "Who's Afraid of Critical Race Theory?," *Race, Racism and the Law*, July 3, 2021, https://racism.org/articles/law-and-justice/405-law-policies-and-race/critical-race-theory/9591-who-s-afraid.

25. KK Ottesen, "An Architect of Critical Race Theory: 'We Cannot Allow All of the Lessons from the Civil Rights Movement Forward to Be Packed Up and Put Away for Storage,'" *Washington Post*, January 19, 2022, https://www.washingtonpost.com/lifestyle/magazine/an-architect-of-critical-race-theory-we-cannot-allow-all-of-the-lessons-from-the-civil-rights-movement-forward-to-be-packed-up-and-put-away-for-storage/2022/01/14/24bb31de-627e-11ec-a7e8-3a8455b71fad_story.html.

Chapter 4

1. Using data from Emmanuel Sikali, NAEP 1971–2012 National Mathematics and Reading Long-Term Trend Restricted-Use Data Files, National Center for Education Statistics, June 20, 2016, https://nces.ed.gov/pubsearch/pubsinfo.asp?pubid=2016102.

2. Eric A. Hanushek et al., "The Achievement Gap Fails to Close," *Education Next* 19, no. 3 (Summer 2019): 8–17, https://www.educationnext.org/achievement-gap-fails -close-half-century-testing-shows-persistent-divide/.

3. "Program for International Student Assessment (PISA)," National Center for Education Statistics, accessed November 27, 2022, https://nces.ed.gov/surveys/pisa/.

4. National Center for Education Statistics, "Program for the International Student Assessment (PISA) 2018 Public Use File (PUF)," https://nces.ed.gov/pubsearch/pubsinfo .asp?pubid=2021019.

5. Daniel Patrick Moynihan, "The Negro Family: The Case for National Action," Office of Policy Planning and Research, United States Department of Labor, accessed December 10, 2022, https://www.dol.gov/general/aboutdol/history/webid-moynihan.

6. Richard J. Herrnstein and Charles Murray, *The Bell Curve: Intelligence and Class Structure in American Life* (New York: Free Press, 1996).

7. Charles Murray, *Facing Reality: Two Truths About Race in America* (New York: Encounter Books, 2021), 38.

8. Andrew J. Coulson, "State Education Trends: Academic Performance and Spending over the Past 40 Years," *Policy Analysis* 746 (March 18, 2014), CATO Institute, https:// www.cato.org/sites/cato.org/files/pubs/pdf/pa746.pdf.

9. Victoria Sosina and Ericka S. Weathers, "Pathways to Inequality: Between-District Segregation and Racial Disparities in School District Expenditures," *AERA Open* 5, no. 3 (September 4, 2019), https://journals.sagepub.com/doi/full/10.1177/233285841 9872445.

10. "Every Student Succeeds Act (ESSA)," US Department of Education, accessed November 27, 2022, https://www.ed.gov/essa.

11. "Per Pupil Expenditures: Maryland," Database, Office of Elementary and Secondary Education, https://oese.ed.gov/ppe/maryland/.

12. "Maryland Still Has No Idea How to Fix Its Public Schools," editorial, *Washington Post*, March 9, 2019, accessed December 8, 2022, https://www.washingtonpost .com/opinions/maryland-still-has-no-idea-how-to-fix-its-public-schools/2019/03 /08/60ec4b10-41b2-11e9-a0d3-1210e58a94cf_story.html.

13. "2018 Bridge to Excellence Annual Update," Montgomery County Public Schools, https://www.boarddocs.com/mabe/mcpsmd/Board.nsf/files/B5TPWY601A02 /$file/Tab%201%20-%202018%20Annual%20Update.pdf.

14. Nicole Asbury, "Montgomery Students of Color Lack 'Equitable Opportunities,' Audit Finds," *Washington Post*, October 11, 2022, https://www.washingtonpost.com /education/2022/10/11/montgomery-schools-antiracist-audit/.

15. "The Educational Opportunity Project at Stanford University," Stanford, accessed January 25, 2023, https://edopportunity.org/.

16. Larry Abramson, "McCain, Obama Offer Dueling Education Plans," *All Things Considered*, NPR, July 28, 2008, accessed December 8, 2022, https://www.npr.org/templates /story/story.php?storyId=93004032.

17. "Section 3: Issues and the 2008 Election," Pew Research Center, August 21, 2008, accessed December 8, 2022, https://www.pewresearch.org/politics/2008/08/21/section -3-issues-and-the-2008-election/.

18. "Race Relations," Gallup, https://news.gallup.com/poll/1687/race-relations.aspx.

19. "Full Text of Obama's Education Speech," *Denver Post*, May 28, 2008, accessed December 8, 2022, https://www.denverpost.com/2008/05/28/full-text-of-obamas -education-speech/.

20. "National Student Group Scores and Score Gaps," NAEP Report Card: Mathematics, National Assessment of Educational Progress, National Center for Education Studies, accessed December 8, 2022, https://www.nationsreportcard.gov/mathematics /nation/groups/?grade=8.

21. Libby Nelson and Dara Lind, "The School-to-Prison Pipeline, Explained," *Vox*, updated October 27, 2015, accessed December 8, 2022, https://www.vox.com/2015 /2/24/8101289/school-discipline-race.

22. David Simson, "Exclusion, Punishment, Racism and Our Schools: A Critical Race Theory Perspective on School Discipline," *UCLA Law Review* 506 (2014), https:// www.uclalawreview.org/pdf/61-2-5.pdf.

23. "Joint 'Dear Colleague' Letter," US Department of Education Office for Civil Rights, January 8, 2014, https://www2.ed.gov/about/offices/list/ocr/letters/colleague-201401 -title-vi.html.

24. Alison Somin, "Obama's Education Guidance Was Terrible Policy—and It's About to Come Back," *The Hill*, July 12, 2021, https://thehill.com/opinion/education/562327 -obamas-education-guidance-was-terrible-policy-and-its-about-to-come-back/.

25. Gail L. Heriot and Alison Somin, "The Department of Education's Obama-Era Initiative on Racial Disparities in School Discipline: Wrong for Students and Teachers, Wrong on the Law," *Texas Review of Law & Politics* (forthcoming), San Diego Legal Studies Paper 18-321, updated June 26, 2018, available at Social Science Research Network, https://doi.org/10.2139/ssrn.3104221.

26. Heriot and Somin, "The Department of Education's Obama-Era Initiative on Racial Disparities in School Discipline: Wrong for Students and Teachers, Wrong on the Law."

27. Jim Bacon, "Disorderly-Conduct Complaints in Schools Surge 45% in Past Five Years," *Bacon's Rebellion*, October 25, 2019, https://www.baconsrebellion.com/wp /disorderly-conduct-complaints-in-schools-surge-45-in-past-five-years/.

28. Wyatt Tee Walker and Steve Klinsky, "A Light Shines in Harlem," *Real Clear Politics*, September 24, 2015, https://www.realclearpolitics.com/articles/2015/09/24/a_light _shines_in_a_harlem_charter_school_128189.html.

29. Thomas Sowell, *Charter Schools and Their Enemies* (New York: Basic Books, 2020).

Chapter 5

1. Andrew J. Coulson, "State Education Trends: Academic Performance and Spending over the Past 40 Years," *Policy Analysis* 746 (March 18, 2014), CATO Institute, https:// www.cato.org/sites/cato.org/files/pubs/pdf/pa746.pdf.

2. Will Kenton, "What Is an Economic Bubble and How Does It Work, with Examples," *Investopedia*, October 20, 2022, https://www.investopedia.com/terms/b/bubble.asp.

3. Ibram X. Kendi, *Stamped from the Beginning: The Definitive History of Racist Ideas in America* (New York: Bold Type Books, 2016), 45.

4. Asra Q. Nomani, "Fairfax, Va. School District Spent $24,000 on Ibram Kendi Books for U.S. History Classes," *The Federalist*, September 30, 2020, accessed December 10, 2022,

https://thefederalist.com/2020/09/30/fairfax-va-school-district-spent-24000-on-ibram
-kendi-books-for-u-s-history-classes/.

5. Ann Doss Helms, "Two Top NC Republicans Take Aim at CMS for Paying Anti-
Racism Author Kendi to Speak," WFAE, June 29, 2021, accessed December 8, 2022,
https://www.wfae.org/education/2021-06-29/two-top-nc-republicans-take-aim-at
-cms-for-paying-anti-racism-author-kendi-to-speak.

6. Christopher F. Rufo, "Lie of Credit—American Express Tells Its Workers Capitalism
Is Racist," *New York Post*, August 11, 2021, https://nypost.com/2021/08/11/american
-express-tells-its-workers-capitalism-is-racist/.

7. Pamela Newkirk, "Diversity Has Become a Booming Business. So Where Are the
Results?," *Time*, October 10, 2019, accessed December 8, 2022, https://time.com
/5696943/diversity-business/.

8. Heather MacDonald, "Heather MacDonald: End UC's Diversity Charade," *Orange
County Register*, April 28, 2013, https://www.ocregister.com/2013/04/28/heather
-macdonald-end-ucs-diversity-charade/.

9. Newkirk, "Diversity Has Become a Booming Business. So Where Are the Results?"

10. Dylan Jackson, "The Black Attorney Population Has Not Grown Since 2011," *American Lawyer*, August 2, 2021, https://www.law.com/americanlawyer/2021/08/02/the
-black-attorney-population-has-not-grown-since-2011.

11. Lauren Silverman, "There Were Fewer Black Men in Medical School in 2014 Than
in 1978," *Weekend Edition Sunday*, NPR, October 24, 2015, https://www.npr.org
/2015/10/24/449893318/there-were-fewer-black-men-in-medical-school-in-2014-than
-in-1978.

12. Peter Arcidiacono, V. Joseph Hotz, and Songman Kang, "Modeling College Major
Choices Using Elicited Measures of Expectations and Counterfactuals," *Journal of
Econometrics* 166, no. 1 (January 2012): 3–16, https://www.sciencedirect.com/science
/article/abs/pii/S0304407611001151.

13. Associated Press, "Harvard Pledges $100 Million to Atone for Role in Slavery,"
US News & World Report, April 26, 2022, accessed December 9, 2022, https://
www.usnews.com/news/us/articles/2022-04-26/harvard-pledges-100-million-to
-atone-for-role-in-slavery.

14. "Recommendations to the President and Fellows of Harvard College," Harvard-
Radcliffe College, 2022, https://legacyofslavery.harvard.edu/report/recommendations
-to-the-president-and-fellows-of-harvard-college.

15. W. E. B. Du Bois, "The Talented Tenth," in *The Negro Problem: A Series of Articles by
Representative Negroes of To-day* (New York: James Pott, 1903).

16. Kevin Mahnken, "New Research Points to 'Loudoun County Effect': When Parents
Clash over Ideology, Kids' School Performance Suffers," *LA School Report*, May 16,
2022, accessed December 8, 2022, https://www.laschoolreport.com/new-research
-points-to-loudoun-county-effect-when-parents-clash-over-ideology-kids-school
-performance-suffers/.

17. "Analysis: Pandemic Learning Loss Could Cost U.S. Students $2 Trillion in Lifetime
Earnings. What States & Schools Can Do to Avert This Crisis," Center for Education,
Harvard University, December 14, 2021, https://cepr.harvard.edu/news/analysis
-pandemic-learning-loss-could-cost-us-students-2-trillion-lifetime-earnings-what.

Chapter 6

1. WTVD and Associated Press, "Districts Deny That Books Mentioned by Lt. Gov. Mark Robinson Are Taught in Schools," October 12, 2021, accessed December 8, 2022, https://abc11.com/mark-robinson-lgbtq-filth-nc/11116508/.

2. Sydney Franklin, "'Gender Queer' Returns to Wake County Public Libraries While Book Removal Policy Goes Through Revision," WRAL News, updated January 10, 2022, accessed December 8, 2022, https://www.wral.com/gender-queer -returns-to-wake-county-public-libraries-while-book-removal-policy-goes-through -revision/20072136/.

3. Zetta Elliott, review of *Dear Martin*, by Nic Stone, Social Justice Books, accessed December 8, 2022, https://socialjusticebooks.org/dear-martin/.

4. 1 Cor. 6:12.

5. Euell A. Nielsen, "Mark Robinson (1968–)," Black Past, April 20, 2021, https:// www.blackpast.org/african-american-history/people-african-american-history /mark-robinson-1968/.

6. Mark Robinson interviewed by Beverly Hallberg, "She Thinks | Lt. Gov Mark Robinson on CRT, 'Woke' Ideology, and Being a Black Republican," YouTube video, uploaded by Independent Women's Forum, November 19, 2021, accessed December 8, 2022, https://www.youtube.com/watch?v=QOq2tGAIfqk.

7. "The Black Lives Matter Movement," School Qube, accessed from https://s3 .documentcloud.org/documents/20397322/blacklivesmattermovement2020-1-school -qube-worksheet.pdf.

8. Tyler Kingkade, "How One Teacher's Black Lives Matter Lesson Divided a Small Wisconsin Town," NBC News, October 24, 2020, https://www.nbcnews.com/news /us-news/how-one-teacher-s-black-lives-matter-lesson-divided-small-n1244566.

9. Eric Kaufmann, "Media Pushes False Narrative of Racism," *New York Post*, April 15, 2021, https://nypost.com/2021/04/15/media-pushes-false-narrative-of-racism/.

10. Sophie Bethune, "Gen Z More Likely to Report Mental Health Concerns," *Monitor on Psychology* 50, no. 1 (January 2019): 20, https://www.apa.org/monitor/2019/01/gen-z.

11. Nicholas Kristof, "'How Can You Hate Me When You Don't Even Know Me?'," *New York Times*, June 26, 2021, accessed December 9, 2022, https://www.nytimes .com/2021/06/26/opinion/racism-politics-daryl-davis.html.

12. Daryl Davis, "Daryl Davis Explains FAIR's Pro-Human Learning Standards," YouTube video, uploaded by Foundation Against Intolerance and Racism, November 15, 2021, https://www.youtube.com/watch?v=6qDaNDq_9_8.

13. Viktor E. Frankl, *Man's Search for Meaning* (Boston: Beacon Press, 2006).

14. Monitoring Bias (@MonitoringBias), "In the absence of a sufficient supply of actual oppression, the left attempts to generate an artificial supply to meet its demand," Twitter, November 12, 2022, 8:20 a.m., https://twitter.com/monitoringbias/status/1591420547455455234.

15. Jamie Gregory, "Dear Martin Censored in Georgia," *Intellectual Freedom Blog*, January 7, 2020, https://www.oif.ala.org/oif/dear-martin-censored-in-georgia/.

16. Gregory, "Dear Martin Censored in Georgia."

17. Raquel Rivera, "Freedom to Read and the Stories We Need," *Canadian Children's Book News*, Fall 2011, http://raquelriverawashere.com/latest/3FreedomToRead_CCBN_Fall _2011.pdf.

Chapter 7

1. Edie Frederick, "SF School Board Member Apologizes After Racist Statement About Students," KCBS Radio, July 20, 2022, https://www.msn.com/en-us/news /us/sf-school-board-member-apologizes-after-racist-statement-about-students /ar-AAZNi46.

2. Racy Conversations (@FleshmanKaren), "Curious @LondonBreed do you agree w your appointee to #SFUSD Board Ann Hsu that the biggest challenge to educat- ing Black & Brown students is 'lack of family support' 'unstable family environments' & 'lack of parental encouragement to focus on or value learning'?," Twitter, July 16, 2022, 11:57 p.m., https://twitter.com/FleshmanKaren/status/1548517122396934144 /photo/1.

3. Michael Hansen and Diana Quintero, "Analyzing 'the Homework Gap' Among High School Students," *Brown Center Chalkboard*, Brookings Institution, August 10, 2017, https://www.brookings.edu/blog/brown-center-chalkboard/2017/08/10/analyzing -the-homework-gap-among-high-school-students/.

4. Kenny Xu, *An Inconvenient Minority: The Harvard Admissions Case and the Attack on Asian American Excellence* (New York: Diversion Books, 2021), 11.

5. Hansen and Quintero, "Analyzing 'the Homework Gap' Among High School Students."

6. Hansen and Quintero, "Analyzing 'the Homework Gap' Among High School Students."

7. Chacour Koop, "Smithsonian Museum Apologizes for Saying Hard Work, Rational Thought Is 'White Culture,'" *Miami Herald*, July 17, 2020, https://www.miamiherald .com/news/nation-world/national/article244309587.html.

8. Suzanne A. Kim, "'Yellow' Skin, 'White' Masks: Asian American 'Impersonations' of Whiteness and the Feminist Critique of Liberal Equality," *Asian Law Journal* 8, no. 1 (2001): 89–109, https://lawcat.berkeley.edu/record/1117593.

9. Williamson M. Evers, "California Leftists Try to Cancel Math Class," *Wall Street Jour- nal*, May 18, 2021, https://www.wsj.com/articles/california-leftists-try-to-cancel-math -class-11621355858.

10. Alex Zimmerman, "These Four Graphs Illustrate New York City's Stark Achieve- ment Gaps by Race and Income," *Chalkbeat New York*, January 31, 2018, https://ny .chalkbeat.org/2018/1/31/21104265/these-four-graphs-illustrate-new-york-city -stark-achievement-gaps-by-race-and-income.

11. Eliza Shapiro, "City School Test Scores Inch Up, but Less Than Half of Students Pass," *New York Times*, August 22, 2019, https://www.nytimes.com/2019/08/22/nyregion /new-york-city-school-test-scores.html.

12. Susan Edelman, "'Cheating' Maspeth High School Teachers Ousted from Classrooms amid 'Testing Improprieties,'" *New York Post*, October 30, 2021, https://nypost.com /2021/10/30/nyc-cheating-teachers-at-maspeth-high-school-fired/.

13. Cindy Jong and Christa Jackson, "Teaching Mathematics for Social Justice: Exam- ining Preservice Teacher's Conceptions," *Journal of Mathematics Education at Teachers College* 7, no. 1 (Spring 2016), https://journals.library.columbia.edu/index.php/jmetc /article/view/785/231.

14. Richard Reeves et al., "Race Gaps in SAT Scores Highlight Inequality and Hinder Upward Mobility," Brookings, February 1, 2017, https://www.brookings.edu/research/race -gaps-in-sat-scores-highlight-inequality-and-hinder-upward-mobility/.

15. Jong and Jackson, "Teaching Mathematics for Social Justice: Examining Preservice Teachers' Conceptions."

16. Shannon Watkins, "Do the Math...or Not," James G. Martin Center for Academic Renewal, June 8, 2020, https://www.jamesgmartin.center/2020/06/do-the-mathor -not/.

17. Watkins, "Do the Math...or Not."

18. Thomas Sowell, *Is Reality Optional? And Other Essays* (Stanford, CA: Hoover Institution Press, 1993).

19. Gloria Ladson-Billings, "Just What Is Critical Race Theory and What's It Doing in a Nice Field like Education?," *International Journal of Qualitative Studies in Education* 11, no. 1 (1998): 7–24, https://doi.org/10.1080/095183998236863.

20. Ladson-Billings, "Just What Is Critical Race Theory and What's It Doing in a Nice Field like Education?"

21. Jay Mathews, *Escalante: The Best Teacher in America* (New York: Henry Holt, 1988).

22. "Tom Brady," *Armchair Expert*, September 10, 2020, https://armchairexpertpod.com /pods/tom-brady.

23. *Stand and Deliver*, directed by Ramón Menéndez (1988), https://www.imdb.com/title /tt0094027/.

24. Noah Baustin, "SF Leads the Nation in These Key Demographics," *San Francisco Standard*, September 30, 2022, https://sfstandard.com/research-data/san-francisco-tops -us-income-chinese-older-adults-census/.

25. Thomas Fuller, "'You Have to Give Us Respect': How Asian Americans Fueled the San Francisco Recall," *New York Times*, February 17, 2022, https://www.nytimes .com/2022/02/17/us/san-francisco-school-board-parents.html.

26. Joe Eskenazi, "The Strange and Terrible Saga of Alison Collins and Her Ill-Fated Tweets," *Mission Local*, March 23, 2021, https://missionlocal.org/2021/03/alison -collins-school-board-tweets/.

27. Joe Fitzgerald Rodriguez, "'Stunning Reversal of Fortune': Ann Hsu Voted Off SF School Board Following Racist Comments," KQED, November 17, 2022, https:// www.kqed.org/news/11932210/stunning-reversal-of-fortune-ann-hsu-voted-off -sf-school-board-following-racist-comments.

28. Rodriguez, "'Stunning Reversal of Fortune': Ann Hsu Voted Off SF School Board Following Racist Comments."

Chapter 8

1. Gloria Ladson-Billings, "Just What Is Critical Race Theory and What's It Doing in a Nice Field like Education?," *International Journal of Qualitative Studies in Education* 11, no. 1 (1998): 7–24, https://doi.org/10.1080/095183998236863.

2. "November 8, 2022 General Election," County of Santa Barbara Elections, accessed December 9, 2022, https://www.countyofsb.org/2813/General-Election.

3. "Santa Barbara Unified School District," GreatSchools, accessed December 9, 2022, https://www.greatschools.org/california/santa-barbara/santa-barbara-unified-school -district/#Students.

4. "Santa Barbara Unified Board of Education Appoints Hilda Maldonado as the Next Superintendent," Santa Barbara Unified School District, May 26, 2020, https://pages

.sbunified.org/2020/05/26/santa-barbara-unified-board-of-education-appoints-hilda
-maldonado-as-the-next-superintendent/.

5. *Noozhawk* editors, "From Our Inbox: Letters to the Editor for the Week Ending
Oct. 30, 2020," *Noozhawk*, October 30, 2020, https://www.noozhawk.com/article
/from_our_inbox_letters_to_the_editor_for_the_week_ending_oct._30_2020.

6. Santa Barbara County school board meeting, accessed September 30, 2022, https://
www.youtube.com/watch?v=NXG-R_mxc-8. The video is now private.

7. Jerry Roberts, "Hilda Speaks: SBUSD Superintendent Responds to Onslaught of
Teacher Criticism, Demands and Anger," *edhat*, June 8, 2022, https://www.edhat
.com/news/hilda-speaks-sbusd-superintendent-responds-to-onslaught-of-teacher
-criticism-demands-and-anger.

8. Roberts, "Hilda Speaks: SBUSD Superintendent Responds to Onslaught of Teacher
Criticism, Demands and Anger."

9. Interview with Rosanne Crawford by the author, conducted November 11, 2021.

10. Interview with Rosanne Crawford.

11. Lillian K. Durán, Cary J. Roseth, and Patricia Hoffman, "An Experimental Study
Comparing English-Only and Transitional Bilingual Education on Spanish-Speaking
Preschoolers' Early Literacy Development," *Early Childhood Research Quarterly* 25, no. 2
(2nd Quarter 2010): 207–17, https://www.sciencedirect.com/science/article/pii/S088
5200609000714.

12. Delaney Smith, "McKinley Elementary to Launch Dual-Language School," *Santa
Barbara Independent*, March 22, 2021, https://www.independent.com/2021/03/22
/mckinley-elementary-to-launch-dual-language-school/.

13. Smith, "McKinley Elementary to Launch Dual-Language School."

14. Interview with Rosanne Crawford by the *Santa Barbara Independent*, n.d., http://
inconvenientminority.com/wp-content/uploads/2023/02/Newsmckinley041621.mp4.

15. Roberts, "Hilda Speaks: SBUSD Superintendent Responds to Onslaught of Teacher
Criticism, Demands and Anger."

16. "Approval of Memorandum of Understanding between AHA! and GVJH for 2021–
2022 School Year (Wageneck)," https://santabarbara.novusagenda.com/AgendaPublic
/CoverSheet.aspx?ItemID=8438&MeetingID=295.

17. "Approval of Memorandum of Understanding between AHA! and GVJH for 2021–
2022 School Year (Wageneck)."

18. Joshua Molina, "Santa Barbara Teachers Protest Outside District Offices; 2 More Schools
Send Demand Letters," *Noozhawk*, May 24, 2022, https://www.noozhawk.com/article
/santa_barbara_teachers_protest_outside_district_headquarters_two_more_schoo.

19. Luke Rosiak, "This Is a Cult," *Santa Barbara News-Press*, May 16, 2022, https://news
press.com/this-is-a-cult/.

20. Bobby Seale, *Seize the Time: The Story of the Black Panther Party and Huey P. Newton*
(New York: Random House, 1970).

21. "Ethnic Studies Model Curriculum," California Department of Education, March 18,
2021, accessed November 26, 2022, https://www.cde.ca.gov/ci/cr/cf/esmc.asp.

22. "Ethnic Studies Model Curriculum."

23. "Ethnic Studies Model Curriculum."

24. Erika Carlos, "Ethnic Studies Now to Be Required in Santa Barbara High Schools," *Santa Barbara Independent*, November 29, 2018, https://www.independent.com/2018 /11/29/ethnic-studies-now-be-required-santa-barbara-high-schools/.

25. Coleman Hughes, "The Case for Black Optimism," *Quillette*, September 28, 2019, accessed December 9, 2022, https://quillette.com/2019/09/28/the-case-for-black-optimism/.

26. John Creamer, "Inequalities Persist Despite Decline in Poverty for All Major Race and Hispanic Origin Groups," United States Census Bureau, September 15, 2020, https:// www.census.gov/library/stories/2020/09/poverty-rates-for-blacks-and-hispanics -reached-historic-lows-in-2019.html.

27. Matef Harmachis, letter to superintendent of Santa Barbara schools, November 20, 2020, http://inconvenientminority.com/wp-content/uploads/2023/02/Harmachis-anti -Semitism.pdf.

28. Catherine Gewertz, "Ethnic Studies Curriculum Deemed 'Anti-Jewish,'" *Education Week*, August 27, 2019, https://www.edweek.org/policy-politics/ethnic-studies -curriculum-deemed-anti-jewish/2019/08.

29. Anonymous video recording of B'nai B'rith synagogue meeting, October 2021.

30. Sherman Alexie, "Inside Dachau," *Beloit Poetry Journal* 46, no. 4 (Summer 1996): 12–16, https://warwick.ac.uk/fac/arts/history/research/centres/ehrc/research/current_research /memory/sherman_alexie_-_inside_dachau.pdf.

31. Theodor W. Adorno, *Prisms: Essays on Veblen, Huxley, Benjamin, Bach, Proust, Schoenberg, Spengler, Jazz, Kafka*, trans. Samuel and Shierry Weber (Cambridge, MA: MIT Press, 1983), https://www.google.com/books/edition/Prisms/f1y_dX04yBgC?hl=en &gbpv=1&bsq=barbaric.

32. Kenny Xu, "California's 'Ethnic Studies' Gold Rush," *Wall Street Journal*, July 12, 2021, https://www.wsj.com/articles/californias-ethnic-studies-gold-rush-11626129598.

33. Annie Gilbertson, "Ethnic Studies Projected Costs Pegged at $73 Million for LAUSD," KPCC, May 22, 2015, https://www.kpcc.org/2015-05-22/ethnic-studies-projected -costs-pegged-at-73-millio.

34. "Ethnic Studies Model Curriculum, Chapter 4: Sample Lessons and Topics."

Chapter 9

1. "Approval of Memorandum of Understanding between AHA! and GVJH for 2021– 2022 School Year (Wageneck)," https://santabarbara.novusagenda.com/AgendaPublic /CoverSheet.aspx?ItemID=8438&MeetingID=295.

2. "How Does SEL Support Educational Equity and Excellence?," CASEL, accessed December 9, 2022, https://casel.org/fundamentals-of-sel/how-does-sel-support-educational -equity-and-excellence/.

3. Jennifer Freed, "What Is Psychological Astrology?," JenniferFreed.com, accessed December 9, 2022, https://www.jenniferfreed.com/what-is-psychological-astrology.

4. Karen de Sá, "Retreat's Risky Lessons," *San Francisco Chronicle*, June 14, 2018, accessed December 9, 2022, https://www.sfchronicle.com/bayarea/article/Leadership-camps -unproven-painful-12985044.php.

5. "How Many People Died on November 18?," last modified July 24, 2021, San Diego State University, https://jonestown.sdsu.edu/?page_id=35368.

6. Jane OB Doe v. Santa Barbara Unified School District et al., 20CV03946, hearing date July 19, 2021, http://inconvenientminority.com/wp-content/uploads/2023/02/TR-of-7.16.21-re-Mx-Quash.pdf.
7. Jane OB Doe v. Santa Barbara Unified School District et al.
8. Mitchell White, "Teacher Banned from Santa Barbara Unified School District," *Santa Barbara News-Press*, January 18, 2021, accessed December 9, 2022, https://newspress.com/teacher-banned-from-santa-barbara-unified-school-district/.
9. "Barbara Dalton," T9 Mastered, https://t9mastered.com/about-t9-mastered/team-t9-mastered/barbara-dalton/.
10. Jennifer Freed, "What Does AHA! Do?—Jennifer Freed, PhD," YouTube video, uploaded by Jim Peal, May 11, 2020, https://www.youtube.com/watch?v=xqkbCL4DP_s.
11. "June 11 2019 Board Meeting, Santa Barbara Unified School District," YouTube video, uploaded by SBUnified, June 13, 2019, https://www.youtube.com/watch?v=c4DJzjwWOfs&t=131s. Timestamp 1:30:00.
12. "June 11 2019 Board Meeting, Santa Barbara Unified School District."
13. "Approval of Memorandum of Understanding between AHA! and GVJH for 2021–2022 School Year (Wageneck)."
14. Harriet Alexander, "California School District Will Spend $40M Making 'Ethnic Studies' MANDATORY for High School Students Sparking a Woke Gold Rush for Consultants Who Charge $1,500 an HOUR to Train Teachers in CRT," *Daily Mail*, updated July 14, 2021, https://www.dailymail.co.uk/news/article-9785805/Small-California-school-district-spend-40m-ethnic-studies-semester-high-school-students.html.
15. "November 13, 2018 Board of Education Meeting, Santa Barbara Unified School District," YouTube video, uploaded by SBUnified, November 15, 2018, accessed December 9, 2022, https://www.youtube.com/watch?v=EdPLKh192D0, timestamp 24:00.
16. Marcia Heller, "Fund for Santa Barbara Gives AHA! $5,000 to Assist Latinx Families," *Noozhawk*, September 16, 2020, accessed December 9, 2022, https://www.noozhawk.com/article/fund_for_santa_barbara_gives_aha_5000_to_assist_latinx_families.
17. Blanca Garcia, "Ethnic Studies Now Coalition Hosts Block Party," *Santa Barbara Independent*, June 1, 2018, accessed December 9, 2022, https://www.independent.com/2018/06/01/ethnic-studies-now-coalition-hosts-block-party/.

Chapter 10

1. Lauren Fruen, "Cops Investigate Virginia Teachers' Facebook Group for Naming Parents Who Were 'Against Critical Race Theory' and Urging Members to 'Gather Information' on Them," *Daily Mail*, updated March 30, 2021, https://www.dailymail.co.uk/news/article-9415407/Cops-investigate-Facebook-group-named-parents-against-critical-race-theory.html.
2. Ellie Bufkin, "Virginia Parents Threatened After Criticizing Critical Race Theory," WRGB Albany, updated May 7, 2021, accessed December 9, 2022, https://cbs6albany.com/news/nation-world/virginia-parents-threatened-after-criticizing-critical-race-theory.
3. Megan VerHelst, "No Charges Filed Against Loudoun County Anti-Racist Group," Leesburg, Virginia, *Patch*, July 31, 2021, accessed December 9, 2022, https://patch.com/virginia/leesburg/no-charges-filed-against-loudoun-county-anti-racist-group.

4. Fruen, "Cops Investigate Virginia Teachers' Facebook Group for Naming Parents Who Were 'Against Critical Race Theory' and Urging Members to 'Gather Information' on Them."

5. Bufkin, "Virginia Parents Threatened After Criticizing Critical Race Theory."

6. Michael Ruiz, "Virginia Mom Who Survived Maoist China Eviscerates School Board's Critical Race Theory Push," Fox News, June 10, 2021, https://www.foxnews.com /us/virginia-xi-van-fleet-critical-race-theory-china-cultural-revolution-loudoun.

7. Drew Wilder, "'The Meeting Has Degenerated': 1 Arrest, 1 Injury at Loudoun Schools Meeting on Equity," June 23, 2021, 4Washington, https://www.nbcwashington.com /news/local/northern-virginia/loudoun-school-board-transgender-student-policy -race-equity/2708185/.

8. "Critical Race Theory: Virginia Parents Slam School Board | NewsNOW from FOX," YouTube video, uploaded by LiveNOW from FOX, June 21, 2021, https:// www.youtube.com/watch?v=htkIs8ogWhI.

9. "Retired Senator Dick Black Rebukes Virginia School Board," *Christian News Journal*, July 2, 2021, https://christiannewsjournal.com/retired-senator-dick-black-rebukes -virginia-school-board/.

10. Hannah Natanson, "Loudoun School Board Cuts Short Public Comment During Unruly Meeting; One Arrested," *Washington Post*, June 23, 2021, accessed December 6, 2022, https://www.washingtonpost.com/local/education/loudoun-school-board -closes-meeting/2021/06/22/30493128-d3ad-11eb-9f29-e9e6c9e843c6_story.html.

11. Jeremy Bauer-Wolf, "The Public Comment Period for Biden's Title IX Proposal Is Over. What's Next?," *Higher Ed Dive*, September 15, 2022, accessed December 9, 2022, https://www.highereddive.com/news/the-public-comment-period-for-bidens-title -ix-proposal-is-over-whats-nex/631847/.

12. House Judiciary GOP (@JudiciaryGOP), "FROM THE WHISTLEBLOWER," Twitter, November 16, 2021, 3:12 p.m., accessed December 9, 2022, https://twitter.com /JudiciaryGOP/status/1460702256601444352.

13. House Judiciary GOP (@JudiciaryGOP), "FROM THE WHISTLEBLOWER."

14. Merrick Garland, "Memorandum for Director, Federal Bureau of Investigation; Director, Executive Office for U.S. Attorneys; Assistant Attorney General, Criminal Division; United States Attorneys," October 4, 2021, https://www.justice.gov/d9/pages /attachments/2021/10/04/partnership_among_federal_state_local_tribal_and_territorial _law_enforcement_to_address_threats_against_school_administrators_board_members _teachers_and_staff_0_0.pdf.

15. Viola Garcia, "Re: Federal Assistance to Stop Threats and Acts of Violence Against Public Schoolchildren, Public School Board Members, and Other Public School District Officials and Educators," September 29, 2021, http://inconvenientminority.com /wp-content/uploads/2023/02/NSBA-Letter.pdf.

16. Jordan Boyd, "Garland Admits Federal War on Parents Sprang from School Boards Letter, Not Evidence," *The Federalist*, October 21, 2021, accessed December 9, 2022, https://thefederalist.com/2021/10/21/ag-merrick-garland-admits-federal-war-on -parents-sprang-from-school-boards-letter-not-evidence/.

17. Beverly Slough, "Re: NSBA Letter to President Biden on Threats [to] School Boards Members and Public Schools," Parents Defending Education, October 11, 2021,

accessed December 9, 2022, https://defendinged.org/wp-content/uploads/2021/10
/Email-Correspondence_NSBA-Letter-to-President-Biden_Redacted.pdf; also see
Wall Street Journal Editorial Board, "About Those Domestic-Terrorist Parents," *Wall
Street Journal*, October 26, 2021, accessed December 9, 2022, https://www.wsj.com
/articles/about-those-domestic-terrorists-national-school-boards-association-merrick
-garland-memo-fbi-11635285900.

18. Viola Garcia, "Update and Action Items on Addressing the Needs of State Association Members," October 12, 2021, Parents Defending Education, accessed December 9, 2022, https://defendinged.org/wp-content/uploads/2021/11/Communication
-to-Members-Final-10.11.2021.pdf.

19. Mark Lungariello, "FBI Created 'Threat Tag' to Track Alleged Harassment of Educators:
Whistleblower," *New York Post*, November 16, 2021, https://nypost.com/2021/11/16
/fbi-created-threat-tags-over-alleged-harassment-of-educators-whistleblower/.

20. Sam Dorman, "Parents Respond to DOJ, School Boards' Statements: 'I Am What
a Domestic Terrorist Looks Like?,'" Fox News, October 5, 2021, https://www
.foxnews.com/politics/parents-respond-doj-nsba-domestic-terrorist.

21. Robert Farley, "Attorney General Never Called Concerned Parents 'Domestic Terrorists,'" FactCheck.org, April 22, 2022, https://www.factcheck.org/2022/04/attorney
-general-never-called-concerned-parents-domestic-terrorists/.

22. Talia Kaplan, "Whistleblowers Saying FBI Targeted Parents via Terrorism Tools
'Scary Stuff': Rep. Jordan," Fox News, May 15, 2022, accessed December 9, 2022,
https://www.foxnews.com/media/whistleblowers-saying-fbi-targeting-parents-via
-terrorism-tools-scary-stuff-rep-jordan.

23. Kerry Picket and Joseph Clark, "Biden Accused of Pressuring FBI to Fabricate
'Extremist' and 'White Supremacist' Cases," *Washington Times*, September 12, 2022,
accessed December 9, 2022, https://www.washingtontimes.com/news/2022/sep/15
/biden-accused-pressuring-fbi-fabricate-extremist-a/.

24. Ruth Marcus, "Merrick Garland Is No Cowboy," *Washington Post*, August 11, 2022,
accessed December 9, 2022, https://www.washingtonpost.com/opinions/2022/08/10
/merrick-garland-trump-search/.

25. Christy Lozano, "Christy Lozano: Password-Protected Portal: Culturally Responsive Curriculum—What Parents Should Know," YouTube video, January 15, 2022,
https://www.youtube.com/watch?v=5WZ4JLQ0WnA.

26. "Wonder Bree activist Bree Newsome art print 5x7 inches," Etsy, https://www
.etsy.com/listing/239272122/wonder-bree-activist-bree-newsome-art.

27. "California Teacher Exposes School's Woke Agenda," YouTube video, uploaded by
Fox News, February 12, 2022, https://www.youtube.com/watch?v=gEiIbHirqZU.

28. Starshine Roshell, "Santa Barbara School Teacher's Rant Is All Wrong," *Santa Barbara Independent*, February 14, 2022, https://www.independent.com/2022/02/14/santa
-barbara-school-teachers-rant-is-all-wrong/.

29. Jerry Roberts, "Why County Schools Supe Challenger Lozano Wants Race, LGBTQ,
and Transgender Issues Out of Classrooms," *Santa Barbara Independent*, May 2, 2022,
https://www.independent.com/2022/05/02/why-county-schools-supe-challenger
-lozano-wants-race-lgbtq-and-transgender-issues-out-of-classrooms/.

30. Roberts, "Why County Schools Supe Challenger Lozano Wants Race, LGBTQ, and Transgender Issues Out of Classrooms."
31. Bill Cirone, "Susan Salcido: A Born Leader," *Santa Barbara Independent*, May 26, 2022, https://www.independent.com/2022/05/26/susan-salcido-a-born-leader/.
32. Nick Welsh, "The Fight for Santa Barbara's Superintendent of Schools Heats Up," *Santa Barbara Independent*, March 30, 2022, accessed December 9, 2022, https://www.independent.com/2022/03/30/poodle-the-fight-for-santa-barbaras-superintendent-of-schools-heats-up/.

Chapter 11

1. Julie Carey, "Virginia Democrats Reflect on Inauguration Day, Moving Forward," 4Washington, January 20, 2021, accessed December 9, 2022, https://www.nbcwashington.com/news/local/virginia-democrats-reflect-on-inauguration-day-moving-forward/2547591/.
2. Jonathan Martin, "Terry McAuliffe Will Not Run for President," *New York Times*, April 17, 2019, accessed December 9, 2022, https://www.nytimes.com/2019/04/17/us/politics/terry-mcauliffe-president.html.
3. Carey, "Virginia Democrats Reflect on Inauguration Day, Moving Forward."
4. Mark Caputo, "School Sexual Assault Roils Virginia Governor's Race," *Politico*, October 28, 2021, accessed November 26, 2022, https://www.politico.com/news/2021/10/28/sexual-assault-schools-virginia-governor-race-517481.
5. Ryan Lizza, "The Surprising Strategy Behind Youngkin's Stunner," *Politico*, November 5, 2021, accessed December 9, 2022, https://www.politico.com/news/magazine/2021/11/05/youngkin-mcauliffe-politics-virginia-strategy-2021-upset-analysis-519622.
6. Dan Merica, "McAuliffe Says Virginia Election 'Is Not About Trump' After Making Former President Central Figure in Campaign," CNN, October 30, 2021, accessed December 9, 2022, https://www.cnn.com/2021/10/30/politics/terry-mcauliffe-donald-trump-virginia-governor-race/index.html.
7. Lizza, "The Surprising Strategy Behind Youngkin's Stunner."
8. Trip Gabriel, "Glenn Youngkin's Journey from the Heights of Finance to the Top Tier of G.O.P. Politics," *New York Times*, November 3, 2021, accessed December 9, 2022, https://www.nytimes.com/2021/11/03/us/elections/glenn-youngkin.html.
9. "Virginia Gubernatorial Debate," timestamp 28:00, C-SPAN, September 28, 2021, accessed February 4, 2022, https://www.c-span.org/video/?514874-1/virginia-gubernatorial-debate.
10. Emily Guskin and Madison Dong, "Exit Poll Results from the 2021 Election for Virginia Governor," *Washington Post*, updated November 3, 2021, accessed December 9, 2022, https://www.washingtonpost.com/elections/interactive/2021/exit-polls-virginia-governor/.
11. Rick Hess, "What Youngkin's Virginia Win Means for Education," American Enterprise Institute, November 3, 2021, https://www.aei.org/op-eds/what-youngkins-virginia-win-means-for-education/.
12. Lauren Camera, "Democrats Cede 'Party of Education' Label to GOP: Poll," *U.S News & World Report*, July 20, 2022, accessed November 27, 2022, https://www.usnews

.com/news/education-news/articles/2022-07-20/democrats-cede-party-of-education
-label-to-gop-poll.

13. "Virginia Gubernatorial Debate," timestamp 37:20.

14. Stephen Sawchuk, "What Is the Purpose of School?," *Education Week*, September 14, 2021, accessed December 9, 2022, https://www.edweek.org/policy-politics/what -is-the-purpose-of-school/2021/09.

15. "Henrico County Public Schools Specialty Centers," Henrico County, https:// henricoschools.us/wp-content/uploads/SpecialtyCentersBooklet20232024.pdf.

16. Larry Abramson, "Sputnik Left Legacy for U.S. Science Education," *All Things Considered*, NPR, September 30, 2007, accessed December 9, 2022, https://www.npr .org/2007/09/30/14829195/sputnik-left-legacy-for-u-s-science-education.

17. Senate Historical Office, "Sputnik Spurs Passage of the National Defense Education Act," United States Senate, December 12, 2019, accessed December 9, 2022, https:// www.senate.gov/artandhistory/history/minute/Sputnik_Spurs_Passage_of _National_Defense_Education_Act.htm.

18. "Elementary and Secondary School Emergency Relief Fund," Department of Education, Office of Elementary and Secondary Education, accessed December 9, 2022, https://oese.ed.gov/offices/education-stabilization-fund/elementary-secondary -school-emergency-relief-fund/.

19. "Frequently Asked Questions: Elementary and Secondary School Emergency Relief Programs; Governor's Emergency Education Relief Programs," Department of Education, Office of Elementary and Secondary Education, May 2021, accessed December 9, 2022, https://oese.ed.gov/files/2021/05/ESSER.GEER_.FAQs_5.26.21_745AM _FINALb0cd6833f6f46e03ba2d97d30aff953260028045f9ef3b18ea602db4b32b1d99.pdf.

20. "Equity in CCS," Cumberland County Schools, accessed December 9, 2022, https:// nc50000603.schoolwires.net/Page/3801.

21. "Cumberland County Diversity, Equity, and Inclusion Advisory Committee (CCDEIAC)," Cumberland County, https://www.cumberlandcountync.gov/docs/default -source/commissioners-documents/dei-committee/2022/ccdeiac-charter-and-term -commitments.pdf.

22. Montgomery County Public Schools, "2018 Bridge to Excellence Annual Update," https://www.boarddocs.com/mabe/mcpsmd/Board.nsf/files/B5TPWY601A02/$file /Tab%201%20-%202018%20Annual%20Update.pdf.

23. "Santa Barbara Talks: Dale Francisco Talks Elon Musk, Carbajal, Hart, Lozano, Mansur, school boards!," timestamp 17:00, YouTube, November 6, 2022, https://www .youtube.com/watch?v=9gp-P1IECZ8&t=979s.

24. Joshua Molina, "Santa Barbara Teachers Protest Outside District Offices; 2 More Schools Send Demand Letters," *Noozhawk*, May 24, 2022, https://www.noozhawk.com/article /santa_barbara_teachers_protest_outside_district_headquarters_two_more_schoo.

25. Derrick A. Bell Jr., "*Brown v. Board of Education* and the Interest-Convergence Dilemma," *Harvard Law Review* 93, no. 3 (January 1980): 518–33, https://doi.org /10.2307/1340546.

Index

About the Author

Kenny Xu is a renowned public commentator on education, minority achievement, and Critical Race Theory. He is the author of *An Inconvenient Minority: The Attack on Asian American Excellence and the Fight for Meritocracy,* and has written for the *Wall Street Journal, City Journal, National Review, Newsweek,* the *New York Post, New York Daily News, The Federalist, The Daily Signal, Quillette,* and the *Washington Examiner,* and appeared on the *Honestly with Bari Weiss* podcast, among others. He is the president of Color Us United and the current recipient of the prestigious Robert Novak Journalism Fellowship and the Government Accountability Institute Fellowship, which allowed him to begin the research for this book.